"If we are truly desiring God's kingdom on earth as it is in heaven, we will encounter persecution and trial in the workplace. When this time comes, will you be ready? With the help of this unique, step-by-step, "home run" book, *Christians on the Job*, by Dr. David Goetsch, you can be. Let Dr. Goetsch counsel and guide you with his thought-provoking case studies and questions. Run the race to win!"

—Gregory Parry, Department of Defense Contracting Officer
and Chief, Policy, Pricing and Support Division

"In his new book, Dr. David Goetsch draws on his decades of leadership experience, an in-depth knowledge of the Word, and his love of Jesus Christ to provide insightful, practical guidance for Christians seeking to live faithfully in the workplace. Replete with real-life examples to which most of us can relate, *Christians on the Job* is an excellent resource for teaching Christians how to honor God in their vocation—highly recommended!"

—Mike Ruff, biblical counselor

"There has never been a greater need for this timely book. Working Christians struggle to strike the right balance between being "in the world" without becoming "part of it." David Goetsch has brought his four decades of experience practicing and coaching techniques that can help Christians in the professional world successfully navigate these thorny issues. This book will make a great graduation gift for seniors in high school and college."

—Michael Mosley, Ph.D., Superintendent, Rocky Bayou Christian School

"*Christians on the Job* is a book that has been needed for a long time. Dr. Goetsch is a fresh and exciting new voice in Christian publishing. I look forward to using this book myself and sharing it with my children when the time comes for them to enter the workforce."

—Caroline Fleetwood McCoy, Director of Business Expansion,
Okaloosa Economic Development Council

"Physicians face many professional challenges, ranging from the expectations of staff, patients, and various organizations, that stretch one's ability to maintain the proper witness for Christ. In *Christians on the Job*, Dr. Goetsch equips Christians to face these challenges in ways that honor God. This book puts into practice the admonition of Ephesians 6 to put on the whole armor of God."

—Donald E. Hamilton, MD, ear, nose, and throat surgeon

"Dave Goetsch is dedicated to helping Christians succeed in secular careers, and this excellent new book, *Christians on the Job,* does just that! He demonstrates that working with excellence in the workplace is a way for Christians to value God above all things and at the same time enable them to more effectively share the Good News of Jesus Christ with their coworkers!"

—William Berry, computer scientist and independent filmmaker

"We have always believed we are blessed with our business success and that we are charged to be good stewards as explained in this excellent new book. Employers dream of hiring people who exhibit the kind of work ethic and stewardship espoused in *Christians on the Job.* Dr. Goetsch demonstrates that honesty, integrity, diligence, and dependability are still the formula for building a successful career."

—Tom and Peggy Rice, owners, Magnolia Grill, Fort Walton Beach, FL

"As a Christian, I render much of my ministry and service unto the Lord in the workplace. However, I often find myself questioning how my faith should best be put into practice at work. Dr. Goetsch's excellent new book, *Christians on the Job*, frames a practical approach to being, as Christ said, "both innocent and wise," and has provided me valuable application of faith on the job."

—Brooke Cosby, teacher, Rocky Bayou Christian School, Niceville, FL

CHRISTIANS ON THE JOB

CHRISTIANS
ON THE JOB

*Winning at Work
without Compromising
Your Faith*

DAVID GOETSCH

SALEMBOOKS
an imprint of Regnery Publishing

Regnery® is a registered trademark of Salem Communications Holding Corporation

Salem Books™ is a trademark of Salem Communications Holding Corporation

Cataloging-in-Publication data on file with the Library of Congress

ISBN: 978-1-62157-793-5
Ebook ISBN: 978-1-62157-859-8

Library of Congress Cataloging-in-Publication Data

Published in the United States by
Salem Books, an imprint of
Regnery Publishing
A Division of Salem Media Group
300 New Jersey Ave NW
Washington, DC 20001
www.Regnery.com

Manufactured in the United States of America

2019 Printing

Books are available in quantity for promotional or premium use. For information on discounts and terms, please visit our website: www.Regnery.com

*"Behold, I am sending you out as sheep
in the midst of wolves, so be wise as serpents
and innocent as doves."*

Matthew 10:16

"To my beloved wife, daughter, son-in-law, and grandson: Deby, Savannah, Ethan, and Matthew. May God bless you richly."

CONTENTS

TEMPTATION, REJECTION, AND PERSECUTION IN THE WORKPLACE

"Be sober minded; be watchful. Your adversary the devil prowls around like a roaring lion, seeking someone to devour."

1 Peter 5:8

When Gary approached me at a Chamber of Commerce meeting, he was distraught. Once we found a private place to talk, Gary unloaded a burden he had been carrying for some time. I thought his career was going well. He was certainly making a name for himself in the local business community. In fact, just twenty minutes earlier Gary was recognized as "Business Leader of the Quarter" by the Chamber. He should have been a happy man, but I could see he wasn't. Gary was doing well at work, but he had begun to compromise his faith to get along with his unbelieving coworkers. Like so many other Christians in the workplace, Gary felt he had to hide his beliefs to avoid being rejected by his coworkers.

In recent months, he found himself being pulled into a circle of unbelieving coworkers whose lives were characterized by self-interest, fast living, misguided ambition, and a win-at-any-cost mentality. They worked hard, if not always ethically, and played even harder. In short, they were like the wolves Christ warned the Apostles about in Matthew 10:16. They completely rejected Christianity. At first, it was just little things. Gary stopped giving thanks before meals, even silently, when in the company of his coworkers. Then he began skipping his weekly prayer breakfast for business leaders, an activity he hosted for two years. Before long, Gary was following in the wayward footsteps of his coworkers, even to the point of taking unethical shortcuts to enhance his job performance.

Gary started joining his coworkers for happy hour at a local tavern. Before long, happy *hour* was lasting two and sometimes three hours. Predictably, Gary soon found himself neglecting his family. He even began skipping church on Sundays to get in a few extra hours of work. Gary's coworkers were leading him down the wrong path, and he was going along to get along. He wanted to put the brakes on before it was too late but feared doing so would harm his career.

Gary felt trapped in the web of an intractable dilemma. On the one hand, he wanted the acceptance of his coworkers as well as their support in climbing the career ladder. He understood work relationships were an important aspect of career advancement. His relationships with coworkers could help or hinder him. On the other hand, going along to get along was causing him to compromise his faith, and he feared where that might lead. These concerns were why Gary approached me for counsel.

During our discussion, Gary asked me a lot of questions, but what he really wanted to know was how to stand firm in the faith when working with wolves. This is the classic dilemma of Christians in today's workplace. As Gary learned the hard way, secular humanism and misguided political correctness are the new normal in the workplace. Gary's story is one that occurs every day for Christians at work. That is why it is so important for believers to understand how to apply Matthew 10:16 in the workplace.

As a Christian in the workplace, do you sometimes feel like a sheep working among wolves? Do you ever feel you are working with predators and you are the prey? I have felt this way many times over the course of my career. Consider how Paul describes unbelievers in 2 Timothy 3:2–4: ". . . lovers of self, lovers of money, proud, arrogant, abusive, disobedient to their parents, ungrateful, unholy, heartless, unappeasable, slanderous, without self-control, brutal, not loving good, treacherous, reckless, swollen with conceit, lovers of pleasure rather than lovers of God . . ." I have worked with people who fit Paul's description. I suspect you have too.

Having worked in the private and public sectors, served in the military, and worked as a college professor and counselor for more than fifty years now, I have seen the best and worst of people in the workplace. There have been times I felt not just ill-at-ease among my coworkers, but completely out of place. You will not work long before learning the truth of 1 Peter 5:8. As this verse states, the devil is indeed prowling around seeking someone to devour, and the workplace is one of his favorite hunting grounds. Every day he uses temptation and pressure from coworkers, superiors, and subordinates to challenge your faith. Sometimes he even stoops to persecution. The devil is a predator who views you as his prey. Consequently, as Paul warns in 2 Timothy 3:12, we can expect to be tempted, pressured, and even persecuted for our faith.

Persecution of Christians is nothing new, of course. Throughout history, Christians have been subjugated, abused, and abased because of their faith. Many have become martyrs. Historically, we have suffered comparatively little for our faith in the United States, but that is changing. Over the years, opposition to Christianity in America has grown steadily. In drafting the First Amendment, our Founders sought to guarantee freedom OF religion. But in recent years, opponents of Christianity have made progress in transforming this guarantee into freedom FROM religion, or at least freedom from the Christian religion. Aided and abetted by progressives in the government, courts, entertainment industry, and media, secular humanists are gaining the upper hand in

American society. Because the workplace reflects contemporary societal standards, secular humanists have gained the upper hand there, too. Unbelievers of all stripes are determined in their opposition to Christianity. This fact is making the workplace an increasingly challenging environment for Christians.

Christians I have counseled in the past several years have complained about coworkers labeling them "fanatics," "misogynists," "extremists," "fundamentalists," and "bigots." What could possibly cause these kinds of attacks? The answer is simple: The Christians in question were *guilty* of openly living their faith in the workplace. Several were asked to remove Bibles from their desks as well as framed Bible verses from their office walls. One was chastised by his boss for silently praying before a business meal. Another was told to stop saying "God bless you" in conversations with coworkers.

Unfortunately, instances of hostility toward Christianity are becoming increasingly common in the workplace. This hostility can and does sometimes cross a line and become persecution. Instances of outright persecution make the headlines and garner the most attention, but—in reality—they represent only a small percentage of faith-related challenges Christians face on the job. The majority of faith-related challenges in the workplace are subtler in nature and more difficult to defend against. In fact, unbelievers often like to disguise their hostility toward Christianity in a cloak of neutrality. They attempt to sound reasonable by arguing that work and religion do not mix. But there are two problems with this argument. First, the only religion they attack is Christianity, and second, Christianity is a worldview encompassing all aspects of life, including our work. As Christians, we cannot separate our beliefs from our work, nor can we leave our beliefs on the doorstep of the office.

Here are just a few examples of subtle attacks experienced by Christians I have counseled: being excluded from important meetings; seeing promotions, salary increases, and recognition go to less deserving coworkers; cyber-bullying including offensive emails, negative posts on social media, and spreading of hurtful gossip and lies via email and social media; coping with snide comments; seeing plum assignments go to less experienced coworkers; having one's work sabotaged by teammates; and seeing credit for their work go to an undeserving coworker. In all these cases, the individuals who sought my counsel felt strongly they were mistreated for one reason and one reason only: their Christianity.

The devil can be slyly subtle when preying on Christians in the workplace. For example, as a college professor in a secular institution, I was once called on to play the role of *designated Christian*. It happened like this: There was a luncheon meeting. The organizers felt there should be a prayer before we ate, so they looked around for someone to do the deed. It was not long before all heads turned to me. I was asked by the politically correct organizers to pray but to keep it "brief, generic, and non-offensive." This is an example of the devil's subtle, but sly handy work. One of the most effective ways to attack Christianity is to water it down over time until our prayers become empty words and our beliefs hollow tenets.

In response to their request for a "non-offensive" prayer, I prayed fervently in the name of Jesus. Predictably, some members of the audience shifted uncomfortably in their seats. Then, for the remainder of the meeting I was treated like a leper by most participants, including those who asked me to pray. This type of scenario, though uncomfortable, is really nothing more than a bump in the road for committed Christians. I am sure you have experienced situations in which standing firm in the faith led to worse repercussions than being scorned by an audience of secular humanists. In all likelihood, that is why you are reading this book.

There are a lot of us out there: working Christians who face faith-related challenges in our jobs on a regular basis. I am sure there are times when you feel like a sheep among wolves. I know this because, as a professor of business, management consultant, corporate trainer, and counselor, I interact frequently with Christians who are struggling with faith-related trials in their jobs. In fact, for the past thirty years, my ministry has been to provide free-of-charge counseling for Christians who are facing workplace dilemmas testing their faith.

Hardly a day goes by that I am not approached for help by Christians who are struggling with faith-related issues in their jobs. While working on this book during a lunch break in a coffee shop, a waiter approached me and asked for advice concerning a dilemma he was facing right then. Unbeknownst to me, this waiter had been reading over my shoulder. The subject of this book emboldened him to ask for help. I am glad he did. As the head waiter, he was responsible for dividing up the cash tips left in a jar on the counter. He tallied up the cash tips at closing and divided them equally among all waiters who worked that shift.

Drowning in debt, this waiter was looking for ways to increase his income. Lately, he was tempted to keep more than his share of the daily tips, something he probably could have gotten away with if he was careful. When we talked, he was trying to rationalize this nefarious scheme based on financial need. Ironically, he was trusted to oversee the distribution of tips because he was known to be a Christian. He knew keeping an unequal share of the tips would be wrong, but the financial dilemma he faced was clouding his judgment. Thankfully, it took nothing but a few words of prayer to bring him to his senses.

Many years ago, this kind of situation cropped up so often I returned to college at night and completed a graduate degree in counseling. I'm glad I did. Christian counselors provide invaluable help to believers who have lost their way or are struggling with the challenges of living faithful lives in a sinful world. Individually and collectively, counselors do a commendable job and serve a worthy purpose. But an important point to remember is this: We are not the source of the answers you seek. God is. The answers you seek will be found in His Word. Our job is to guide you to the appropriate verses in the Bible and assist you in applying those verses in practical, helpful ways. The value of the counseling we provide is it guides Christians to the right places in the Bible and helps translate that guidance into practical action. That is also the goal of this book.

Christians struggling in the workplace approach me at Chamber of Commerce meetings, during breaks in college classes I teach, after seminars or speeches I have given, during conferences, in businesses when

I am consulting, in airports, and, yes, even in coffee shops and restaurants. What all these Christians have in common is they are experiencing faith-related dilemmas that make them feel like sheep working "in the midst of wolves." As Christians working in a setting where secular humanism is the norm, a dilemma we face is the same one Gary faced earlier in this chapter: How can I stand firm in the faith when working with wolves. This is an important question. I hope this book helps you answer it.

YOUR FAITH IS GOING TO BE CHALLENGED IN THE WORKPLACE—COUNT ON IT

The majority of Christians work not in the ministry or on the mission field but in secular careers. We are doctors, lawyers, professors, teachers, engineers, architects, scientists, sales representatives, accountants, investment brokers, bankers, project managers, journalists, editors, military personnel, computer programmers, police officers, firefighters, nurses, emergency medical technicians, restaurant owners, hotel managers, cashiers, entertainers, and on and on. Christians can be found working in most jobs that exist in the private, public, and nonprofit sectors. This is good news because consistent Christians who work in these settings can be emissaries for Christ among their coworkers. As Christians, we can and should set examples of working in ways consistent with the teachings of Scripture and that reflect the image of Christ. But there is also bad news.

There was a time when Christianity was the norm in America and correspondingly in the workplace. However, over time the workplace has become less friendly to Christian believers. Secular humanism has muscled its way into society and become the norm. Because of this, Christians often find themselves confronting faith-related dilemmas in the workplace. Every day working Christians must fight a two-pronged battle. On one hand, there is the personal battle to avoid succumbing to the temptations so prevalent in the workplace. Even as Christians, we are still sinners. This means we are still susceptible to greed, lust, self-adulation, envy, jealousy, ego, misplaced ambition, idolatry, lying, cheating, stealing, and more. Our unbelieving coworkers have no monopoly on sin.

On the other hand, we must also battle against the pressures of the workplace to engage in sinful behavior in the name of competitiveness, the bottom line, success, career advancement, job security, salary increases, bonuses, recognition, perquisites, making quotas, meeting deadlines, and a host of other pressure-inducing factors. For example, you may have worked with people whose focus on the bottom line was so intense they were willing to push the boundaries of ethical behavior in the name of profits. People who are willing to do that are usually not averse to pressuring others to follow suit. You may have felt the sting of rejection or even hostility from coworkers when you resisted their pressure to behave unethically. Christians in the workplace often feel this kind of pressure. There is no question today's fast-paced, hypercompetitive workplace can be a minefield of moral dilemmas for Christians.

However, in spite of the faith-related challenges so prevalent in today's workplace, not only can Christians survive in this environment, we can thrive. Further, we can thrive not by hiding our faith but by living it in ways that reflect the image of Christ for our colleagues. The key for Christians in secular careers can be found in Matthew 10:16: "*Behold, I am sending you out as sheep in the midst of wolves, so be wise as serpents and innocent as doves.*" Matthew 10:16 is the theme of this book. As Christians in secular careers, we must be both "wise" and "innocent," or we risk being devoured by predatory coworkers.

Helping Christians accomplish this difficult but critical challenge is the purpose of this book. Those who learn the lesson contained in Matthew 10:16 will, in turn, be better equipped to follow the admonition of Christ set forth in Matthew 5:16. In the latter verse, we are told to shine our lights before others, so they may see what it means to be a Christian and so that we, by our examples, give glory to God.

CHAPTER 1

KNOW HOW TO RESPOND WHEN YOUR FAITH IS CHALLENGED AT WORK

"The Lord is my light and my salvation; whom shall I fear? The Lord is the stronghold of my life; of whom shall I be afraid?"

Psalm 27:1

When your Christianity is challenged at work, it is important to stand firm in the faith but to do so without becoming like those who oppress you. Mike had to learn this difficult lesson. Anytime Mike's faith was challenged by coworkers, his immediate response was to attack. As a former Marine, Mike's idea of a good defense was a strong offense. Mike knew his Bible well and was a talented, assertive debater. The problem with Mike's approach was he used the Bible as a weapon for defeating naysayers rather than a tool for defending his faith. He liked to claim his attacks on unbelievers were justified by righteous anger like that shown by Christ when He threw the moneychangers out of the Temple. Mike did not understand his coworkers are not moneychangers, the workplace is not the Temple, and he is not Christ.

Although he always argued the biblical perspective effectively, Mike never seemed to change the minds or hearts of unbelieving coworkers. That is what brought him to me. When Mike came in for counseling, I complimented him for standing firm when coworkers challenged his faith but suggested he consider a different approach. Rather than use his debating skills to verbally slay those who reject Christianity, why not use them to edify unbelievers and show them a better way?

This can be difficult advice for Christians to accept, especially when their faith is regularly challenged, belittled, or rejected by coworkers. It was for me when a pastor first suggested it many years ago. It is only human to want to strike back at those who attack us, particularly when they attack our faith, but being human means being sinful. Christ does not call us to verbally smite those who reject His Word. We are supposed to use the Word of God to show unbelievers the ways of Christ, not to boost our egos by bettering them in arguments. I told Mike he would enjoy better results by leading coworkers to Christ than by arguing them into submission.

It took Mike a while to accept my advice. Just as I did years ago, he resisted this approach, at least in the beginning. But, to his credit, Mike finally came around. When he did, his knowledge of the Bible gave him the depth needed to patiently deal with even the most vociferous attacks on his faith. Rather than counterpunch those who challenged his faith, Mike began to calmly offer another point of view—the biblical point of view. Mike was surprised to observe his new approach was well-received. As a result, Mike started a Bible study in his home one night a week and invited coworkers to join him. Over time, Mike's Bible study became quite popular with his coworkers. It had the effect of improving the work environment for everyone in Mike's department. Mike felt particularly blessed one day when a former naysayer defended him after a coworker from another department chided Mike for having a framed copy of John

3:16 on his cubicle wall. That former naysayer became a regular at Mike's Bible study and later gave his life to Christ.

For Christians, the modern workplace can be a stormy sea to navigate. Secularism coupled with the day-to-day pressures of the job can create situations challenging your faith. To review, secular humanism is a worldview that rejects the God of Holy Scripture. In this worldview, man is god. Political correctness is societal pressure to avoid offending anyone, particularly when it comes to matters of diversity (e.g., age, race, sex, body size, etc.). Although Christians should be concerned about offending people, the problem with political correctness is it can be taken to extremes that limit free speech and effective communication. As Christians, we should always make an effort to be tactful, kind, and considerate when interacting with others. If the dictates of political correctness stopped at tact, there would be no controversy surrounding it. Unfortunately, political correctness does not stop at tact. Rather, it has morphed into a kind of speech control reminiscent of George Orwell's book, *1984.*

As Christians in the workplace, a dilemma we often face is how to be faithful to our beliefs when working with people who don't share those beliefs and when confronted with situations that challenge those beliefs. That is what concerned Phyllis when she sought me out for counseling. She was upset and even a little angry because her Christianity seemed to be fair game among the people she worked with, including her supervisor. What frustrated her most was Phyllis did not know how to respond when her beliefs were attacked. She wanted to defend her faith, but she did not want to damage her career. To make matters worse, Phyllis felt like an island in a river of unbelievers. A lot of Christians feel the same way.

NAVIGATING THE STORMY SEAS OF THE MODERN WORKPLACE

The fact we as Christians encounter faith-related trials in the workplace should come as no surprise. Rejection of God started in the Garden of

Eden. It can be difficult for Christians to live their faith among coworkers who reject Christ. Christians in the workplace often feel pressured to take part in the inappropriate behavior of coworkers and, in some cases, fear that refusing to go along will have bad repercussions. But Christians who learn to apply Christ's admonition in Matthew 10:16 can successfully navigate even the stormiest seas. To meet the challenge of wisely and innocently working among wolves without being devoured, it will be necessary to understand several key principles emphasized throughout this book:

- As a Christian in the workplace, your faith is going to be challenged. Count on it and do not be surprised or shocked when it happens. The devil is a predator who never stops hunting, and you, like all Christians, are his prey. Further, the workplace is one of his favorite hunting grounds. When your faith is challenged and you find your resolve weakening, remember suffering for your beliefs in the short run is better than suffering in eternity for compromising them. Also, remember unethical coworkers who appear to win in the short run almost always come to grief in the long run. If we refuse to compromise our Christian values, we may have to endure some rough sledding for a time. However, unlike our predatory coworkers, we never have to worry about our sins catching up with us in the long run. And remember this: One way or another, sins always catch up with the sinner.
- No matter how successful you may be in your job, you have failed if your success comes by compromising your faith. Success built on sin is not success at all. In fact, it will be only temporary, no matter how long it lasts in human terms.
- No matter where you work or what kind of job you have, as a Christian you work first for the Lord and second for your employer. Colossians 3:23 tells us to work hard but

for God rather than for men. No matter how your job description at work reads, you have a bigger job description: This Christian represents Christ in the workplace.

- Quitting your job when the faith-related trials you are experiencing seem overwhelming should be viewed as an option of last resort, at least in most cases. There are two reasons for this. First, what is needed most in a sinful workplace is people like you who are willing to set a Christ-like example for their coworkers. Christians who reflect the image of Christ for people who don't know Him or, worse yet, reject Him make an important contribution to the Kingdom of God. Second, you cannot escape the predatory behavior of sinful people by changing jobs. There are wolves in most every organization.

THE ULTIMATE CHALLENGE FACED BY CHRISTIANS IN THE WORKPLACE

When you are confronted with faith-related dilemmas, problems, and frustrations, remember this: They all grow from the same root—sin. The real challenge you face in the workplace and elsewhere is your own human propensity for sin, which is the ultimate weapon of the ultimate predator: Satan. Our battles in the workplace may appear to be with unscrupulous bosses or unethical coworkers, but in reality, they are with our own sinful nature. The devil simply uses unscrupulous bosses and unethical coworkers as his instruments to lure, pressure, or coerce us into sinning. The real battle we face as Christians occurs not in the workplace per se, but in our own hearts. We can stand firm against the temptations and pressures of the workplace, but only if we stand firm against our own propensity for sin.

Sin can manifest itself in many ways in the workplace including laziness, bad attitudes, self-promotion, discontentment, pride, selfishness, ego, boasting, idolatry, office politics, rumor-mongering, lying, cheating, stealing, adultery, pornography, coarse language, impatience, irritability, bullying, exploitation, envy, jealousy, passing the buck, taking credit for the work of others, poor self-control, and anger, to name just a few. Regardless of how it manifests itself, sin is what clogs up the gears of human interaction in the workplace. Consider some actual examples of situations experienced by Christians I have counseled over the years and see if they sound familiar:

- An assistant manager learned a colleague sometimes falsified monthly reports to exaggerate his performance.
- An accountant knew one of his team members routinely overcharged customers for the work he did on their accounts.
- A college professor found his continued employment challenged when a homosexual student learned of his biblical views on same-sex marriage and filed a complaint with the administration.
- A sales manager for an automobile dealership became frustrated and wanted to resign because his peers who cheated, lied, and exploited seemed to benefit from these sins when it came to bonuses, recognition, and promotions.
- A sales representative was pressured by her boss to make false claims about their company's product during sales calls. Her boss implied there might be repercussions if she refused.
- An inventory manager observed an executive taking office supplies from the company for his personal use.
- An attorney learned a colleague was watching Internet pornography at his desk for hours at a time rather than doing the work his clients were paying for.
- A project manager learned a friendship between two members of his team developed into an adulterous affair.
- A construction supervisor was pressured to cut corners on safety measures to get a project back on schedule.

- A construction foreman knew his company was improperly disposing of hazardous materials in ways that could harm the community.
- An administrative assistant knew her boss was running an Internet business on the side out of his office and during work hours.
- A college professor was pressured to give students grades they did not earn to improve student retention in his department.
- An administrative assistant was harassed continually by an unbelieving coworker who sent her offensive emails and posted offensive comments about her on social media sites.

In these examples, the individuals who approached me seeking counsel shared a common dilemma: They were Christians confronted with challenges to their faith, and they were unsure how to respond. These Christians feared speaking up might cause problems for them at work or even jeopardize their careers. At the same time, they also feared ignoring what they knew would compromise their beliefs. Unfortunately, this kind of dilemma is common among Christians in today's workplace.

Christians just like you must cope with faith-related dilemmas in their jobs more frequently than one might think. At the very least, the workplace is a worldly environment littered with moral potholes. It follows, then, the workplace is not always the friendliest environment for those of us who have given our lives to Christ. John 15:18–19 reminds us the world hated Christ first, so it should come as no surprise the world also hates those who follow Christ. It also reminds us if we were of the world, our unbelieving coworkers would accept us as one of their own. However, because we follow Christ, the world rejects us and our beliefs. In other words, John is telling us we should not be surprised when our beliefs are not welcomed by those who do not share them. This brief but profound lesson from the Gospel of John illustrates why it is important to be both wise and innocent when we go to work each day.

For Christians such as you and me, John 15:18–19 is borne out all too frequently in the workplace. Most working Christians have had or will have their faith tested by pressure, rejection, temptation, or even persecution. This is the bad news. The good news is those of us who shine the light of Christ in the workplace while consistently, firmly, and adroitly applying Matthew 10:16 will typically win in the long run. Granted, the victory may not always come when we would like it to, but it will come in God's time and it will be a victory.

Angela, a college professor, learned this lesson when she refused her dean's demands to give college students better grades than the ones they earned. The dean was trying to improve the university's declining graduation rate, but at the expense of academic and professional integrity. When Angela would not budge on the issue of grades, the dean responded by assigning her to a remote branch campus in another city far from her home. The assignment required Angela to drive an extra ninety roundtrip miles every day, miles that detracted from her family and free time. But Angela persevered, even after the dean began to openly and contemptuously criticize her "arcane and outmoded Christian beliefs." After two years of making the long drive to the university's branch campus, Angela woke up one morning to read in her hometown newspaper about her antagonist being fired for unauthorized tampering with student grades. After the dean's ignominious departure, Angela was restored to her old position at the university's main campus. Angela eventually won out because she persevered in the faith.

PERSEVERING IN THE FAITH IS ALWAYS THE RIGHT RESPONSE

Persevering in the faith is no guarantee you will be spared from the temptation, pressure, rejection, or persecution of unbelieving coworkers or, in some instances, even fellow believers. One of the most disillusioned Christians I ever counseled approached me because his boss, a professing

Christian and church deacon, was pressuring him to engage in unethical behavior to increase his department's sales volume. My friend was resisting the pressure but feared his refusals might bring punishment. Appeals to his supervisor's Christian faith did no good. His boss played the role of a Christian on Sunday but was one of Satan's minions the rest of the week.

Consistently living your faith in the workplace is almost guaranteed to cause you problems from time to time. Nevertheless, maintaining your faith when others are pressuring you to sin is always the right choice. Consider what is written in Hebrews 12:3. This verse reminds us that Christ suffered for us, and there has never been a time when Christians did not suffer for their faith. Consequently, we should not grow weary when we have to suffer. Suffering for our faith is part of being a Christian.

Examples of Christians who suffered for their faith abound. You are familiar with the story of Job. Put to the test by Satan, he became so distraught over the suffering inflicted on him he wanted to die. Then there was David who, even after being chosen by God and anointed as king, had to run for his life. Another example is the prophet Jeremiah. Jeremiah wept in frustration because he was ignored. His life was threatened because he spoke the truth, a truth the people of Judah did not want to hear. There are plenty of people in the workplace who, like the people of Judah, do not want to hear God's truth. But reflecting God's truth in your actions, behaviors, and decisions is always the right choice, even when others do not appreciate your choice.

When it comes to the story of Job, even unbelievers typically know it. The phrase *he has the patience of Job* is widely used in contemporary American society. Ironically, it is used even by unbelievers who have never read the biblical account. Of course, those who have studied Job know patience is only part of what the story teaches. Job is about persevering in the faith no matter what trials one faces. Over the course of my career, I have come to know several modern-day Jobs who persisted in difficult situations by clinging to their Christian faith as a drowning man clings to a life preserver.

Cindy was a Christian who worked as a paralegal at a large law firm. She had an associate degree and was good at her job. Over the years, other paralegals less capable than Cindy were promoted, recognized, and given salary increases. Meanwhile, Cindy languished at the same level and same pay grade. Why? Several years earlier Cindy blew the whistle on a lawyer in her firm (I will call him Don) who was engaged in unethical behavior. Don was consistently claiming more hours than he worked on his client's cases and, as a result, overcharging them. This behavior had been going on for months and Cindy, who worked closely with Don, cautioned him on numerous occasions about it. But each time Cindy raised the issue, Don brushed her off and told her to mind her own business. When she finally went to someone in authority with what she knew, Don was forced to resign.

Rather than appreciate Cindy's honesty, many in the firm who were friends of Don's resented her. Several coworkers even called her a "rat." Others shunned her. But their law firm had a whistle-blowing policy. This policy required any employee who became aware of unethical behavior to report it. In fact, the policy had a provision for punishing employees who knew of unethical behavior and failed to report it. The policy ensured Cindy's job was safe, but those who resented her whistle-blowing made a point of finding ways to make her work life miserable.

Cindy was given projects to complete with deadlines nearly impossible to meet, left out of important meetings, no longer invited to join her coworkers for lunch, and shunned when she entered the break room. Her immediate supervisor, a close friend of Don's, was especially hard on Cindy when conducting annual performance appraisals. Despite doing an excellent job, Cindy was rated as just "average" on performance appraisals. Over time, Cindy began to wonder if she should have blown the whistle on Don after all. It was beginning to appear that trying to do the right thing was the wrong thing.

By the time she approached me for counseling, Cindy was at rock bottom. She was ready to pack up her desk and quit, even before finding another job. In fact, Cindy was convinced her supervisor would seek retribution by making it difficult for her to secure a new job. At the very least, he would give her a poor recommendation. Consequently, she felt trapped. To make matters worse, as a single mother—she lost her husband in an automobile accident—Cindy needed her job. She had a little money set aside for emergencies, but it was only enough to sustain her for a couple weeks if she quit.

After talking with Cindy for a while, I recommended she take the long view, be patient, and wait the situation out. My thought was the normal personnel changes that occur in big firms, coupled with her excellent work, would eventually set Cindy's situation right. I also recommended that in the meantime she sustain herself with prayer and Bible reading, pointing out how certain individuals in the Bible had persevered through hard times and came out well in the end. Cindy did not share my optimism, but with no other options, she felt compelled to accept my advice. Fortunately, about a year later the advice paid off, but not in the way I anticipated. Ironically, Cindy got some help from her old nemesis, Don.

When Don was forced to resign, he was hired immediately with a competing law firm. Don did well at his new firm. Although some clients complained they were being overcharged, Don's new superiors thought little of the complaints. To them, he appeared to be a sharp young attorney who worked hard and consistently exceeded his quota on billable hours. But Don's image with his new employer was all smoke and mirrors. In reality, Don picked up where he left off at his old firm. He was once again engaged in the unethical practice of padding his billable hours. When an administrative assistant in his new firm turned him in, the word got around and several major clients sued. When the controversy was picked up by the local newspapers, Don lost his job and his firm lost its credibility with clients. In fact, so much business was lost because of the scandal, the firm eventually had to reduce its workforce to avoid bankruptcy.

In the aftermath of Don's disgrace, Cindy began to notice subtle changes. Nobody came forward and admitted she was right to blow the whistle on Don. Nobody thanked her for sparing their firm from Don's destructive behavior. But coworkers did start talking to Cindy again and inviting her to join them for lunch. What really surprised Cindy was her boss quietly submitted amended performance appraisals for her to the firm's Human Resources Office. These amended performance appraisals, which rated her work as "excellent," soon resulted in a promotion and substantial raise for Cindy. Cindy's quiet but firm perseverance in the faith paid off. In the beginning, she persevered because there appeared to be no other choice. But after much prayer, Cindy decided to do her job to the best of her ability and leave the rest in God's hands. Her faith, coupled with perseverance, eventually paid off.

WORK FIRST FOR CHRIST AND SECOND FOR YOUR EMPLOYER

In the example of Cindy, things worked out well in the end. But this kind of outcome is not guaranteed, even for the most faithful Christians. There may be times when remaining faithful to your beliefs will jeopardize your job security or, at the very least, cause you emotional distress, a hard fact Christians must understand. Consequently, it is important to remember when facing moral dilemmas on the job as Christians we work first for Christ and second for our employers.

Colossians 3:23–24 tells us to work for the Lord, not for men. It reminds us, as believers, we serve the Lord, and ultimately, our reward comes from God. As Christians, our reward may not always come when we would like, but even when this is the case we should not despair. We may have a plan for our career, but God has an even bigger plan encompassing every aspect of our lives. It is possible our career plan may not match God's plan. When this is the case, it must be enough to know God has a plan for each of us, and His plan is better than ours. Understanding and accepting God has a plan for us is part of our Christian faith. It is why we are told in Scripture to wait patiently on the Lord.

Some moral dilemmas in the workplace may turn out to be so intractable we have no alternative but to resign. When we cannot continue in a job without denying our faith, we must be prepared to make the hard choice. Remember what Christ said about plucking out your eye and cutting off your hand if they cause you to sin (Matthew 5:29). However, in most cases, resigning should be the option of last resort. After all, the more sinful the workplace, the more it needs the leavening influence of a good Christian example. You can provide that example, but only if present.

PRESSURE, REJECTION, AND TEMPTATION ENCOURAGE SIN IN THE WORKPLACE

Most of the manifestations of sin observed in the world at large are present in the workplace. To complicate things further, factors such as global competition, human ambition, and the ever-increasing demands of customers, magnify the pressures Christians often feel on the job. Worse yet, Christians in the workplace sometimes feel subtle and even not-so-subtle pressure from superiors and coworkers to engage in sinful behavior. Then they feel the lash of rejection when they don't give in to the pressure. Add to the job pressures Christians often face at work the usual temptations experienced by all human beings, and the modern workplace becomes a difficult environment for the faithful.

What Christian has not been tempted by power, money, and status in the workplace? What Christian has not wanted to fit in with coworkers even though they reject Christ? What Christian has not witnessed the devastation to lives brought on by adulterous office affairs? What Christian has not been tempted to express jealousy or envy over a coworker's promotion? What Christian has not felt resentment when a less deserving coworker received a raise or special recognition? What Christian has not observed coworkers padding their expense accounts? What Christian has not observed colleagues taking home office supplies for personal use? In short, what Christian does not observe sinful behavior in the workplace every day and feel tempted to join in?

As Christians, we are different from our worldly coworkers in some important ways, but we are still human. Thus, we are still sinners. We feel all the temptations and pressures present in the workplace. But as Christians, we have prayer, Scripture, the counsel of Godly men and women, and the guidance of the church to help us respond to temptation, rejection, and pressure. For every kind of pressure or temptation, we are subjected to on the job, there are appropriate responses, responses that align with the teachings of Scripture and are appropriate in a work setting. The key to responding to pressure, rejection, and temptation in a biblical manner is to use an approach I call the *First-Response Model*.

FIRST-RESPONSE MODEL

The remaining chapters in this book provide specific strategies you can use for responding to the faith-related dilemmas you confront in the workplace and for preventing such dilemmas. But before getting into specific strategies for specific situations, it is important to review what we, as Christians, should do first when facing moral dilemmas. The *First-Response Model* summarizes the first steps we, as Christians, should take when facing faith-related dilemmas in the workplace.

1. *Avoid responding out of anger, fear, or frustration.* Not only is it important to say "no" to sin in the workplace, it is important to respond to sin in a Christ-like manner. Remember, when Satan tempted Christ in the wilderness? Jesus responded with the authority of His Father rather than out of anger, fear, or frustration. Christ is our example. Thus, our responses to sin should be Christ-like. Responses driven by anger, fear, or frustration are not likely to be Christ-like responses. Consequently, when you feel like responding in a way Christ would frown on, take a deep breath and don't respond at all, at least not in the moment. Follow the guidance provided in Psalms 37:8 where we are told to refrain from anger because it leads only to evil. Instead of responding out of anger, fear, or frustration, step back and give yourself time to complete the remaining steps in this model.

2. *Pray for guidance.* Never try to deal with faith-related trials in the workplace without enlisting the help of God. In 1 Thessalonians 5:17, Paul says we are to pray

constantly. Remember, no matter how helpless you may feel, all things are possible with God. The Holy Spirit is right there with you. He will be there at your side as you confront faith-related trials in the workplace. Seek God's guidance through prayer. Proverbs 20:24 makes it clear we cannot understand even our own way without the help of the Lord. This is another reason we should heed Paul's admonition to pray constantly. Ask Christ what He would have you do. Then listen. Never make the mistake of trying to go it alone or of thinking you are self-sufficient when confronted by Satan. Without the help of God, Satan will win, and you will lose. Satan's power compared with yours is that of an elephant trampling a flea. But compared with Christ, Satan is powerless. With God's help, you will win, and Satan will lose.

3.   *Seek guidance in Scripture.* There is no situation you will ever face at work or in any other setting not spoken to in the Bible. Holy Scripture provides God's guidance concerning how we should live, interact with others, face dilemmas, and solve problems, as well as how we should honor Him in how we do these things. Consequently, when facing trials at work, it is both wise and innocent to consult Scripture before taking action of any kind. A word of caution is appropriate at this point. When you consult Scripture, do so to determine what God would have you do in a given situation, not to validate what you have already decided to do. Using the Bible to rationalize decisions you have already made is neither wise nor innocent. The Bible does not always tell you what you want to hear, but it does tell you what you need to hear.

4.   *Seek the counsel of Godly men and women.* One of the many benefits of being a Christian with a church family is you have a lot of brothers and sisters in Christ to help you face trials in the workplace. Asking for help is not a

sign of weakness. It is a sign of wisdom. The Bible is clear in its admonition that Christians are to seek the counsel of Godly men and women. Proverbs 12:15 makes clear the wisest among us listen to good counsel. Seeking wise counsel can involve talking to your pastor, a Christian counselor, fellow believers, or all of these. Never skip this step. God works through individual Christians. Hence, He might use one of your brothers or sisters in Christ to help you deal with the dilemma you are facing.

5. *Translate Scriptural guidance and wise counsel into workplace-appropriate practical action.* I have stressed that your best guidance for confronting faith-related dilemmas on the job will come from prayer, reading the Bible, and seeking the wise counsel of Christian brothers and sisters. The answers you need are in Scripture, but it will not be enough to simply read pertinent verses relating to the trials you face. To overcome faith-related dilemmas at work, you are going to have to translate the Scriptural guidance and wise counsel you receive into both biblically sound and workplace-appropriate action. Philippians 4:9 makes clear what we have learned and heard from God is to be put into action. How to put Scriptural guidance and wise counsel into action in a work setting will not always be obvious. Consequently, in all cases it is important to remember the theme of this book as stated in Matthew 10:16. In the current context, that verse means Christians should be both wise and innocent when translating Scriptural guidance and wise counsel into practical action. This book is replete with examples of how to accomplish this.

When confronting faith-related dilemmas, it is only natural to want solutions right now. The temptations and pressures you are subjected to can seem unbearable at times. Consequently, you may feel like skipping the first four steps in the First-Response Model and going directly to the final step. <u>Do not do this</u>. Go through each step in the model in the order recommended. Approaching faith-related dilemmas in the manner prescribed in the model is the best way I know to produce positive results for yourself while honoring God in how you do it.

DISCUSSION CASE 1.1: "I'M NOT SURE I CAN DO THIS . . ."

When Martha returned to the classroom after being out of teaching for more than twenty years, she was shocked to learn how much things had changed. Martha was a math professor before her first child was born but resigned to stay home and raise a family that quickly grew to three children. With the children grown and in college, Martha agreed to fill an unexpected vacancy in the math department of her old university.

Martha had fond memories of the university. She completed her Ph.D. in math there many years before. As an award-winning student, Martha was immediately snapped up by the math department and made an assistant professor. By the time she resigned to raise a family, Martha was well on her way to becoming a tenured professor. Her memories of teaching and of her relations with other faculty members were all positive. Consequently, it was a shock for Martha to learn how much the university and the makeup of its faculty changed during her absence.

More than twenty years earlier, the university maintained an active, vibrant Christian student group. Martha was its faculty sponsor. But recently, a politically correct administration forced the group off the campus. As a result, its membership dwindled to a small handful of resolute young students. In those earlier years, Martha's faculty colleagues included a strong contingent of professing Christians. Her Christian colleagues were gone. Worse yet, they were replaced by ardent atheists and humanists who sneered at Christianity. Her atheist colleagues made it clear they refused to accept the existence of the God. Her humanist colleagues claimed the values of man predominate, not the principles of Scripture.

Where she once felt comfortable and accepted among her faculty peers, she now felt like an outcast. Further, she was an object of derision for the most vocal of her anti-Christian colleagues. When Martha approached her pastor for counseling, she began by telling him going to work every day felt like going to a funeral. Martha wasn't sure she could continue to work under the circumstances or that she even wanted to. She told her pastor, "I'm not sure I can do this anymore."

Discussion Questions

1. Have you ever been in a situation such as Martha's where being a Christian made you an outcast? If so, what were the circumstances?
2. If Martha came to you for help, what would you advise her to do? Should she just quit, or are there other things she might try first?

DISCUSSION CASE 1.2: "IT IS LIKE BEING PECKED TO DEATH BY DUCKS."

Devin liked his job and was good at it. However, as a Christian he often felt like a sheep among wolves. On one hand, his colleagues were not vocally opposed to Christianity. But on the other hand, they were not supportive of it either. There was nothing major Devin could put his finger on that made him uncomfortable at work. Rather, it was a thousand little things such as the snide comments, jokes, and lack of respect for his beliefs that bothered Devin. Describing his work life to a friend from church Devin said, "It is like being pecked to death by ducks."

Discussion Questions

1. Have you ever worked in a setting where your coworkers made it uncomfortable to be a Christian? If so, describe the situation and how you were made to feel uncomfortable because of your faith.

2. Explain how Devin could use the *First Response Model* to cope with his situation at work.

REVIEW QUESTIONS FOR GROUPS AND INDIVIDUALS

1. Explain why it is important to be willing to suffer for your faith in the short run.Explain what is meant by the following statement: *Success built on sin is not success at all.*
2. What does it mean to work for God first and your employer second?
3. Why should quitting your job when faith-related challenges arise at work typically be a last-resort option?
4. What is the ultimate challenge faced by Christians in the workplace?
5. Why is persevering in the faith always the right answer for Christians in the workplace?
6. What are some common forms of temptation and pressure Christians might confront in the workplace?
7. List and briefly explain each step in the *First-Response Model.*

CHAPTER TWO

DO NOT HIDE YOUR FAITH AT WORK—LIVE IT

"Keep your conduct among the Gentiles honorable, so that when they speak against you as evil doers, they may see your good deeds and glorify God on the day of visitation."

1 Peter 2:12

Some Christians who work in the midst of colleagues who reject their beliefs respond by hiding their faith. This is what Jan's friend and fellow Christian, Neesha, did. Jan wasn't sure what to do. Neesha was the only person on her work team who shared her Christian beliefs, but she was reluctant to admit it. Jan and Neesha attended the same church. Neesha even led a women's Bible study. But at work, Neesha hid her beliefs from her coworkers. In fact, she counseled Jan to do the same thing. According to Neesha, Jan would never be included in company social events or off-site business meetings if it got around she was a religious "fuddy-duddy." With no other Christians on her work team to turn to, Jan was beginning to feel like a sheep "in the midst of wolves." She wanted to stand firm in the faith on the job but was afraid doing so might undermine her career. After all, her boss had a reputation for being a "party animal." Jan was at a loss. She didn't know what to do.

The fact you are reading this book suggests you sometimes feel like a stranger in a strange land at work. Perhaps you are struggling with temptation. Maybe you are being pressured by coworkers to join them in questionable activities. Possibly your boss is trying to coerce you into doing things that would compromise your faith. Maybe you are feeling the lash of rejection from coworkers who do not share your beliefs. It could be you have a coworker who is struggling with a faith-related dilemma on the job and you would like to help. The workplace, with its many temptations and pressures, has always been fertile ground for Satan. He is the predator, you are his prey, and the workplace is one of his favorite hunting grounds.

As human beings, we are sinners. As sinners, we need little encouragement when it comes to acting out of hubris, self-interest, ego, envy, greed, misguided ambition, or other nefarious motives. Consequently, when we work in a hypercompetitive environment that only encourages these things, sin is going to be a problem. This is why the Bible warns us about what can happen when misguided competition brings out the worst in people. For example, recall in Mark 10:35–45 when James and John, the sons of Zebedee, got carried away by the temptation to compete for Christ's favor. Out of self-interest, ego, and misguided ambition, they wanted to sit with Christ on his glorious throne, one on his left and one on his right.

If the other disciples resented the presumptuousness of James and John, they need not have worried. Jesus quickly brought his two wayward disciples to heel when he told them if they wanted to lead they must first learn to be servants. He reminded them He, the son of God, came to serve, not to be served (Mark 10:42–45). Not surprisingly, the ways of Jesus are the opposite of what comes naturally to sinners, and we are all sinners. I am not criticizing when I refer to you, me, and everyone else as sinners. Rather, I am just stating a fact of which we must all be cognizant. Of course, even though we are sinners, there is an important difference between those of us who are in Christ and our unbelieving coworkers. As believers, we admit to being sinners in need of forgiveness and the saving grace of Christ. We also know we are to reflect the image of Christ, not the sinful nature of man, in how we work and live.

As Christians, we are not immune to sin. We are tempted to act just like James and John, to behave in ways at odds with the teachings of Scripture. Temptation is not just ever-present in the workplace, it is magnified by it. Rejecting sin in the workplace involves more than just struggling against temptation. It also involves (1) standing firm against pressure from coworkers and superiors to engage in sinful behavior, (2) bearing up when coworkers reject you because of your faith, and (3) continuing to treat coworkers in a Christ-like manner even when they do not reciprocate. The hard truth is, as Christians in the workplace, we face the daily challenge of trying to do our jobs in ways that reflect the image of Christ while working with people who reject Christ. In fact, some of the people you work with every day might even abhor your faith.

Added to the challenge of working in such an environment is the fact God expects us to do more than just hunker down and survive among unbelieving coworkers. He expects us to shine the light of Christ among them. It is not enough for us to just cope with the pressure, rejection, and temptation we are exposed to in the workplace. It is not enough for us to just defend our faith. We are supposed to be proactive and set an example that shows our coworkers a better way, the way of Christ.

The strategies presented in this book are provided to help you remain faithful to your Christian beliefs while working with people who don't share those beliefs. Staying faithful to your Christian beliefs in a setting that does not encourage or appreciate those beliefs will require sacrifice. Sacrifice, of course, is a fundamental aspect of Christianity. In fact, being willing to sacrifice for our faith is a form of worship. This is the message of Romans 12:1, where we are admonished to offer ourselves as living sacrifices to God. Consequently, it is important for you to be prepared to sacrifice for your beliefs, just as Christ sacrificed for us. However, as you ponder the frustrations and challenges of being a Christian among unbelievers, take comfort from what is written in Psalm 1:5–6. In these verses, we are told the Lord knows who is righteous and who is not and that the unrighteous will surely perish.

You have probably seen the warning in Psalm 1:5–6 come true many times over the course of your career. I certainly have. There have been many times when coworkers I knew for years saw their careers crash and burn because of their sinful actions, decisions, or behaviors. As sad as it is to observe an individual suffering the consequences of self-destructive choices, it is even sadder to contemplate that individual perishing for all eternity by rejecting the saving grace of Christ. That is why I stress throughout this book the need for you to set a consistent Christ-like example that shows your coworkers a better way, a way that can save their lives on earth and their souls for eternity.

The strategies provided in this book are based on the teachings of Scripture. In addition, they have been put to the test in the workplace and proven to be effective for use by Christians facing the kinds of trials, tribulations, and dilemmas you may be facing in your job. They include strategies I have used myself as well as strategies shared by Christians who have used them effectively in their jobs. However, before learning specific strategies, you have an important choice to make: In responding to the pressure, rejection, and temptation always present in the workplace, are you going to hide your faith or live it? Answering this simple but profound question is half the battle for Christians who work among people who do not share their faith.

THE COVERT CHRISTIAN

Covert Christians are what I call believers who hide their faith when working among unbelievers. Covert Christians avoid pressure, rejection, and persecution in the workplace by hiding their Christianity. They go along to get along. In this way, they avoid having their faith become an issue when working with unbelievers. They respond to pressure, rejection, and temptation in ways that don't rock the boat. Their approach to working with people who don't share their faith is to pull back into their shells and do whatever is necessary to fit in. The mistake covert Christians make is trying to please superiors, coworkers, and subordinates instead of Christ. Their attempts to please coworkers may be motivated by a desire to fit in, but more often than not they are motivated by fear, comfort, or ambition.

When Mark sought me out for counseling, he was embarrassed and ashamed. He had just returned from a business trip with his new boss, someone he hoped to impress for the purpose of career advancement. Unfortunately, to impress his boss Mark hid his Christian beliefs and did some things he later regretted. While on the trip, Mark learned his boss was a much different person out of town than when at home. Feeling pressure from his boss, Mark swallowed his objections and joined him in some questionable activities. Mark was feeling the pangs of remorse and guilt.

By putting coworkers ahead of God, covert Christians run afoul of Matthew 5:14–16. In these verses, we are admonished to let our light shine in ways that allow others to see our good works and how we use those good works to glorify God. As Christians, we are to shine our light, not hide it. This is not to say we are to spend our time at work sermonizing or handing out tracts. We are not. Rather, we are to shine our light in the workplace by setting a Christ-like example for our coworkers, one that shows them a better way. Our beliefs should be apparent in how we treat others, make decisions, do our work, and respond to adversity.

Before continuing, a caveat is in order. In referring to them as covert Christians, it is not my intention to belittle fellow believers who feel compelled to hide their faith in favor of social acceptance, job security, or career advancement. I understand how difficult it can be to excel at work without fitting in. Further, there is certainly nothing wrong with wanting to protect one's job security. I have worked in less-than-friendly environments to Christianity for many years. There have been times when my beliefs resulted in being left out of meetings, problem-solving sessions, and social activities that might have been career enhancing. Consequently, I understand the fears and frustrations of Christians who work with people who do not share their faith or, worse yet, are hostile to it.

Further, no one should be criticized for wanting to keep a job that provides for the material needs of a family. However, the ways in which we go about achieving job security and career success do matter. One of the goals of this book is to demonstrate it is possible for you to not just survive but thrive when working in the secular workplace and without being compromised. As Christians, we can excel while maintaining our faith. The key is to heed the admonition in Matthew 10:16. Another goal of this book is to demonstrate you don't have to adopt the covert approach to keep your job or to build a successful career. In fact, in the long run your Christian principles—if faithfully applied—will actually help you excel in your career.

I received some invaluable advice from a faithful Christian man when I first started my career. He could tell I felt like a fish out of water among my coworkers, all of whom were unbelievers. He invited me into his office for a chat. I told him I felt out of place and I didn't know how to act. He gave me some of the best advice I have ever received. He said, "You don't have to act. You are a child of God. No matter where you are or what you are doing, be who you are."

My final word on being a covert Christian is this approach can lead to some heart-breaking situations. A Christian I will call Andrew went out of town on a business trip that extended over a weekend. On Sunday, he sought out a church in his denomination and attended the 11:00 a.m. service. After the service, Andrew bumped into a coworker who was on the same business trip. Upon seeing Andrew coming out of church, the man made a comment no Christian would want to hear. He said: "I didn't know you are a believer." This comment struck Andrew like a sledgehammer. He later confided to his pastor the shame and embarrassment he felt over what his coworker's comment implied.

THE OVERT CHRISTIAN

I call Christians who consistently live their faith in all situations, *overt Christians*. Overt Christians choose what can be a difficult route when confronting the pressure, rejection, and temptation of the workplace. They choose to act in ways consistent with their faith. Overt Christians are guided by such Scriptural admonitions as 1 Corinthians 11:1, where Christ tells us to be imitators of Him. Imitating Christ means setting a Christ-like example in all we do. How we work, treat others, make decisions, and respond to challenges should reflect the image of Christ.

For overt Christians, appropriate responses to temptation, rejection, and pressure are those exemplifying the teachings of Scripture. They are responses that illustrate what is written in Titus 2:7. In this verse, we are told to show ourselves to be models of "good works." The verse also admonishes us to demonstrate "integrity" and "dignity" in our teaching.

Responding to temptation, rejection, and pressure in ways consistent with the example of Christ can be difficult, especially when working with people who don't share your beliefs. Secular humanism and its adjunct, political correctness, permeate the workplace. Admittedly, swimming upstream against the current of secular humanism is not easy. It can require sacrifice. I don't want to understate this fact. Although it is certainly true you must be prepared to sacrifice for your beliefs—even if this means losing or quitting your job—it is also true sacrificing your job should be the last option exercised in most cases. This is because what is needed more than anything in a sinful workplace is the leavening influence of faithful Christians.

Your coworkers, particularly the wolves, need to be exposed to a Christ-like example on a regular basis. You can be their example, but only if you are present among them. The importance of setting this kind of example is stressed in Philippians 3:17, where we are told to imitate Christ and follow the examples of others who imitate Christ. Your example might well be the only sermon some of your coworkers ever hear. Setting a consistent Christ-like example can be an effective way to evangelize on the job without violating the secular-humanist policies of a politically correct employer.

John was an overt Christian and an excellent certified public accountant (CPA) for a highly rated accounting firm. His boss, the firm's chief executive officer (CEO), liked John and knew he was someone who could help the company compete. But there was a problem. Many of the firm's larger clients liked to sample the nightlife when they were in town reviewing their accounts and they expected John and his colleagues to join them. John had no problem treating clients to a nice meal, but he drew the line at some of their more raucous activities. When his clients hit the nightclubs and bars, John bowed out and went home. When a large client complained about John's reluctance to join him for some after-hours partying, this committed believer found himself in the crosshairs of an angry boss.

By the time he was called on the carpet, John had prayed, sought Scriptural guidance, and discussed the situation with his pastor. Now all that remained was for John to respond to his boss in a manner both wise and innocent. In the meeting with his boss, John was respectful and humble, but firm. He explained that the types of things some of the firm's clients liked to do for fun violated his Christian beliefs. But he didn't stop there. He also explained the type of behavior the client in question liked to engage in would not pass the *front-page test*.

When his boss looked confused, John explained the front-page test was a simple method he used for evaluating all of his activities and decisions. The test amounts to asking yourself just one question: If your behavior in a given situation were to be reported on the front page of the local newspaper, complete with photos, would you be proud of yourself or embarrassed? John expressed doubt that the company's top CPA's being seen carousing in bars like college students on spring break would pass the front-page test. He also expressed doubt it would help the firm's image with the majority of its clients or the public in general. John explained the issue was bigger than just his personal beliefs. It was a matter that could affect the firm's credibility and corporate image.

The CEO listened to John but didn't respond. Saying only they would talk again later, he ended the meeting. After several days passed, the

CEO asked John to stop by his office. John, who had been waiting on pins and needles, didn't know if he was going to be reprimanded, demoted, or sacked. But he was determined to be steadfast. Regardless of what came next, he intended to remain faithful to his Christian beliefs. As soon as John was seated, the CEO handed him a document. Certain it was a letter of reprimand or worse, John began reading with trepidation. When John's face registered confusion, his boss—with just the hint of a smile—explained the document was a new corporate policy he was going to enact right away. The policy required all employees to apply the front-page test to their behavior when representing the firm in any capacity, during work and after hours.

John prevailed in this situation not just because he was resolute in defending his Christian beliefs, but because he was wise in how he did it. Rather than restrict his concerns to his religious beliefs, John showed how the issue was also about the credibility and image of the CPA firm. He explained his reservations against forays into bars and nightclubs in terms his CEO, an unbeliever, could understand. John's boss might not have appreciated the CPA's Christian beliefs, but he did appreciate how adhering to those beliefs could help the company he ran. By explaining his personal beliefs in terms to which the CEO could relate, John helped himself, but he also helped his employer.

There is a lesson in the example of John the CPA for all Christians who feel pressured by superiors or coworkers to compromise their beliefs. One of the keys to maintaining your faith without suffering repercussions is learning to be wise in how you respond when pressured to act inappropriately. Of course, you must also be innocent in how you respond. John was wise in how he responded to his boss, but he was also innocent. In this example, John was never dishonest or haughty. Everything he said to his boss was true and helpful. He stated his case humbly. Further, everything he recommended accorded with his Christian beliefs.

When responding to faith-related dilemmas in the workplace, remember Christ's admonition in Matthew 10:16. In defending his beliefs, John took this verse to heart. He was wise and innocent. John's was a biblically sound, workplace-appropriate response to faith-related pressure on the job. John's story demonstrates something working Christians should remember when trying to respond to faith-related dilemmas: Coworkers will not always respect your Christian beliefs, but they will respect their own self-interest. Ironically, their self-interest and your Christian beliefs often coincide. Sometimes being wise means showing others how their self-interest and your Christian beliefs correspond.

HOW YOU RESPOND TO FAITH-RELATED CHALLENGES MATTERS

There is one more point about responding to workplace temptation, rejection, and pressure that is important to understand. Being an overt Christian does not mean going to the opposite extreme of being a covert Christian. The opposite extreme of the covert response to workplace temptations and pressures is for the Christian to go on a vocal crusade, loudly condemning sinful behavior. Please understand that I am not making light of Christians who are vocal about their beliefs. After all, in Philippians 4:9, Christ tells us we are to practice the things we have learned from Him. As Christians, we are supposed to confront and reject sin wherever it occurs, including the workplace. But how we go about confronting and rejecting sin does matter, especially in the workplace.

When responding to faith-related challenges, the key is to make your point without making an enemy. When we interact with unbelievers, Christ wants us to be truthful and straightforward concerning His Word. But He also wants us to drive in the nail without breaking the board. Unbelievers are not likely to accept the teachings of Christ when they are delivered as an accusatory tirade. Setting a consistent Christ-like example for unbelievers in the workplace is more likely to bear fruit than upbraiding them.

Providing a consistent example of living out what the Bible teaches is a powerful response to workplace temptation, rejection, and pressure. Further, a good Christian example is an appropriate response in any setting. There may be organizational policies against openly evangelizing on the job, but there can be no policies against setting a good Christian example. Further, those who consistently model the Word of God are more likely to be invited by their coworkers to explain what the Word says about difficult situations arising on the job. Remember, although what you say to others about your Christian beliefs is important, your words will have more credibility when they are supported by your example.

The most effective approach for showing others a better way is to do just that: show them. People respond more positively to actions than to words. Your colleagues are more likely to be *led* into the arms of Christ than *talked* into them. Christians who spend their time on the job vocally evangelizing while neglecting their work set the wrong example for those who, if shown a better example, might see the light.

DISCUSSION CASE 2.1: "I WANT TO SHINE MY LIGHT AT WORK BUT . . ."

Jane knew she owed her life to Christ. Upon losing her husband to cancer, she suddenly found herself not just a widow but the sole breadwinner for a family of three young boys. Her grief and despair were beyond anything she could have imagined. Six months after her husband's death, she hit rock bottom emotionally. Not only did Jane feel like she could no longer go on, she didn't even want to. In despair, she contemplated suicide. At this low point in her life, she had nothing left to hold onto but her faith in Christ, so Jane held onto that with every ounce of strength she could muster. With the help of prayer and the support of her church, Jane finally turned a corner and started rebuilding her life.

Just before the life insurance money ran out, Jane was able to find a job. To her surprise, she also found she was good at the job and liked doing it. Things began to look up for her, but there was one fly in the ointment: The company she worked for did not provide the most welcoming environment for her Christian beliefs. In fact, her supervisor's oft-stated motto was, "At ABC, Inc. we work hard, and we play hard." It was the playing hard part of the motto causing Jane problems. It sometimes created situations that ran counter to her Christian beliefs.

Jane was torn. Her faith was important to her, but so was her job. She needed the job to support her family. Consequently, when her boss became angry because she begged off joining her coworkers in some questionable after-hours activities, Jane became concerned. Although her boss didn't say anything, Jane could tell from his attitude her refusal to participate was not appreciated. She also began to receive some not-so-subtle ribbing from her coworkers about not being a team player.

Before long Jane found herself hiding her Christianity at work. She began to go along with the crowd, all the while feeling guilty about compromising her beliefs. When the double life became too much of a burden, Jane scheduled a meeting with her pastor. She told him frankly, "I want to shine my light at work, but every time I refuse to go along with my boss, I get serious pushback. I want to model my beliefs at work, but I can't afford to lose this job or to run the risk of not getting future raises or promotions. I am barely making ends meet as it is."

Discussion Questions

1. Have you ever felt pressured to hide your Christian beliefs at work? If so, how did this pressure manifest itself? How did you deal with the pressure?
2. If Jane came to you for counsel, what advice would you give her?
3. How could Jane apply the *First-Response Model* from Chapter 1 in this case?

DISCUSSION CASE 2.2: "WHAT YOU ARE ASKING ME TO DO IS WRONG"

Most of the school's faculty members agreed with their principal's proposed solution to the intractable problem they all faced. It would be more accurate to say some faculty members agreed with the principal while others agreed, out of desperation, that there was no choice but to go along with his proposal. However, Mack was a minority of one. He disagreed strongly with what the principal was asking the faculty to do. In fact, Mack not only disagreed, he openly opposed the principal's plan.

What the principal wanted the faculty to do violated Mack's most deeply held beliefs about right and wrong, not to mention the Ninth

Commandment. The principal's plan put Mack in a difficult position. The rest of the teachers at his school were tired of being penalized for things they could not control. In addition to making things better, the solution their principal was recommending would allow the teachers to get back at the State Department of Education for creating an unrealistic, unfair accountability system.

The Department of Education, in passing the "School Accountability Bill," created an impossible situation for teachers in the state's poorer school districts. As part of the School Accountability Bill, student performance on standardized tests taken at the end of the seventh and tenth grades was being used to rate local schools as A, B, C, D, or F institutions. Schools rated D or F were penalized financially. Schools rated A or B were rewarded financially. Schools rated C received neither penalties nor rewards.

To the Department of Education and the general public, the rating system seemed fair and appropriate. On the surface, it appeared to be a system of accountability based on merit. Greater performance meant greater rewards. Correspondingly, lesser performance meant lesser rewards or even penalties. But what the rating system did not take into account was socioeconomic factors that introduced bias into the system. It was well known among teachers, as a general rule, that students who came from highly educated families in the more affluent neighborhoods did better in school than those who came from less educated, poorer families.

Consequently, not all first graders were at the same level academically when they began school, nor did they receive the same amount of help or quality of support from parents as they progressed through school. These inherent inequities tended to carry through each grade level throughout school. Accordingly, the rating system based on student performance was biased in favor of schools located in the more upscale, affluent communities where the better-educated families lived. It was biased against schools in the poorer neighborhoods.

During a meeting with Department of Education officials, teachers argued schools should be rated on the basis of progress made by students, not their relative performance on standardized tests. They argued teachers who taught students who started below their grade level faced a bigger challenge than those who taught students who were ahead of it the day they started school. Unfortunately, their arguments fell on deaf ears. Consequently, the sole criterion for ranking schools was the average performance on standardized tests of all students tested in a given year for a given school.

Mack's school was located in a poor community where most families were headed by single parents with less than a high school education. The school dropout rate was high, crime was common, and drug use was epidemic. Consequently, as a rule, the students at Mack's school did not fare well on the standardized tests given at the end of the seventh and tenth grades. After two years of seeing funding lost because of his school's F rating, Mack's principal was growing despondent. He tried to explain to state legislators the inherent unfairness of the rating system they enacted but to no avail. Finally, in an act of desperation he called an off-the-record meeting of the school's faculty and suggested they "give their students some help" during the tests.

Some faculty members were so angry over the unfairness of the accountability system they agreed with the principal. Others were simply willing to go along because they didn't know what else to do. All faculty members were tired of missing out on raises and having their instructional budgets cut because of the financial penalties assessed against D and F schools. Consequently, Mack—the lone dissenter—stood out like a sore thumb among his colleagues. Mack's fellow teachers, many of them close friends, tried to persuade him to join them in carrying out the principal's recommendation, but Mack steadfastly refused. His response was always the same: "This is wrong. There must be a better way."

The principal was reluctant to go forward with his solution unless the faculty was unanimous in accepting his recommendation. Consequently, the pressure on Mack from the principal and his fellow teachers was intense. When the principal asked for a private meeting with him, Mack knew things would not go well. The principal could not fire Mack, but he did have the power to make his life miserable. In addition to giving Mack the bulk of the distasteful extracurricular assignments normally rotated among the faculty, he could recommend to the superintendent that Mack be transferred to another school—one farther from his home.

After listening to the principal explain how the financial penalties from being rated an F school hurt students, Mack became too confused and tongue-tied to give a coherent response. He faced a real dilemma. On the one hand, he was sure what the principal was asking the faculty to do was wrong. On the other hand, he did not want to be the cause of his school having to close down music, art, and sports programs in order to balance a declining budget. Nor did he want to be the cause of his fellow teachers being denied a badly needed salary increase. As a Christian, Mack knew cheating was wrong, even if done for the right reasons.

All Mack could manage to say to the principal was, "What you are asking me to do is wrong. There must be a better way." Consequently, for the remainder of the meeting, Mack sat mute while his principal portrayed him as disloyal and stubborn. The strongest point the principal made was he would agree with Mack if the accountability system imposed on them was fair, but it wasn't, and Mack knew it wasn't. He told Mack that by refusing to go along with the plan he was hurting the school, the faculty, and the students. He also told Mack his "antiquated views of right and wrong" were naïve and they had no place in the real world the principal was forced to work in. Confused and torn, Mack decided to schedule an appointment with his pastor. He needed help. He prayed often and sought guidance in Scripture, but Mack still did not know what to do.

Discussion Questions

1. Have you ever found yourself in a situation such as Mack's where you felt it was you against the world because of your religious beliefs? What was the moral dilemma you

faced and how did you respond? Looking back on this experience, are you satisfied with your response? If not, what should you have done?

2. Mack did not handle his meeting with the principal well. What advice would you give Mack for handling a follow-up meeting better?

3. Does Christ's admonition to His disciples in Matthew 10:16 apply in Mack's case? If so, how?

REVIEW QUESTIONS FOR INDIVIDUALS AND GROUPS

1. What are some of the pressures in the workplace that might lead people to hide their Christianity, to be covert Christians?

2. Have you ever worked with someone and been surprised to learn he or she is a believer? How did this make you feel about the individual in question?

3. Are there any consistent Christians in your workplace? How do they *let their light shine*? How do others in the workplace respond to these Christians?

4. Have you ever been pressured by coworkers to join them in sinful endeavors? How did you respond?

5. Have you ever felt pressured by a superior to do something that violates your conscience? How did you respond?

6. Does your organization have corporate policies that discourage open displays of Christianity on the job?

7. Does your organization have a corporate ethics statement or a statement of core values? If so, what principles are covered by these statements? Can these principles be traced back to Scripture?

8. Has your job security ever been jeopardized because of your Christian beliefs? If so, how?

9. Have you ever had to be "wise as serpents" when responding to pressure from coworkers or superiors to act inappropriately? Explain.
10. What is the biggest challenge you have faced in trying to be a consistent Christian in your workplace?

CHAPTER 3

SET A 1 CORINTHIANS 13 EXAMPLE FOR YOUR COWORKERS

"So now faith, hope, and love abide . . . but the greatest of these is love."

1 Corinthians 13:13

Maria's father was a pastor who raised her to treat people the way she wanted to be treated. Up to now, she always followed her father's advice and benefitted from doing so. But having to deal with a coworker who was self-serving, dishonest, and manipulative was testing her faith. Maria was finding it difficult to show Christian love to someone who was so unlovable. Her coworker was a master of office politics who used manipulation, spreading of rumors, and lying to curry favor with her supervisor while undermining the work of her teammates. Maria knew she was supposed to be long-suffering, kind, and patient with this wolf in sheep's clothing, but what she wanted to do was give her coworker a piece of her mind. If not that, she wanted to at least avoid her. When Maria discussed the problem with her father, he took out his well-worn Bible and read 1 Corinthians 13 to her. Then he told her, "Maria, you haven't really given biblical love until you have given it to the unlovable."

As human beings, it is tempting to associate only with people whose worldviews agree with ours. It's is only natural. After all, there is comfort in common ground. However, as Christians, you and I are called to interact positively with people of all worldviews, believers and unbelievers. Associating positively with unbelievers does not require you to condone inappropriate behavior, nor does it mean compromising your faith in order to get along with them. Rather, it means interacting in ways that reflect the image of Christ rather than segregating yourself from those who don't know Him.

Ideally, when our coworkers see us in action, they will see Christ in us. Think of it this way. We are children of God the Father. Shouldn't there be a family resemblance? As children of God, we should reflect the image of Christ in all we do. The Bible is replete with guidance concerning the importance of setting a good example. In fact, James 4:17 makes clear that knowing the right thing to do but failing to do it is a sin. Therefore, not only is setting a Christ-like example the right thing to do, failing to set such an example is a sin.

For Christians, doing the "right thing" as stated in James 4:17 means doing what is pleasing to God. This verse makes no exceptions for the times when you are dealing with unbelievers. Unfortunately, you cannot count on your coworkers being Christians. Inevitably, some are going to be agnostics, some will be unbelievers, and some will be *wolves.* Wolves in the workplace, like their namesakes in the wild, are predatory. They are concerned only about satisfying their appetites, ambitions, and self-interest. Those who do not follow the pack or, worse yet, get in the way of it sometimes become the prey. When you are attacked by a coworker who is a wolf, it is only natural to want to respond in kind. I fully understand the bite-back impulse. In fact, I struggle with it myself. In situations such as this, the Marine in me comes out and I want to counterattack. Not only do I want to bite back, I want to bite harder.

As appealing as this kind of response can be when you are attacked by a predatory coworker, it is the opposite of how we, as Christians, should respond. A better response is one pleasing to Christ, one that reflects His love as defined in 1 Corinthians 13. Learning to respond in this way will not be easy. If you are like me, it will be downright difficult. However, it might make you feel better to know that setting a Christ-like example does not mean allowing predatory coworkers to use you as a doormat, as is demonstrated throughout the remainder of this book. Rather, it means standing firm in your faith and setting the type of example that might convince your coworkers there is a better way.

Misty was especially good at showing 1 Corinthians love to customers as well as to coworkers, even those who were determined to be unlovable. She worked in a competitive business—new car sales—where her coworkers were the competition. The owner of the dealership had a rule that almost guaranteed sales personnel would poach customers from each other, lie to customers, and engage in other nefarious acts. It was known as the *up-or-out rule*. When quarterly sales figures were reviewed, those in the top quartile of sales were given bonuses. Those in the bottom quartile were given pink slips. The rule created a dog-eat-dog environment at the dealership. Surprisingly, Misty thrived in this environment, and not by poaching customers from her coworkers or lying to buyers. In fact, just the opposite.

Misty treated her fellow sales representatives the way she wanted them to treat her. In addition, she was honest, forthright, and helpful to customers. She worked hard and smart at keeping her own sales numbers up, but she also helped coworkers who were struggling. Misty understood that much of the bad behavior she witnessed in her fellow sales representatives was driven by desperation. Like her, they needed their jobs to support themselves and their families. As a result, she would occasionally hand off customers to fellow sales representatives who were in danger of receiving a pink slip. Misty's kindness did not go unnoticed.

In fact, Misty's commitment to demonstrating the kind of love described in 1 Corinthians 13 insulated her from the bad behavior of her fellow sales representatives.

When Misty was the top sales representative four quarters in a row, the owner of the dealership asked her, "What is your secret?" She explained her approach to dealing with customers and coworkers. Shocked by what he heard, the owner questioned the other sales representatives. Each of them had a story to tell about how Misty was not just a good sales representative but also a good coworker. When Misty was top sales representative for the fifth quarter in a row, the owner decided to change his approach. He would get rid of the up-or-out rule and replace it with a sales approach based on collaboration, cooperation, and mutual assistance. In other words, he implemented Misty's approach to sales. Within six months of implementing the new approach, the dealership increased its overall sales by 17 percent.

1 CORINTHIANS 13 AS THE FOUNDATION OF YOUR CHRIST-LIKE EXAMPLE

1 Corinthians 13 is the Bible's classic exposition on the subject of love. Consequently, when trying to set a Christ-like example in the workplace, this chapter of Scripture is an essential reference. A Christ-like example must rest on a foundation of biblical love, and 1 Corinthians 13 contains Christ's definition of the concept. Any other foundation will crumble like sand. Only if your example is based on the kind of love described in 1 Corinthians 13 will you be able to endure the inevitable faith-related trials that crop up in the workplace. Further, only if your example is based on this kind of love will it pass the test of James 4:17 (knowing the right thing to do but not doing it is a sin).

The type of love described in 1 Corinthians 13 has nine characteristics, all of which have specific application in the workplace. These nine characteristics are:

- Long-suffering
- Kindness

- Not jealous or envious
- Not boastful
- Not arrogant
- Becoming in its actions
- Seeks the good of others rather than seeking its own
- Not provoked
- Keeps no records of wrong done by others

Setting an example that exemplifies these characteristics will be difficult in the best circumstances. However, it will be especially difficult when working with wolves in sheep's clothing who wouldn't think twice about devouring you if doing so served their perceived self-interest. However, the closer you come to incorporating the love of 1 Corinthians 13 into the example you set for coworkers, the more effective your example will be. Even more important, the closer you come to incorporating the love of 1 Corinthians 13 into your example, the more pleasing your example will be to Christ.

The best advice I ever received concerning setting a Christ-like example in the workplace came from a wise Christian friend. He was a colleague who enjoyed a long and successful career. My friend was finishing his career as I was starting mine. Frustrated by the behavior I observed in some of my new coworkers, including my boss, I sought this good man's counsel. He told me in the long run the best way to deal with the sinful behavior of coworkers was to (1) refuse to participate in it and (2) show them a better way by setting a consistent Christ-like example.

When I responded that setting a Christ-like example among my new coworkers would be difficult, he didn't argue. In fact, he agreed with me. Then he asked me if I was familiar with 1 Corinthians 13. When I commented 1 Corinthians 13 was about love, he just smiled and nodded. He was silent for what seemed a long time. Finally, my friend told me something I have never forgotten. He said, "There are going to be people who will treat you poorly on the job no matter what you do. But, it is harder for people to treat you poorly when you treat them with love." As things turned out, he was right. Not everyone responds positively to a good example, but many do. In fact, my experience has been that more will respond positively than won't.

Lessons abound in 1 Corinthians 13 for those of us who are called to set a Christ-like example in the workplace. Verse 1 tells us no matter how well or how truthfully we speak, if our words are not spoken in love, they are like a "noisy gong" or a "clanging cymbal." When you disagree with colleagues, doing so in a considerate, caring, and respectful manner will provide a powerful example of Christian forbearance for others. It will, no doubt, also be a welcome change for people who are accustomed to being attacked by those who disagree with them. The number of people who have learned to disagree without being disagreeable is, unfortunately, small.

All too often workplace disagreements go awry as the volume increases and the narrative becomes personal. Those who disagree in a disagreeable manner often sound like a noisy gong or a clanging cymbal. Learning to disagree without being disagreeable is a prerequisite for those who want to set a Christ-like example. Your ability to do this will be welcomed by your coworkers, even those who don't practice it themselves. Learning to disagree without being disagreeable is so important to Christians in the workplace it is treated in more depth later in this book.

Verses 4–6 describe love as being "patient and kind." These verses also explain what love is not. It is not envious or boastful, "arrogant or rude," set on getting its own way, or "irritable or resentful." Further, love rejoices in the truth rather than "wrongdoing." Few among us, regardless our religious convictions, are averse to receiving this kind of love. The reason Paul's words resonate even today is that in the workplace, as in life, there are likely to be impatient, unkind, jealous, boastful, arrogant, and rude people who insist on getting their way and who seem to take pleasure in behaving badly. These are the *wolves* in the workplace. They are the types of people Paul wrote about in Romans 1:29–31, where he mentions "gossips," "slanderers," "haters of God," "insolent," "haughty," "boastful," "inventors of evil," "disobedient to parents," "foolish," "faithless," "heartless," and "ruthless." I cannot read these verses without thinking Paul must have somehow worked in some of the organizations where I have worked.

By setting a Christ-like example personifying 1 Corinthians 13, you can be a welcome antidote to people who seem to take pleasure in behaving badly. Ironically, even those who are impatient, unkind, jealous, boastful, irritable, arrogant, and rude themselves do not like to work with others who are guilty of the same sins. Likewise, those who insist on having their own way and who become irritable when their selfish actions are thwarted do not like to work with selfish people. When people set themselves up as little gods, they tend to overlook their own transgressions while condemning the same transgressions in others. This is an easy trap to fall into, which is why we were given the admonition in Matthew 7:5 to take the log out of our own eye before condemning someone else for the speck in theirs. It is always easier to recognize faults in others than in ourselves. Remembering this biblical truth will set you apart from your unbelieving coworkers in ways even they will appreciate.

In committing to model Christ in ways that exemplify 1 Corinthians 13, you are agreeing to demonstrate a love that serves others before self. But how does one translate this kind of love into practical action in the workplace? The following list contains examples of specific things you can do to translate 1 Corinthians 13 into practical action on the job:

- Help others who need help
- Listen attentively to others when they need to talk
- Be willing to forgive and ask for forgiveness
- Rejoice in the successes of others
- Be humble and share the credit when receiving recognition for a job well done
- Support others who are right even when doing so is difficult
- Be willing to sacrifice to help coworkers, your team, and the organization
- Refuse to mistreat others

- Refuse to encourage others to do wrong
- Refuse to take pleasure in the misfortune of others
- Refuse to embarrass others by saying or doing things that make them look or feel foolish
- Refuse to abuse others emotionally or physically
- Refuse to wish misfortune on others
- Refuse to take part in office gossip

As you can see from these examples, being a 1 Corinthians 13 Christian will never be easy. The most difficult part, of course, is to be loving, patient, and kind to those who do not reciprocate. However, although it is true exemplifying the behaviors recommended in verses 4–6 is no guarantee of reciprocal treatment, it is also true that it is harder for people to treat you poorly when you treat them well. Patience and long-suffering will no doubt be necessary as you struggle to set a Christ-like example day after day. When you become frustrated with setting a good example in an environment where people do not reciprocate, think of what is written in Galatians 6:9, where we are told to avoid becoming weary in doing good because our reward will come in God's good time if we persevere.

A caveat is in order here. As was mentioned earlier, setting a 1 Corinthians 13 example in the workplace does not require you to meekly allow people to abuse you. As Christians, we are not called to be helpless dupes. Rather, setting a Christ-like example means showing others the image of Christ in how you respond when they treat you badly. In workplace disagreements, those who fight fire with fire just make a bigger fire. As Christians, we are to confront and reject sin in any setting. But how we go about this is important. When responding to those who treat you badly in the workplace, remember the admonition in Proverbs 25:21–22, where we are told to feed our enemy if he is hungry and give him water if he is thirsty. This verse reminds us doing these things will "heap burning coals" on the head of our adversary on the one hand and bring us rewards from God on the other.

HEAPING BURNING COALS ON THE HEAD OF YOUR ADVERSARY

Susan was rude to everyone in her department to the point of belliger-ence. She was loud, pushy, and insistent on getting her way. In fact, Susan could be downright obnoxious. As a result, her coworkers avoided her. Susan was good at her job and at hiding her negativity from the depart-ment's supervisor. Consequently, she received excellent performance appraisals. Her boss thought she was great, but her coworkers dreaded even being around her. For some reason, which was unknown to her coworkers, Susan was an angry, bitter person.

The only individual in the department who seemed able to cope with Susan was Melinda. Susan treated Melinda the same way she treated everyone: badly. But unlike their coworkers, Melinda never lost her temper with Susan and never responded in kind. Instead, she quietly but firmly stood her ground with Susan while treating her with kindness. Melinda, a devout Christian, sensed Susan's gruff exterior was just an act to cover up insecurity or, perhaps, problems in her personal life. Susan never mentioned problems at home or anything else about her life, but Melinda had seen this kind of behavior before. In her experience, it almost always signaled personal problems or insecurity or both.

In addition to avoiding Susan, her coworkers shunned her. They refused to sit with her in the break room or invite her to join them for Friday lunches, a popular office tradition. When Susan's coworkers grumbled among themselves about her negativity, Melinda always encouraged them to try to see beyond her outward rudeness and be patient with her. Melinda was certain that beneath Susan's gruff exterior there was a different person, one who needed help. Melinda's idea of how to deal with difficult people was to treat them well and let God do the rest.

In an attempt to break through Susan's gruff façade, Melinda tried to engage her in conversation during breaks. She also made a point of inviting her to lunch on Fridays, just the two of them. But Melinda's efforts bore no fruit. With every attempt at reaching her angry coworker,

Melinda was rudely rebuffed. This continued for months with no change. Frustrated but undeterred, Melinda prayed continually for Susan and for her own forbearance. She also sought out helpful Scripture verses about persevering in the faith. Melinda's favorite verse, one she went back to again and again, was Romans 5:3–4. This is the classic biblical passage on persevering in the faith. In these verses, we are admonished to actually rejoice in suffering because suffering builds endurance that, in turn, builds character. Further, character gives us hope, and hope is most needed most in times of suffering.

Melinda also sought advice from her pastor and other members of her church. Her pastor shared the words of James 1:12 with her. This verse offers comfort when we are facing difficulties, reminding us to remain "steadfast under trial" for by doing so we will "receive the crown of life" as God has promised. Then he told Melinda she should be thankful God chose to use her as His emissary in this situation and that she should remember God never gives His children more than they can handle. Renewed in hope, Melinda continued to patiently absorb the anger seeping out of Susan like steam from a broken pipe.

After a full year of absorbing angry rebuffs and rude put-downs, Melinda's Christian forbearance was beginning to wear thin. Frankly, she felt like grabbing Susan by the shoulders and shaking her. But praying and reading Scripture always gave her renewed hope and the will to persevere. Then one day, out of the blue, Susan stopped by her desk and asked if she was free for lunch on Friday. Masking her surprise, Melinda quickly accepted. She and Susan had lunch together that Friday and for many Fridays thereafter. At one point, Susan asked Melinda how she managed to persevere so steadfastly through the rudeness and anger she directed at her. That was the opening Melinda prayed for, the opening that allowed her to share her faith with Susan, which she did.

Over time, as she became more and more comfortable with Melinda, Susan began to open up. She eventually explained why she was so bitter. Predictably, her negative attitude was just a defense for feelings of insecurity tied to family problems she had growing up in a home with an abusive father and an alcoholic mother. To escape the toxic environment of her home, Susan moved out and married at a young age. The marriage soon ended in divorce, leaving Susan alone and the sole breadwinner for two young children. With no family support, Susan faced the difficulties that go with working full-time while still trying to be both mother and father to her young children. The more problems she had in her personal life, the angrier she became. The angrier she became, the more bitterness she displayed at work.

Sensing an opportunity, Melinda invited Susan to come to church with her. Melinda explained her most reliable support base was her church family. Susan surprised her by accepting the invitation. By God's grace, Susan eventually became a committed Christian. Her personal problems did not just go away, but as a member of a church family, she did at least have more support in dealing with them. At long last, she also had the help needed to cope when things were not going well. The more engaged she became in church, prayer, and reading the Bible, the more her attitude improved at work. Susan eventually became one of the best-liked employees in her company. She and Melinda remain fast friends and Christian sisters.

Of course, situations of this nature will not always turn out as well as Susan's did, but one thing is certain: Susan's situation would not have turned out the way it did without the consistent example and steadfast perseverance of a committed Christian. The positive outcome in Susan's case was possible because Melinda committed to setting a Christ-like example of caring, kindness, and forbearance rather than responding in-kind to a bitter person whose anger was a cry for help.

Melinda evangelized by example long enough to convince Susan to ask about the source of her forbearance, commitment, and positive attitude. Once Susan asked, Melinda was able to share her faith as the source of her strength. That was the message Susan needed all along. What was missing in Susan's life was someone willing to look past her gruff exterior to the real Susan, the one who was hiding her pain and frustration behind a façade of anger.

AN OUNCE OF PREVENTION CAN BE WORTH A POUND OF CURE

The story of Susan and Melinda demonstrates how setting a Christ-like example based on 1 Corinthians 13 can be an effective response to sin in the workplace. But there is another side to setting a Christ-like example. A consistent example of demonstrating the kind of love described in 1 Corinthians 13 can also be an effective preventive measure for warding off temptation, rejection, hostility, and even persecution. Setting a Christ-like example in how you treat people, do your work, make decisions, face adversity, solve problems, and conduct yourself—even when no one in authority is watching—can help minimize your exposure to faith-related dilemmas in the workplace.

Those who set a consistent example of integrity, honesty, trustworthiness, fairness, self-discipline, commitment, sacrifice, service, caring, perseverance, and love are less likely to be tempted or pressured to do things that would violate their faith. A Christ-like example based on 1 Corinthians 13 will not exempt you from the temptations and pressures of the workplace, but it can reduce your exposure to them. The good news is the fewer faith-related dilemmas you face at work, the more mental energy you can devote to doing your job well and evangelizing by example and word when appropriate.

Setting a consistent example of living and working in accordance with your professed beliefs can be that ounce of prevention worth a pound of cure. This is yet another reason why we, as Christians, should shine our lights in the workplace. In many cases, superiors, coworkers, or subordinates who would otherwise pressure or tempt you to sin will either respect the Christian beliefs you model every day or be sufficiently forewarned by them to leave you out of their nefarious shenanigans. Of course, not everyone will respond in this way. Otherwise, there would be no need for this book. Consequently, as Christians, we should understand although setting a Christ-like example in the workplace will help reduce the number of faith-related challenges we must face, it is not likely to eliminate them altogether.

A Christian professional I will call Luke once told me he had to deal with temptation, rejection, and persecution only rarely at work. He attributed this welcome circumstance to his steadfast commitment to setting a Christ-like example for his coworkers. Because of his consistent example, coworkers knew who Luke was and what he believed. They also knew he worked and lived in accordance with his beliefs. On business trips, Luke was never invited to join his coworkers in their bar-hopping forays. In the office, he was never invited to join others in questionable activities that distracted from the jobs they were supposed to be doing. Coworkers never asked Luke to look the other way so they could sneak out of the office early while claiming to have worked a full day. Luke was simply excluded when his coworkers planned to engage in questionable activities.

There were times, of course, when Luke's example did not spare him from faith-related trials. He once had a supervisor who wanted his direct reports to inflate their sales figures to make the department's monthly performance reports look more impressive. Luke was the only member of the department who refused to go along. The pressure on him to join in distorting sales figures was intense. As a result, Luke endured some rough sledding at work. The bad times lasted for several months. However, in the end the supervisor thought better of the idea and simply dropped it. It probably didn't hurt that Luke gave his supervisor a copy of a business article about the highly publicized downfall of a once-successful sales manager. The sales manager in the article saw his credibility, and eventually his career, undermined as a result of playing fast and loose with the numbers in his monthly sales reports.

On another occasion, Luke was invited to lunch repeatedly by a female colleague with who he worked closely for several years. This colleague—I will call her Julie—was attractive, smart, and successful. She and Luke made a good team at work and were known by others in their department as the "dynamic duo." Luke felt a strong attraction to Julie and wanted badly to accept her invitations to lunch. He was single, so the allure of a relationship with this attractive, successful woman was strong. But there was a problem. Julie was married.

Luke knew Julie's marriage was in trouble and her husband was being unfaithful to her. He empathized with Julie and felt a strong sense of protectiveness and compassion toward her. But Luke was a committed Christian whose views on adultery were carved in stone when Moses received the tablets. He knew if he and Julie started seeing each other outside work the relationship would probably become increasingly intimate. Although Julie's invitations tormented him for weeks, Luke persevered in kindly and gently refusing them. In the meantime, he prayed, read his Bible, and even discussed the situation with his pastor. Finally, Luke talked openly and forthrightly with Julie about why he felt compelled to turn down her invitations. To his surprise, she accepted the explanation graciously, saying she understood. As a result, they were able to continue working well together as the dynamic duo.

Like all Christians in the workplace, Luke's beliefs were tested from time to time. But by standing firm in his faith and setting a consistent Christ-like example, Luke managed to limit the number of occasions when he was tempted, rejected, or persecuted. His Christ-like example was the ounce of prevention worth a pound of cure. Some of his colleagues respected his example, whereas others simply chalked him up to being, in their words, "a lost cause." In any case, the number of times he had to cope with faith-related dilemmas was minimized because his Christ-like example showed coworkers where he stood and what he stood for.

Unfortunately, even those Christians who consistently set a positive example of shining their lights in the workplace will still face challenges. As Luke's story shows, there will still be occasions when Christians, in spite of their examples, will be pressured and tempted to engage in behaviors that would compromise their beliefs. There may even be times when Christians will have to endure persecution for refusing to compromise. When these things happen, it is important to avoid rash responses fueled by anger, frustration, or fear. The more often we, as Christians, respond to sin-related dilemmas calmly, systematically, and biblically, the better the eventual results will be. The *First-Response Model* explained in Chapter 1 coupled with a consistent Christ-like example will help you respond to temptation, rejection, and persecution at work in ways that will improve your chances of enjoying a positive outcome.

DISCUSSION CASE 3.1: "I DIDN'T KNOW IT WOULD BE LIKE THIS."

Lois was an alumna of a well-known Christian college with a reputation for turning out excellent graduates, particularly in the field of finance. Consequently, she was aggressively recruited by numerous financial management companies and several banks. When she accepted her job as a financial manager and advisor for a nationwide investment firm, Lois thought she had embarked on an interesting career with a worthy employer. She particularly liked the company's corporate culture statement that emphasized such values as honesty, integrity, trust, and dependability.

Unfortunately, her supervisor and several investment brokers in the office Lois was assigned to treated the company's corporate culture statement like a suggestion rather than a policy. Lois barely completed her orientation before her supervisor began to casually suggest she adopt some questionable practices for managing client accounts, strategies Lois viewed as unethical. When she asked several others in her office about the questionable practices, Lois was told they were often used by most of the financial managers who worked for the supervisor in question. Lois learned her supervisor did not insist his team members engage in these practices, but rewards and recognition always seemed to go to those who did. As she walked back to her office after discussing the situation with another member of her team, Lois thought to herself, "I didn't know it would be like this."

Discussion Questions

1. Have you ever felt subtly pressured to engage in work practices that would compromise your faith?

2. Do you think Lois could help her situation by setting a
   1 Corinthians 13 example for her supervisor and teammates?

3. If Lois came to you for wise counsel, what would you
   advise her to do?

DISCUSSION CASE 3.2: "YOUR EXAMPLE IS THE BEST DEFENSE . . ."

Mike had not been a construction foreman long before the pressure to
cut corners on safety began to rear its ugly head. The construction company Mike worked for had a reputation for completing projects right,
on time, and within budget. This reputation made the company competitive and brought it plenty of work, even in recessionary times. Consequently, the company's higher management team guarded its reputation
assiduously. When a project fell behind schedule, the company's management team was willing to do almost anything to get it back on track,
including cutting corners on safety. So far there were no major injuries
or deaths as a result of ignoring safety procedures, but Mike knew it was
only a matter of time. After all, there were several near-miss
events recently.

   So far Mike was able to keep all his projects on schedule and under
budget, but he was hearing some disturbing stories from his fellow foremen whose projects fell behind. Mike knew it was only a matter of time
before some factor completely out of his control caused one of his projects
to fall behind schedule. When it happened, would the construction
superintendent pressure him to ignore safety procedures? He hoped not
but wanted to be prepared just in case. In truth, Mike wasn't sure what
he could do to prevent this eventuality. However, he did remember being
told by a fellow Christian years earlier when he first began his career,
"Your example is the best defense you have against the pressures and
temptations you are going to be subjected to on the job."

Discussion Questions

1. Have you ever been in a situation in which you were pressured to cut corners to get your work done on time? If so, how did you respond?
2. Do you think Mike could use setting a 1 Corinthians 13 example as an ounce of prevention in this case?
3. If Mike came to you for wise counsel, what would you advise him to do?

REVIEW QUESTIONS FOR INDIVIDUALS AND GROUPS

1. Why is it important for 1 Corinthians 13 to be the starting point for setting a Christ-like example in the workplace?
2. How does 1 Corinthians 13 apply to those who are trying to learn how to disagree without being disagreeable?
3. What is meant by the phrase ". . . a love that does not seek its own"? How does this phrase apply to setting a consistent Christ-like example?
4. What is typically the most difficult aspect of applying the kind of love described in 1 Corinthians 13 in the workplace?
5. Explain how the phrase "An ounce of prevention is worth a pound of cure" applies to setting a consistent Christ-like example in the workplace.

CHAPTER 4

BE A SERVANT LEADER AMONG YOUR COWORKERS

"... If anyone would come after me, let him deny himself, and take up his cross and follow me."

Matthew 16:24

Mack grew up watching John Wayne movies with his father. To him, John Wayne was the personification of leadership. Consequently, when Mack was promoted to supervisor, he knew just how he was going to lead. Jenny was promoted to supervisor on the same day as Mack, but she had a different idea of what it meant to lead. Jenny's role model was Christ. Like Christ, Jenny led by serving. After Mack and Jenny were supervisors for six months, they had to undergo a comprehensive evaluation process. The evaluation was based primarily on the performance of their respective teams. Had the evaluation been a test in school, Mack would have made a C and Jenny would have made an A. Mack was flabbergasted. He couldn't believe Jenny's team outperformed his. After all, in his mind she wasn't even a leader. He never once heard

Jenny give an order or even raise her voice to an employee. How could her team have possibly outperformed his?

Good leadership can transform the world. Christ proved that. No person in any field of endeavor even approaches Christ in personifying what it means to be a leader. All the most widely advocated leadership traits found in business literature were personified in Christ. In fact, Christ not only personified these leadership traits, He is the source of them. Consequently, when you are looking for an example of leadership to emulate, look no further than Christ. When you understand how Christ led His followers, you will understand how you can lead your coworkers.

Leadership is about setting an example that inspires others to commit to not just doing their best but being their best. A good leader will influence people to go beyond just being better employees to being better people. If you are an effective leader among your coworkers, your example will encourage them to continually improve their work skills while also improving their character. Supervisors want peak performance and continual improvement from their subordinates. Businesses want to maximize and continually enhance their bottom lines. These things are important, but what is even more important is how individuals and organizations go about accomplishing them. This is where Christ-like leadership becomes critical, and Christ-like leadership is servant leadership.

Your goal as a Christ-like leader is to help coworkers adopt the teachings of Scripture and apply them in all their actions. You want to interact with coworkers in ways that will influence them for good. By "good" I mean influencing coworkers in ways that will cause them to adopt the teachings of Scripture and apply them on the job. Over time, the individuals and organizations that enjoy sustained success are those that most consistently apply the principles taught in Scripture. Those who get ahead in the short run by nefarious means invariably crash and burn in the long run. Quinton was such an individual.

Quinton was the most ambitious person I have ever known. He didn't want to just climb the career ladder, he wanted to vault up it, skipping as many steps as possible. Unfortunately, his career vision quickly morphed into misguided ambition, and Quinton started taking liberties with professional standards and good engineering practices. For a while, Quinton seemed to prosper. He went from being a project engineer to chief engineer for his company in a period of just two years. But then one day problems started to crop up. It began to appear as if every engineering project Quinton worked on had flaws—some of them serious. After a section of the seating for a stadium Quinton designed collapsed, investigators began to look into his other projects. They found he was guilty of taking dangerous shortcuts, acting on incomplete calculations, and saving money by using substandard materials. The cost to his company to renovate and repair all of Quinton's projects was enormous. As a result, Quinton lost not just his job but his professional engineering license. Had Quinton's mentors and supervisors been servant leaders, his career trajectory might have been much different.

When employees behave in ways that accord with Scripture, they are also behaving in ways that make them more productive and more valuable to their employers. Further, when organizations behave according to Scripture, they typically perform better, at least in the long run. Of course, the obverse is also true in both cases. This is why good leadership is so important in the workplace. Every organization—public, private, nonprofit, or military—needs its personnel to do their best every day and continually improve over time. This is the only way an organization can excel in a competitive environment. Anyone who can lead employees to do their best will be a valuable asset to an employer. You can be this kind of asset. You can serve Christ while also serving your employer.

CHRIST-LIKE LEADERS ARE SERVANT LEADERS

Servant leadership is the kind of leadership personified by Christ. The foundation of servant leadership can be found in Philippians 2:3, where it is written that we are to avoid selfishness and conceit in all we do. Rather we are to be humble and regard serving others as more important than serving self. Not surprisingly, servant leadership involves leading by serving. It is an approach to leadership that emulates Christ's example.

Servant leadership is about upholding and uplifting others rather than self, a concept antithetical to our sinful nature and to contemporary societal norms.

Servant leadership is not the kind of leadership usually portrayed in the movies or on television. A lot of people my age grew up believing John Wayne exemplified leadership. Not to take anything away from the Duke, but the better example to emulate when it comes to leadership is Christ. Christ is the ultimate example of servant leadership. Consequently, as a Christian, it is important for you to understand the concept of servant leadership and how to apply it in the workplace. However, before getting into the details of servant leadership, a caveat is in order.

Leadership is not about the position one holds. Granted, there are leadership positions in every organization. But being in a leadership position does not make one a leader. Unfortunately, in many organizations, there are people in positions of authority—leadership positions—who are not good leaders. On the other hand, there are people with little or no authority who are excellent leaders. The ideal is for people in leadership positions to be good leaders, but many fall short of the ideal. Leadership is about influencing people for good, something that can be done by any person in any position who is willing to set the right kind of example and interact with others in a Christ-like manner. This is important to note because, even if decision makers in an organization are averse to Christianity, they will value Christians who can lead others to be more productive and more committed to the organization's success.

Jane held a low-level position in her company but was an excellent leader. She led by serving. Jane cared about the people she worked with, a fact she demonstrated daily in practical, helpful ways. She helped those who were hurting, listened when coworkers needed to talk, and remembered important dates and events in the lives of those she worked with. Jane never forgot a coworker's birthday, and she always brought in a cake to celebrate. She also got to know her coworkers on a personal level. Consequently, she knew when they had needs, fears, and frustrations she could help with. Jane also excelled in her job. She had an outstanding work ethic. Because of her positive influence, Jane's coworkers tried hard to be better employees and better people. Jane felt especially blessed one day when she overheard a coworker say, "If the supervisors in this company would be more like Jane, our productivity would triple."

Jesus explained what He meant by servant leadership in Mark 10:42–45 when He reined in two of His Apostles, James and John, for wanting to exalt themselves. He told them if they wanted to be great they had to be servants. He told them further that He came to serve, not to be served, and they should follow His example. Christ's message to James and John was clear. If you want to lead, you must serve. This message is just as valid in the modern workplace as it was when Christ conveyed it to His Apostles. Every time I read Mark 10:42–45, I think of a former colleague—I will call her Jennifer—who made the same mistake as James and John. She tried to exalt herself by lobbying for proximity to the boss.

Our workspaces were cubicles. Jennifer schemed, plotted, and maneuvered to be assigned the cubicle next to our supervisor's office. In meetings, Jennifer arrived early to make sure she was seated next to him. In publicity photographs, Jennifer would push, shove, and elbow if necessary to be the one seen standing next to our boss in brochures and other marketing publications. Because Jennifer professed to be a Christian, I once tried to caution her about using proximity *to the throne* to exalt herself, but my words fell on deaf ears. She was convinced being seen with the boss would improve her chances of winning a promotion in the future. Consequently, when an opportunity for a promotion arose, Jennifer was shocked when it went to someone else.

The individual who got the promotion was the most humble but most capable person in our department. Rather than trying to exalt himself by proximity to the boss as Jennifer always did, this individual followed the admonition of Luke 14:10 to always take the lower place at the table. This allows the host or, in this case, the boss to move you to a higher place should he or she deem it appropriate. This is exactly what happened when the opportunity for a promotion arose. The boss moved our humble colleague—who also happened to be an outstanding servant leader— to the higher position by giving him the promotion Jennifer craved. The rest of us in the department breathed a sigh of relief over the decision.

To be a servant leader, regardless of your position or level of authority in an organization, you must do at least three things: (1) help others in ways that help them perform better and, in turn, help the organization perform better, (2) be a good steward of the resources entrusted to you, and (3) do the first two things in ways that reflect the image of Christ for your coworkers. Helping others might involve pitching in and assisting when they are overloaded, listening when they need to talk, taking notes for them when they have to miss a meeting, offering to take their place when work interferes with family obligations, mentoring, keeping them informed about issues that arise, and helping secure the resources and information they need to get their jobs done right, on time, and within budget.

Being a good steward is an important part of being a servant leader. It means taking care of the resources entrusted to you and making efficient and effective use of them. Good stewards are not wasteful, nor do they misuse or abuse the equipment, machinery, technology, supplies, funds, or people entrusted to their care. Good stewards are like the manager spoken of in Luke 12:42–43 who was faithful and wise. The master in these verses from Luke, no doubt, appreciated having such a manager over his household. Like the master in these verses, employers will appreciate having leaders who are faithful and wise. In other words, leaders who are good stewards of the resources entrusted to them. Servant leaders are valuable assets to employers. The more valuable you are to your employer, the less likely it is you will be subjected to temptation, rejection, or persecution by your coworkers.

SERVANT LEADERSHIP PERSONIFIED

When I think of servant leadership, the first example that comes to mind is the one in John 13:1–17, where Christ washes the feet of His disciples. I know of no more poignant example of servant leadership. There is also an example closer to home that comes to mind. One of the best servant leaders I have ever known was a janitor at the college where I served as vice-president. He was a humble, unassuming man and a committed

Christian. I will call him Tom. Tom was certainly not in a leadership position in our organization, nor did he have any authority. Nevertheless, he was an excellent servant leader and, in turn, a valuable employee. His example of servant leadership was a daily sermon for all of us who worked with him.

Tom was a good listener, and he was perceptive enough to sense when someone needed to talk. This was important to me because employees were willing to share things with Tom they might have been reluctant to share with me or someone else in a position of authority. People tend to be more guarded when talking to those in positions of authority over them. The number of personnel issues defused and problems prevented because Tom was willing to listen to people vent would be too many to count. There were a lot of them.

Tom could tell when someone just needed to vent, as well as when small problems might become big problems if left unattended. In the latter case, he always let me know, so I could take appropriate preventive action. There were many times when he let me know one of our employees needed help or additional resources to do his or her job better. When employees suffered personal trials or tragedies, Tom was always the first to console and comfort them. If an employee was having a bad day, Tom made a point of doing something nice for that individual. He would also let me know when a kind word from me might be helpful. When batteries died, keys got locked in cars, or tires went flat, Tom was always quick to come to the rescue.

Tom was also a good steward. He never wasted anything. In fact, he was one of the most rare of breeds: an organized pack rat. As a result, he could usually be depended on to come up with that badly needed supply item somebody forgot to order. On occasions when someone inadvertently made a mess, Tom would put aside whatever he was doing and take over the cleanup operation. His comment was always the same: "Let me clean this up. You have more important things to do." Further, it was not uncommon for Tom to work late because he put his normal duties aside to help other people with theirs.

Few people did more to influence our employees for good than Tom, a janitor. Because of his example of servant leadership, our personnel not only worked better, they tried to be better people. This, in turn, made our personnel a tight-knit group that functioned at a high level and whose members took care of each other. If a janitor can have that much influence for good by being a servant leader, how much more influence for good can you have in your organization?

CHARACTERISTICS OF SERVANT LEADERS

For years I have advised working Christians to become servant leaders among their coworkers. Invariably, those I advise ask, "How do I become a servant leader?" To help answer that question, I developed a list of characteristics common to servant leaders. I call them the *Seven Characteristics of Servant Leaders* or the *Seven Cs*. By developing, internalizing, and applying these characteristics, Christians can become servant leaders in the workplace regardless of their relative authority and status. The *Seven Cs* are:

- Caring
- Character
- Communication
- Clarity
- Commitment
- Courage
- Competence

Each of these concepts is solidly grounded in Scripture. In fact, all seven could be summarized with just one "C": Christ. Applying these concepts consistently in the workplace will help protect you from the temptation, rejection, and persecution of unbelieving coworkers, but their application is more than just a defensive strategy. Applying the Seven Cs is an effective way to take the initiative in leading unbelievers to Christ while also advancing your career.

SETTING AN EXAMPLE OF CARING

As Christians, we are expected to care about other people. Christ made this clear in the Second Greatest Commandment when he told us to love our neighbors as ourselves (Matthew 22:37–39). This is a powerful message, and it leaves little room for misinterpretation. But how do we show our neighbors in the workplace we care about them, particularly those who don't seem to care about us? I am often asked this question by Christians who feel like sheep working among wolves. I tell Christians they can demonstrate caring by consistently exemplifying the following traits: honesty, empathy, interest, patience, and servanthood.

Honesty as Evidence of Caring

One way to show coworkers you care is to be honest with them. For example, when you have a message to convey to coworkers, whether it is good news or bad, the best way to show you care is by telling the truth. Lying, dissembling, and distorting—even if your intention is to shield the listener from disappointment—are signs you do not care. Why? Because you do not lie to people you care about. But what about well-intended distortions meant to soften the blow of bad news? In such cases, do not confuse honesty with tactlessness. We should be tactful when delivering bad news, of course. But tact does not mean dissembling or distorting. It means being considerate in how you deliver the message. Think of tact as driving in the nail without breaking the board.

Once when I was serving in the Marine Corps many years ago, I received a note from the mother of one of my men. His father died, but his mother did not want him to know until he returned from overseas. She was afraid the death of his father added to all he was coping with being deployed might be too much for him. I was torn. I knew my friend would want to attend his father's funeral, and I knew the Red Cross could make that happen. But his mother asked me not to tell him, so I complied. That was a mistake. I should have helped his mother realize it would be better to tell him the truth.

When my friend finally rotated back to the United States and took leave to visit his family, his father had been dead for six months. When he found out his mother and I purposefully withheld the information from him, my friend refused to speak with me for years. He loved his father and felt betrayed by our well-intentioned mistake. All he could think of was we caused him to miss the funeral. Although our motives were well-intentioned, they did not alleviate his disappointment or feelings of betrayal.

Honesty is one of the most fundamental Christian values, a value set in stone as the Ninth Commandment. Not surprisingly, the Bible is replete with admonitions to be honest. For example, Zechariah 8:16 tells us to speak the truth to our neighbors. Telling the truth is fundamental to being a Christian. Being honest with people is an effective way to show them you care. Tactfully and kindly speaking the truth, even an unwelcome truth, is a sign of caring. To do otherwise is to withhold information recipients could use to respond to bad news in a timely and helpful manner. For example, if several of your team members are going to be laid off, you don't help them by conveying the message in a way that creates false hope. If they know the hard truth, they can start looking for another job right away. But if a distorted message gives them false hope, they might wait until it is too late to find another job in a timely manner. Telling the truth about the situation, even though the message may be unwelcome, shows you care.

Looking back over my career, one of the people I admire most was my supervisor in the first job I had after graduating from high school. It was a good job, but more importantly, it was a flexible job that allowed me to schedule work around my college classes. I will call this individual Charlie. Charlie was a committed Christian who cared about those he supervised. One of the ways he showed us he cared was by being scrupulously honest with us. We knew whether the news was good or bad, if we heard it from Charlie we could count on its veracity. Consequently, when Charlie called all of us on his work team together one day and informed us layoffs were coming in the near future, we knew the situation was serious.

Charlie cared about the work he was responsible for getting done. Consequently, he did not want to lose any of his team members by frightening us into seeking other jobs. But, on the other hand, he cared enough about his team members he did not want us to be unaware of the possibility of losing our jobs. At the point when he delivered the bad news, Charlie's team was a strong and cohesive group with an outstanding performance record. In fact, Charlie often told us we were the strongest team he ever led. Charlie could have simply kept what he knew to himself and left his team intact until the layoffs occurred. In fact, he was advised to do just that by higher management.

The company's CEO wanted to make sure several important projects were completed before anyone left for a new job or got laid off. He was rightfully concerned that some of our better employees might leave for other jobs if they knew about the layoffs. After all, when layoffs are threatened, it is often the organization's best employees who leave because they are the ones most capable of getting other jobs. Unfortunately, the CEO cared only about the work. He didn't care about us. Charlie cared about the work too, but he also cared about us.

If there was even the slightest possibility any member of his team would be laid off, Charlie wanted that individual to have plenty of time to prepare and take appropriate action. Consequently, not only did he advise us of the possibility of layoffs, he let those of us who were the most junior members of the team know we would probably be the first to go if layoffs became a reality. Charlie told us our company would apply the *last-in-first-out* rule when determining who would be laid off. Later, when layoffs did occur, those of us who were forewarned and, as a result, secured other jobs felt a deep sense of gratitude to Charlie for caring enough to be honest with us. In fact, even after getting new jobs, two of us worked with Charlie at night and on weekends to complete the projects assigned to him. I returned to the company and Charlie's team once work picked up again.

Empathy as Evidence of Caring

Empathy means identifying with and understanding another person's feelings, motives, and circumstances. As Christians, we are called to be empathetic. Empathy is about putting yourself in the shoes of other people and trying to see things through their eyes. 1 John 4:11 makes the point that, because God loved us, we should love one another. This is another way to say, if God can show sinners such as you and me empathy, we should be willing to show empathy to our coworkers. The following story illustrates the value of empathy.

John worked for a waste management company I will call ABC, Inc. He was the company's best and most popular driver. John was respected by his supervisor and liked by his fellow drivers because not only did he do a good job, but he also pitched in and helped other drivers when they got behind in their work. In fact, John trained and mentored most of the company's other drivers. He was never too busy to help other drivers and often filled in when they needed time off.

ABC's drivers dumped their loads in a landfill about ten miles outside town. To encourage productivity, the company awarded a cash incentive bonus to drivers who exceeded their dumping quota during any pay period. John was a no-nonsense worker who hustled from the moment he clocked in until he clocked out. Because he was so efficient at the collection and compacting aspects of the job and because he knew his routes so well, John earned incentive bonuses more often than any other driver. In fact, there were months he earned a bonus almost every payday, quite an accomplishment. One payday, while congratulating John on receiving yet another cash bonus, his supervisor, Benton, noticed signs of discomfort in his star driver. As they talked, John squirmed in his chair and avoided making eye contact. After observing this reaction on several subsequent paydays, Benton began to sense something was wrong.

When he looked into the situation, Benton learned his intuition was right. Something was indeed wrong. In order to surpass his dumping quota and earn cash bonuses, John was skipping the time-consuming compacting step on several loads every week. This was a serious procedural breach because it violated an important municipal statute. The city's landfill was fast reaching capacity, a fact that made the compacting step a critical part of the overall waste management process. The city council and John's company shared a common interest in putting off the expensive development of a new landfill as long as possible. Consequently, John and his fellow drivers were trained to take the extra time to compact their loads as tightly as possible before dumping them in the landfill.

Benton, a committed Christian, was disappointed in his star driver to say the least. However, there were extenuating circumstances complicating what, on the surface, looked like an open-and-shut case of cheating, greed, and fraud. While investigating the situation, Benton learned John's motive for cheating on his quota was not fraud but desperation. John was cheating to increase his income. There was no denying that. But his reason for cheating was need, not greed.

With a critically ill son in the hospital, John turned to cheating on his dumping quota in an effort to pay his family's mounting medical bills. John's son was suffering from an extended illness, his treatment was so expensive even with health insurance, and the bills were piling up faster than John could pay them. Clearly, John was not acting out of a perverse motive. He was acting out of fear and desperation. Knowing this created a heart-wrenching dilemma for Benton.

On one hand, Benton knew the procedural violations were serious and they had to stop. In fact, he planned to put a stop to them right away. But he feared that action alone would not be sufficient to satisfy higher management. In fact, once the violations became known, it was likely John would be fired. Benton cared about his drivers and did not want John to lose his job. He viewed John not as a bad person, but as a good person who was making bad decisions because he was caught in the web of an intractable dilemma. Aware of how his boss was likely to react when informed, Benton prayed about the situation. As he prayed and read the Bible, an idea emerged that could possibly be used to transform this lemon into lemonade. His first step was to develop a plan to preempt any hasty action from higher management, which he did. Benton proposed the following plan to his boss:

- Benton would meet with John privately and put an immediate stop to the procedural violations. Further, he would ask John to cooperate in determining how many times he had received an unearned bonus. Benton knew John did not have the money to simply return the unearned bonuses. Consequently, he would ask him to forgo an equal number of bonus payments as he earned them in the future. If John agreed to this step in the plan, Benton would proceed to the next step.
- Benton would require John to work on Saturdays until the uncompacted material in the landfill had been retrieved and properly compacted.
- Benton would personally organize a companywide fundraiser to help defray the costs of John's mounting medical expenses.
- Benton would limit the punishment John received to a written reprimand placed in his personnel file.

Higher management accepted the plan but made it clear to Benton it had better work. In other words, Benton had to put his own credibility at risk to support his wayward driver. When Benton confronted him that evening, John was contrite, embarrassed, and remorseful. He made a full confession, accepted responsibility, apologized, and even offered to resign. However, when Benton informed John of the proposal he made to higher management, a much-relieved John accepted the plan immediately. John promised to be at the landfill every Saturday morning at 7:00 until he retrieved all the improperly dumped material and compacted it. He was as good as his word.

The following Saturday he showed up at the landfill at 6:45 a.m. To his surprise, John found Benton and several other drivers waiting to help him reload and compact the trash. Further, the companywide fundraiser Benton organized caught fire and soon became a community-wide event. In just weeks, the company and community raised enough money to ensure John would no longer have to worry about his son's medical bills.

In this case, Benton showed he cared by being empathetic. By putting himself in John's shoes before taking any action against him, Benton was able to empathize with his driver. As a result, he devised a solution that earned him the appreciation not just of John, but of all the other drivers too. Benton showed John, the employees of ABC, higher management, and the local community an empathetic solution to a problem that might have been handled much differently by someone else. In taking this approach, Benton exemplified what it means to be a 1 Corinthians 13 Christian. He also personified what Christ meant in Matthew 10:16 when he told His disciples to be both wise and innocent.

Interest as Evidence of Caring

One of the best ways to demonstrate you care about other people is to show sincere interest in them. Getting to know your coworkers and learning about their families, fears, ambitions, dreams, and frustrations is an indication you care. A willingness to give people your undivided attention and listen attentively when they need to talk is a sign of interest and, in turn, an effective way to show you care. If we are to love our neighbors as ourselves, we must show sincere interest in them. Therefore, part of setting a Christ-like example is getting to know your coworkers well enough to understand what makes them tick. This means getting to know their dreams, fears, and needs.

A CPA I will call Ann supervised a staff of eight other accountants and an administrative assistant. Ann was a committed Christian who tried hard to exemplify both parts of the Greatest Commandment (Mark 12:30–31). Ann knew if she loved the Lord, she also had to love her neighbors as commanded by the Lord. She tried hard to put love into practice in the workplace.

One of the hallmarks of Ann's approach to being a supervisor was showing sincere interest in her team members. She got to know her team members by taking the time to talk with them and by listening when they needed to talk. At the beginning of every workday, she made a point of greeting her team members individually and asking how they were doing. Many people ask, "How are you doing?" in a perfunctory manner, but Ann's team members soon learned when she asked this simple question she sincerely wanted to know. If a team member was having trouble, Ann was always willing to take the time to listen and help in any way she could.

One of Ann's most effective ways of showing interest in her team members was what she called her "Personal Dream Sheet" or PDS. Once a year, Ann met with her team members individually to develop or update their PDSs. The PDS is a simple single-page document containing the employee's most important career goals and/or personal needs. Most of the entries for her employees were career oriented, but some were not. For example, one year, Ann's administrative assistant said what she really wanted that year was a more flexible work schedule during the high school baseball season, so she could attend some of her son's after-school ball games. Because she was a single mother, it was difficult for the administrative assistant to spend as much time with her son as she wanted. Consequently, the goal of having a flexible schedule during baseball season was important to her. It took some convincing, but higher management eventually approved the flexible schedule Ann proposed for her administrative assistant.

Ann made a point of doing everything within reason to help her team members realize their dreams. As a result, her team members were resolutely loyal to her. They gave her their best every day and worked hard to improve continually. The combination of consistent peak performance and continual improvement on the part of her team members gave Ann the highest-performing department in the company. Her team members worked hard for Ann because they knew she cared about them. Because she cared about them, they cared about her and doing a good job for her.

Patience as Evidence of Caring

People who care about others—those who love their neighbors as themselves—are patient with them. Patience is a willingness to tolerate the human frailties, foibles, quirks, opinions, and personalities of people as well as the petty inconveniences of life while still maintaining a positive attitude. For many people, and this certainly includes me, patience comes hard. Patience can be a difficult state of mind to maintain. For example, have you ever beeped your horn at the slow-to-react driver in front of you when the traffic light changed from red to green? Do you get fidgety when you have to stand in line? Do you interrupt when the person you are talking to doesn't get to the point fast enough? Answering "yes" to these questions means being patient is a challenge for you.

Being patient with others is part of setting a Christ-like example, an example that shows you care. It is an attribute firmly grounded in Scripture. For example, 1 Thessalonians 1:3 encourages us to maintain our patience of hope in Christ. Treating people with patience shows you care. Patience is especially important when you must give constructive criticism to a coworker or subordinate. If not delivered with tact, kindness, and patience, *constructive* criticism can be received as just criticism. Christians who fail to exercise patience with their coworkers and subordinates set the wrong example for them, an example that says, "I don't care about you."

Servanthood/Stewardship as Evidence of Caring

Servanthood involves putting the needs of others ahead of your own. Stewardship involves taking care of the people and resources entrusted to you. The personification of servanthood and stewardship is Christ, and servanthood coupled with stewardship is the ultimate example of caring. In Matthew 20:28, we read Christ came not to be served, but to serve. If Christ, our Lord and Savior, came to serve rather than be served, surely service to others must be important. Further, if serving others is that important to Christ, it should be part of the example we set for coworkers. Christ walked the earth as a servant and good steward. Our calling is to emulate His example in all aspects of our lives, including the workplace.

When He stooped to wash the feet of His disciples, Christ taught them the lesson of service. When He fed the multitudes, gave sight to the blind, healed the sick, and told the lame to arise and walk, Christ exemplified service and stewardship. He demonstrated the importance of taking care of people. Recall what Peter was told by Christ in John 21. Christ told Peter three times to care for and feed His lambs. This was Christ's way of telling Peter to be a good servant and a good steward. Christ's example of service and stewardship has direct application on the job.

In today's fast-paced, pressure-packed workplace, few things are needed more than servant leaders and good stewards. Servant leaders put the needs of others—coworkers, customers, and the organization— ahead of their personal agendas. Good stewards take care of the resources entrusted to them: human, physical, and financial. Consequently, when you set a consistent example of servanthood and good stewardship, it not only shows you care, it helps your organization perform better. Christians who can make their organizations more competitive will be appreciated, even by those who don't appreciate their beliefs.

Few things show others you care more than being a good servant and a good steward. I saw this fact borne out in stark terms when I served in the Marine Corps many years ago. For a short time, our platoon was commanded by an officer whose attitude could be summed up as "rank has its privileges." I will call him Lt. Morgan. He was the polar opposite of most Marine platoon leaders, a breed known for taking care of their troops. Part of the problem was he resented being assigned to ground troops. He joined the Marine Corps to be a pilot but washed out of flight school. As a result, he still owed Uncle Sam four years of service, and his contract specified his service was to be spent in the infantry. Clearly, Lt. Morgan was a fish out of water, one who resented every day he spent mingling with what the Marine Corps affectionately calls "grunts."

Lt. Morgan treated the enlisted Marines in our company like his personal serfs. In the field, while we ate cold C rations out of a can, he ate store-bought delicacies brought along in an extra pack. Then, to make matters worse, he required an enlisted Marine to carry his extra pack for him. He also required an enlisted Marine to prepare and serve his meals. Whenever we were on patrol long enough for our supplies to run low, this officer made sure he ate before anyone else to get the best of whatever was left.

Our loyalty to Lt. Morgan was less than zero, and our performance for him was mediocre at best. As a result, he was soon relieved of command and replaced by another officer. The new platoon leader—I will call him Lt. Murphy—was a committed Christian with a servant's heart and a steward's attitude. In contrast to his predecessor, Lt. Murphy made a point of pitching in and helping us do the dirty work. For example, part of our training involved completing frequent twenty-five-mile forced marches while carrying packs weighing between sixty and eighty pounds. If a Marine fell behind on one of those marches, Lt. Murphy carried his pack until he was sufficiently rested to carry it himself. Whenever we took a break to eat, he made sure everyone else had plenty of food before he took even a bite for himself. When he received goodies from home, this servant-oriented Christian distributed them among the men in our platoon rather than eating them.

Our new platoon commander was the kind of officer more commonly found in the Marine Corps, one who would carry your pack and cover your back. His servant's heart and good stewardship quickly turned things around in our platoon. Morale and performance skyrocketed. He took care of us, so we took care of him. The same thing will happen to you in the workplace when you set a Christ-like example of servanthood and stewardship. When you take care of others, they will be more likely to reciprocate when the pressures and temptations of the workplace become burdensome.

SETTING AN EXAMPLE OF EXEMPLARY CHARACTER

One of the most fundamental aspects of setting a Christ-like example is trust building. Your coworkers will not be influenced for good by someone they do not trust. To win the trust of people, it is necessary to demonstrate exemplary character. Character is the moral strength to reflect God's righteousness, justice, and fairness in all aspects of life, including work. Your character shows through when you not only recognize the right thing to do in a given situation but follow through and do it. As Christians, our character should be a reflection of Christ for those we work with.

Like the other aspects of servant leadership, character is solidly grounded in Scripture. In fact, character is about conforming in all ways to the teachings of Scripture. Proverbs 28:6 makes it clear it is better to be poor and have integrity than to be rich and "crooked." Without character and the wisdom that comes with it, setting a consistent Christ-like example will not be possible. In fact, without character your example will be a charade others easily see through. Even unbelievers understand the importance, if not the source, of character. This is why so many companies adopt codes of ethics and require their personnel to complete mandatory ethics training.

The example you set for coworkers is a reflection of your character. Without character, you will be unable to stand firm in the faith when the temptations and pressures of work press down on you. Character is what helps you withstand the workplace trials and tribulations that test your faith. Observing your example of coping with trials and tribulations in a Christ-like manner sends a powerful message to your coworkers. Why character is so important to Christians in the workplace can be discerned from reading Romans 5:3–5. These verses explain that, as believers, we are to rejoice in suffering because suffering builds character, and character produces hope. Leaders who give their coworkers hope are assets to their organizations, particularly during times of adversity.

It is important to internalize the message in Romans 5:3–5 because people of exemplary character—particularly Christians—are going to occasionally suffer because of their integrity. People of character often find themselves at odds with people who put their personal agendas ahead of character. When this happens, unethical people often respond by attacking those who speak out against their nefarious schemes. Their attacks can be vicious, causing principled people to suffer, at least in the short run. But when we suffer, two good things can happen if we respond properly. First, we can be driven closer to God and thereby enhance our character. Second, we can set an example of how to deal with bullying and other types of adversity that gives others hope. Few people are more valued in the workplace than those who can give their coworkers hope during difficult times and in difficult situations. Giving hope to others is an important aspect of servant leadership.

One of the most important things you can do in leading people is give them hope. People of character give hope to others by treating them with honesty, integrity, fairness, and justice, even when doing so is difficult and even when there is no personal gain to be enjoyed. Letting your Christian character shine through in your everyday example at work is powerful evidence you care. When coworkers see you care, not just about the job to be done, but about them, it will be much easier to influence them for good. Further, it will be less likely they will subject you to temptation, rejection, or persecution.

SETTING AN EXAMPLE OF EFFECTIVE COMMUNICATION

Christ was the ultimate communicator. By His words and example, Christ communicated the most important truths known to man. As Christians, we too need to be good communicators. Even unbelievers recognize effective communication as essential to good human relations. Part of setting a consistent Christ-like example in the workplace is striving to be an effective communicator. Like all the other elements of your example, effective communication is solidly grounded in Scripture. The Scriptural basis for effective communication can be found in several places beginning in Psalm 19, where God is shown to be the Great Communicator.

According to Psalm 19, God communicates with us through both general and special revelation. As to general revelation, Psalm 19:1–4 tells us the heavens and skies declare the glory of God, and there is no one on earth who does not *hear* the message they speak. These verses tell us to know God all we have to do is look around. God communicates with us constantly through His creation. These same verses also tell us we can come to know the existence, power, and glory of God through nothing more than the process of observation.

As to special revelation, the author of Psalm 19:7–9 speaks of the "law," "testimony," "precepts," and "rules" of the Lord, all of which are contained in Holy Scripture. God communicates with us in specific terms through His Word. In Scripture, God communicates special revelation concerning who He is, who we are, and what is expected of us. His communication is effective beyond measure or description.

Because God has given us a powerful example concerning communication and because His is the example we are to follow, communicating effectively must necessarily be part of the example we set for others. That being the case, how should we go about making effective communication part of the example we set in the workplace? Again, God provides the answer. In 2 Timothy 3:16–17, God tells us Scripture is useful for instruction, correction, and training. All these are forms of communication that help equip our coworkers to perform at peak levels and improve continually.

The verses from 2 Timothy show how we should use communication in the workplace. In addition to informing, we communicate to teach, rebuke, correct, and train coworkers, so they are better equipped and better motivated to do their jobs. By communicating effectively with them, we can also equip our coworkers to cope with the fears, frustrations, pressures, and temptations that can impede their performance. The most effective way to teach, rebuke, correct, and train in the workplace is by providing a consistent Christ-like example in how you do your job, make decisions, interact with coworkers, and handle adversity. Your Christ-like example will *speak* even louder than words. Further, when you have the opportunity to use words, your example will multiply their effectiveness.

I once worked with a committed Christian I will call Jeff who did his best every day to communicate the importance and benefits of a good work ethic to all of us who worked with him. I know he was effective at communicating his message because our supervisor used him as a role model for how he wanted the rest of us to work. Once when the supervisor rated me a four out of five on "job performance" during my annual performance appraisal, I asked what I could do to improve on the next appraisal. Rather than provide the constructive criticism I hoped to receive, the supervisor told me to observe Jeff in action for one week. Then he said, "What you will see is what it takes to earn a five."

One final note on communication in the workplace is in order here. It is not necessary that you be an articulate orator or accomplished writer to be a good communicator. However, it is necessary you be a good listener. Listening is the most important communication skill there is and the least practiced. If you do not listen well, you cannot communicate well. By becoming a good listener, you can show people you care. Because listening gives people something they badly need but rarely get: the undivided attention of someone who will let them talk through things troubling them.

LISTENING: THE KEY TO EFFECTIVE COMMUNICATION

The best advice concerning listening comes from Scripture. In James 1:19, it is written we should be quick to listen but slow to speak. Clearly James knew the tendencies of sinners like you and me when he wrote those words. As sinners, we tend to talk more than we listen. I know I do. It is not uncommon for people to interrupt others before they finish speaking, tune out in the middle of a conversation, and allow themselves to be distracted. It is not uncommon for some people to become angry when they don't like what they are being told. People who do these things will be poor listeners and, as a result, poor communicators. Christians trying to set the right kind of example for their coworkers cannot afford to be poor communicators.

To become a good listener, begin by understanding what listening involves. First, listening is not just hearing. Hearing is the physiological process of receiving sound waves. But listening involves much more than just receiving sound waves. It also involves correctly decoding what is heard and accurately perceiving what is meant. Hence, an individual with acute hearing can be a poor listener, whereas an individual with impaired hearing can be an excellent listener. In fact, some of the best, most attentive listeners are deaf.

The next step in becoming a good listener is to practice concentrating on what is said as well as how it is said. In other words, concentrate on both the verbal and nonverbal aspects of the message. Don't be concerned you lack formal training in *listening to* nonverbal communication. You don't need it. People learn to understand nonverbal communication when they are mere infants. A little baby can tell if its mother is angry, happy, stressed, or frightened by the signals she gives off nonverbally. Right now, without any training, you are able to interpret such nonverbal cues as tone of voice, facial expressions, smiles, laughter, scowls, gestures, and so on.

There are two keys to understanding what is being said nonverbally: (1) pay attention to the nonverbal cues people provide (e.g., eye contact or lack of it, tone of voice, facial expressions, nervousness, etc.) and (2) look for agreement or disagreement between what is said verbally and what is said nonverbally. When the verbal and nonverbal messages do not agree, something is wrong. When you observe this kind of discordance in a conversation, wait for an opening and then ask for clarification. You might ask, "What is really going on here—your words say everything is alright, but your body language says the opposite?"

To be a good listener, it is also necessary to discipline yourself to avoid several common inhibitors of effective listening. These include failing to concentrate on what is being said, giving into preconceived notions, getting impatient and thinking ahead to where you assume the speaker is going, allowing interruptions, thinking of what you want to say instead of paying attention to the speaker, and tuning out while the other individual is speaking. In addition to avoiding these common inhibitors, try applying the following listening strategies:

- Remove all distractions so you can concentrate on what the speaker is saying. Turn off your cell phone, do not sneak glances at your watch, and find a private place to talk where the conversation will not be interrupted.

- Put the speaker at ease. If the speaker seems nervous or edgy, talk about a comfortable neutral topic (sports, grandchildren, a hobby, etc.) until the individual relaxes.
- Look directly at the speaker, concentrate on what is being said, and watch for nonverbal cues.
- Be patient. *Do not help* the speaker when he or she is struggling to get the message out. Give the speaker a reassuring look and wait. *Helping* a speaker who is struggling often does more harm than good. It can shut down communication rather than encourage it.
- Ask clarifying questions. If the speaker's message is unclear, wait for a break in the conversation and ask clarifying questions.
- Paraphrase and repeat the message back to the speaker once he or she is finished conveying it. This will show you have heard and understood the message or, if the message is still unclear, it will give the speaker an opportunity to clarify.
- Control your emotions. No matter what the speaker says, control your emotions. Do not become angry, defensive, or argumentative when you don't like what you hear. Let the speaker get it out. People usually settle down once they have had an opportunity to vent.
- In today's fast-paced, high-tech world when people communicate primarily through electronic devices, an important part of your example can be providing the human touch for coworkers who need someone to listen. Listening has become such a rare skill; Christians who discipline themselves to be good listeners will find it easier to influence their coworkers for good. You are also less likely to be confronted by temptation, rejection, or persecution from coworkers who appreciate your willingness to listen.

SETTING AN EXAMPLE OF CLARITY

People need to feel their work has a worthy purpose, that it matters. People who think their work doesn't matter will begin to wonder if they matter. Although this is a misguided frame of mind, it is quite common. Unfortunately, many people in the workplace, including Christians, see no worthy purpose in their work. Over the years, I have counseled many Christians who were unhappy in their work because they felt it had no meaning beyond paying the bills. On the other hand, I have counseled Christian professionals in executive positions whose work—in spite of the inherent money, status, and power—left them feeling hollow and unfulfilled.

When your work seems meaningless, the problem is the same whether you are the CEO or the janitor. Christians who see no purpose in their work are overlooking an important point. They have forgotten whom they work for and why. Hold that thought for the moment. I will return to it shortly. But first, consider the following stories about two Christians I knew. Both have since passed on, but their stories endure as examples of how we should view our jobs and how we shouldn't.

I once ran into an old college buddy and fellow Christian in an airport who by all appearances should have been a happy man but wasn't. After graduation, this friend—I will call him Lloyd—went into banking. Lloyd was ambitious, hard-working, and determined to make it to the top in his profession. By the time we stumbled into each other, he had already accomplished this goal. After beginning a career at the bottom of his profession, Lloyd swiftly ascended through the ranks to become a bank president. That's where things stood when we bumped into each other in the airport.

When I congratulated him on achieving his goals, we discussed so many times as college students, Lloyd just shrugged. In spite of his apparent success, Lloyd was not just unhappy; he was depressed. In fact, he admitted to being on the way to the airport bar when we bumped into each other. It saddened me to learn Lloyd turned to drinking for solace from the depression engulfing him. After working long and hard to enjoy the perquisites of success, Lloyd found his job left him feeling empty. He felt his work lacked a worthy purpose. I never saw Lloyd again but later learned he sunk even deeper into depression and eventually took his own life.

In contrast to Lloyd, Joseph was happy, fulfilled, and satisfied in his work. Joseph was a maintenance worker at the college where I taught early in my career as a professor. He was also a committed Christian. Joseph took great pride in his work and did it well. He always arrived early, worked hard, and usually stayed beyond the end of his shift. He gave everyone he came in contact with a welcoming smile and had the best attitude of any individual I have ever worked with. His was one of the best examples of clarity of purpose I have ever observed. The difference between Joseph and Lloyd is Joseph, a maintenance worker, knew what Lloyd, a bank president, didn't: as a Christian, his goal was to honor God through his work, not to achieve self-gratification. Unlike Lloyd, Joseph saw a worthy purpose in his work.

Although status, money, power, and perquisites may satisfy in the short run, in the long run they rarely do. Our sinful nature is such that enough is rarely enough. We almost always want more. The only way people find true meaning and real purpose in their work is to understand and accept what is written in Colossians 3:23–24. In these verses, we read, whatever our work happens to be, we are to do it well and do it for the Lord, not man. Then we are told through our work we serve the Lord, and it is from the Lord our true rewards will come. Christians who understand the message in these verses can set an example of working as hard in low-level jobs as they would in jobs perceived by society to be more important. Further, they can do this while maintaining a positive, thankful attitude. Christians who know they are pleasing God by how they do their work, do not need the approval of people who believe work is about self-gratification and ego stroking.

In Ephesians 3, we learn our purpose in life is to know God, to make Him known to others, and to live to glorify Him. One of the ways we can glorify God is to do well the work He has given us. Regardless, the kind or level of job we have, as Christians, we work first for God and second for our employers. Knowing this gives meaning to our jobs, regardless the status, salary, or authority we might enjoy. Our work is a gift from God. We show our appreciation for the gift by how we do our job and the attitude we bring to it. This does not mean we shouldn't strive to climb the career ladder. Often the higher you go in your career, the more influence for good you can have. Rather, it means wherever you happen to be on the career ladder, be thankful, be positive, and do a good job.

People at work—whether Christians or unbelievers—need to understand the meaning in their work. They need to know their work is important as well as why it is important. In short, they need to know their work matters. By exemplifying what is written in Colossians 3:23–24, you can help coworkers find meaning in their work no matter what their jobs happen to be. This is why exhibiting clarity of purpose must be part of your Christian example in the workplace.

SETTING AN EXAMPLE OF COMMITMENT

There is a joke that illustrates the difference between being involved and being committed. It goes like this. With a breakfast of bacon and eggs, the chicken is involved but the pig is committed. This is a humorous way to make an important point: commitment means more than just being involved. When it comes to providing breakfast, the chicken gives up an egg or two, but the pig gives up its life. The message in this joke is commitment requires sacrifice. Commitment means more than just getting involved or saying you will try hard. In the workplace, commitment means you are willing to sacrifice to get the job done right, on time, and within budget. For Christians, it also means doing this while standing firm in your faith.

Exemplifying commitment is an important aspect of setting a Christlike example. Christ set the ultimate example of commitment when He went willingly to the cross for your sins and mine. His Apostles set examples of commitment when all of them except John died in the cause of spreading the Gospel. The Apostles didn't just get involved in spreading the Gospel. They sacrificed their lives because they were committed to the task. It is not likely you will be asked to die for a work-related cause. However, you might have to sacrifice time you would like to spend doing something else or give up personal recognition in favor of team recognition.

Perhaps the ultimate Scriptural statement about commitment is found in Matthew 16:24–26 where Christ tells us if we want to follow Him, we must be willing to deny ourselves. Self-denial is a form of sacrifice. As these verses illustrate, just deciding you will try or you will give a good effort is not commitment. When you decide to make all the appropriate sacrifices necessary to set a Christ-like example in how you do your work, you have made a commitment. People admire and respect those who exemplify the concept of commitment.

Joan was a committed Christian. She was also committed to doing a good job in her work. Joan's example of commitment served her well in the workplace. Her coworkers liked to use Sunday as a catch-up day at work. If any important work remained on their desks at quitting time on Friday, they would come in Sunday and finish it, so they could begin Monday with a clean slate. But for Joan, Sunday was a day for worship, rest, and fellowship. She viewed the day as the Lord's Day in the strictest sense. Consequently, Joan was known to come in early on Fridays and even work late on Friday nights to get her work caught up when necessary. Work on Saturdays was not out of the question either. But Joan guarded her Sundays assiduously.

Her coworkers knew of Joan's commitment to the Christian faith, but they also saw she was committed to her work. Joan always did what was necessary to get her work done right, on time, and within budget. Consequently, they never pressured her to join them for work sessions on Sunday mornings. Had Joan been less committed to doing an excellent job, her faith commitment might not have been enough to earn the level of respect she enjoyed. But because her superiors and coworkers knew she was committed to her work and her faith, there was no pressure for Joan to work on Sundays.

SETTING AN EXAMPLE OF COURAGE

It takes courage—moral courage—to set a consistent Christ-like example. This is because doing so often requires swimming against the current of societal norms, norms grown in a secular humanistic worldview. It is not easy or comfortable to swim upstream against peer pressure. Yet this may be necessary at times if you want to reflect the image of Christ in the workplace. As Christians, if we are going to set a consistent example of living our faith among coworkers who do not share that faith, we must have the courage to stand firm in our beliefs, in the face of temptation, rejection, and even persecution. This will never be easy. There are going to be times when you feel overwhelmed, frustrated, and even afraid. When this happens, remember courage is not a lack of fear. Rather, it is a willingness to do what is right in the face of your fear.

As Christians, we could have no better role model of courage in the face of adversity than Christ. We may have to endure many faith-related challenges in the workplace, but we will never face anything even approaching what Christ endured on our behalf. Because He stood firm in carrying out His mission on earth, Christ was given a mock trial, scourged, forced to wear a crown of thorns, insulted, abased, degraded, nailed to the cross he was forced to carry, speared in the side, and crucified. Try to imagine the courage required to go willingly through all that because your faith required it of you.

Finally, imagine you could put an end to the agony and prevent your death at any time by simply striking down your antagonists, but instead, you willingly submit to their brutality. This is the example Christ set for us. As Christians, we need look no further than the life of Christ for an example of courage in the face of adversity, an example exceeding anything we will ever face in the workplace. For additional guidance, we can look to the Psalms. Psalm 31:24 tells us to "be strong" and let our hearts "take courage." Psalm 27:1 asks us who we should fear when the Lord is our "light" and "salvation." These verses and all the many others that speak to taking courage in the Lord make the same point: If you believe, God is with you. When God is with you, you have nothing to fear.

I once counseled a committed Christian whose faith was tested almost daily in his job. Mickey was a college professor. In addition to a Ph.D. in history, Mickey held a master's degree in divinity and served as a fill-in pastor. He was an excellent teacher, popular with his students and colleagues. But there was a problem. Mickey reported to a department chairman who was an ardent atheist. This department chairman—I will call him Edward—delighted in making Mickey's work life miserable.

Frustrated he could not simply fire Mickey, a tenured professor, Edward tried hard to make him resign. For example, Mickey was assigned the smallest office of all the professors in his department in spite of his seniority. His office was located in a different building away from his colleagues, making it inconvenient to interact with them or to get administrative support from the department's secretary. Mickey's requests to attend history conferences were routinely denied, whereas the requests of his colleagues were routinely approved. Mickey was always scheduled to teach the most unpopular classes in the most undesirable locations. Whereas his colleagues enjoyed teaching graduate courses and benefiting from the help of teaching assistants, Mickey was typically assigned freshman and sophomore courses. Further, his requests for a teaching assistant were routinely denied. When departmental meetings were scheduled, Edward often *forgot* to inform Mickey. Then he would berate Mickey for missing meetings.

A major bone of contention between Mickey and his department chair was the Bible verse Mickey displayed on the wall of his office. Sandwiched between his diplomas and various awards, the keen observer would find a framed copy of the 23rd Psalm. Edward attempted to force Mickey to remove the Bible verse from his office. When the faculty council agreed with the department chair, Mickey filed an appeal citing the First Amendment and academic freedom, which he won. Embarrassed and angry to have his efforts thwarted, Edward went on a vengeful tear, and Mickey's work life was miserable ever since.

It was at this point Mickey came to me for counseling. He was on the verge of resigning, but after much prayer and Bible reading, he decided to take my advice and "wait him out." My thought was an administrator who was so blatantly negative would eventually lose credibility with the other professors in the department, even if they did not share Mickey's religious views. It took another two years, but that is exactly what happened. Mickey continued to exhibit the courage of his convictions, and Edward continued to harass, bully, and abuse him. Finally, the other professors in the department got together and approached the dean, demanding something be done. Their show of unity on Mickey's behalf resulted in Edward's being replaced as department chair. Ironically, his replacement was Mickey.

Edward, a tenured professor, was not fired. Rather, he was returned to the faculty as a history professor, a difficult pill to swallow for a man who took great pride in being the department chairman. Some of the other professors in the department hoped Mickey would exact a measure of revenge against Edward by exiling him to a distant office in a different building and assigning him freshman and sophomore courses. They certainly would have supported him. But taking revenge was not in Mickey's Christian make-up. Instead, he did just the opposite. He heaped burning coals upon the head of his adversary by demonstrating how Edward should have treated him when their roles were reversed.

Mickey assigned Edward a regular faculty office. He also made a point of assigning him his share of graduate courses and giving him a teaching assistant. Mickey and Edward worked together for many more years and developed a relationship characterized by mutual respect. It would be nice to report that because of Mickey's example, Edward converted and became a Christian. Unfortunately, that did not happen. Edward remained a committed atheist, but he did acknowledge a newfound respect for Mickey's moral courage in standing firm in his faith.

SETTING AN EXAMPLE OF COMPETENCE

Professional competence must be part of your example. As Christians, we must do what is necessary to become good at our jobs. There is a sense in which every Christian in the workplace is a pastor, and the example we set for others is our sermon. Part of the example we set for coworkers should be professional competence. Ordained pastors use words to share the Gospel. Workplace "pastors" preach by example. Remember, as Christians, we work first for Christ and then for our employer. Further, we are supposed to honor God through our work. This means no matter what kind or level of position we hold, it is important we do the best job possible. Your employer expects this of you, but more importantly, God expects it of you. Further, your coworkers will admire your competence, making it less likely they will tempt, reject, or persecute you.

Consider what is written in 2 Timothy 2:15. As is often the case with Scripture, this verse can have more than one meaning. In the current context, it means we are to present ourselves to God as diligent employees who are committed to doing a good job. The relevant application is this: do well the work God has given you. This is what the great reformer, Martin Luther, meant when he said (in paraphrase) it is better for a Christian cobbler to make good shoes than to put crosses on shoddily-made shoes. I learned the hard way what Martin Luther meant.

Needing a plumber, I once hired a man whose advertisement read "Christian businessman." His truck had John 3:16 painted on the side. Naturally, I expected him to be diligent and honest. He was neither. This supposedly Christian businessman showed up late, did shoddy work, failed to correct the problem, and then charged considerably more than the estimate. When I complained about the work and the exorbitant cost, he told me I shouldn't treat a Christian brother that way. As he walked out the door, the plumber said he would pray for me and dropped a tract on the floor. Not surprisingly, he later went out of business after being sued by a long list of disgruntled customers. Was this plumber really a believer? Only God can answer that question, but there was certainly no evidence to support his claim. Said another way, if he was a child of God, there was no family resemblance.

When counseling Christians who are struggling with faith-related dilemmas in the workplace, one piece of advice I often give is this: No matter what your job happens to be, get good at it. Strive to be the best. If you are an engineer, strive to be the best engineer in your company. If you are in sales, strive to be your company's leading sales representative. If you are an administrative assistant, be highly organized and efficient. No matter what kind of job you have, get good at it. The better you are at doing your job, the more credibility you will have with superiors, coworkers, and subordinates. People in the workplace admire and respect competence. When coworkers respect your competence, they will be more likely to respect your Christianity.

A carpenter I know is a hard worker and a committed Christian. I will call him Mark. Mark is good at his job. At work, he always gives his best and is never idle. If he completes his work ahead of time, Mark pitches in and helps his fellow carpenters with theirs. When there is a new and different situation the other carpenters cannot handle, the foreman relies on Mark to find a solution. Mark's foreman once asked him why he worked so hard. Always ready for this kind of opening, Mark replied: "I work hard because God expects me to. He provided this job for me, so I show my appreciation by working hard and doing it well. Jesus is my role model. Remember, He was a carpenter." This is the kind of opening that can come to Christians who make competence part of their example.

DISCUSSION CASE 4.1: "FOR ME, SOMEONE IS ALWAYS WATCHING . . ."

John was a construction foreman for ten years. During that time, the safety requirements of the federal government's Occupational Safety and Health Administration (OSHA) became increasingly stringent, especially in construction. John knew the increased regulations were in response to the high accident and death rates in the construction industry.

Consequently, he did not agree with some of the other foremen in his company who resented the regulations. But John's strict adherence to safety regulations often put him at odds with his boss, the construction superintendent, who thought John's safety measures slowed down the pace of work.

The superintendent was known to push his foremen hard. They, in turn, pushed their crews hard so the company could earn the cash bonuses that came with completing jobs ahead of schedule. The other foremen in the company not only pushed their crews hard, they cut corners on safety. John pushed his crews hard too but refused to take shortcuts on safety measures. He made sure his crews complied with all applicable OSHA safety regulations and then some. In other words, John set a consistent example of caring about his workers, something they appreciated. As a result of his dedication to safety, the company's employees and subcontractors liked to be assigned to John's crews.

In spite of his popularity with workers, John was not well liked by the company's superintendent. In an attempt to convince John to take shortcuts, the superintendent once commented, "You don't have to worry about taking shortcuts, no one is watching. Nobody will know." John, a committed Christian, responded, "For me, someone is always watching." After trying unsuccessfully for months to pressure John into taking shortcuts with safety measures, the superintendent suspended John without pay and replaced him with a more ethically pliable foreman.

The new foreman simply ignored OSHA regulations, something that pleased the superintendent immensely. In spite of several "near-miss accidents," John's replacement continued to ignore safety regulations. Eventually and predictably, the chickens came home to roost. One day, a bricklayer working on a scaffold four stories high suddenly lost his footing and plunged to his death. The victim was not wearing the required safety harness. The subsequent investigation by OSHA resulted in numerous citations and a heavy fine. As part of the investigation—at the instigation of several of his former crew members—OSHA personnel interviewed John. When John revealed he was suspended without pay for refusing to take safety-related shortcuts, the OSHA inspector recommended increasing the amount of the fine. There was even consideration of filing criminal charges against the superintendent.

The negative publicity generated by the fatal accident cost the construction company even more than the fines levied by OSHA. By the time the dust settled, the construction superintendent was fired, as was the foreman who replaced John. Further, the construction firm was required to submit a plan for improvement to OSHA that clearly demonstrated the steps it would take to prevent future accidents. As part of that plan, the company recommended adding the position of safety manager to the staff.

Once the plan was approved, John was brought back from suspension and given the new position of safety manager. He also received a raise and full back pay. Not surprisingly, in the years following, John helped the company establish an excellent safety record and, in turn, a reputation as a safe employer. Because of his steadfast example, John was never again pressured to take shortcuts on safety measures. This unfortunate situation turned out well in the end because a committed Christian cared enough about his work crews to stand up to higher management on safety issues. John knew bad things happen when good people remain silent. Because of this he spoke out and stood fast in his beliefs.

Discussion Questions

1. Have you ever worked with a supervisor or manager who was willing to stand up to inappropriate pressure from higher management because he or she cared about you and your fellow workers? If so, what effect did that individual's caring attitude have on subordinates?

2. In this case, John stood up to pressure from his boss because he cared about the safety of his work crews. Eventually, things turned out well for John and his employer. However, this may not always be the case. Had things not turned out well, would you still agree John's actions were correct?

DISCUSSION CASE 4.2: "HE BEHAVES WHEN YOU ARE WITH US."

This was the third time her coworkers asked Sally to join them for the team's regular Friday luncheon. In fact, they practically begged her to join them. As a morale booster, the department manager took his team out to lunch at a different restaurant every Friday. The problem was this manager, Jeff, liked to drink during these luncheons. Unfortunately, the more he drank, the more his behavior became coarse and unpredictable. Her coworkers took to pleading with Sally to join them for lunch, something she rarely did because of Jeff's drinking and crude behavior. This time when they asked, one of them said: "Please go with us, Sally. He behaves when you are with us."

This observation was true. Jeff actually drank less, if at all, and behaved better when Sally was present. Although Jeff did not profess to be a Christian, he seemed to respect Sally's Christian values. He also seemed to be influenced positively by her example. If Sally went to lunch with the team, everyone would get back to work on time and, as a result, not have to work late on Friday night to catch up. It was also less likely an inebriated Jeff would cause an embarrassing situation. Such incidents happened several times before and seemed to be happening more often. Finally, after much prodding from her coworkers, Sally relented and agreed to join them for lunch.

Discussion Questions

1. Have you ever worked with someone who did not profess to be a Christian but was respectful of your Christianity? If so, how did this respect manifest itself?
2. Have you ever worked with someone who seemed to be influenced in a positive way by your Christian example? If so, what effect did your influence have?
3. Should Sally participate in the Friday luncheons and apply her positive influence on Jeff or avoid them because of the types of behavior he might engage in?

REVIEW QUESTIONS FOR INDIVIDUALS AND GROUPS

1. List seven characteristics of servant leaders.
2. What are some ways a Christian in the workplace can set an example of caring? Character?
3. What are some ways a Christian in the workplace can set an example of communication? Clarity?
4. What are some ways a Christian in the workplace can set an example of commitment? Courage?
5. What are some ways a Christian in the workplace can set an example of competence?

CHAPTER 5

BE WISE AND INNOCENT WHEN TRANSLATING SCRIPTURE INTO ACTION

"Behold, I am sending you out as sheep in the midst of wolves, so be wise as serpents and innocent as doves."

Matthew 10:16

LaKeesha could not understand why her coworkers didn't get it. She told them numerous times that purposely slowing the pace of work so they could earn extra pay for having to work overtime was wrong. The job she and her teammates were working on was the most important project their firm ever landed. Consequently, higher management was anxious to get it done on time. Which is why LaKeesha's team leader authorized overtime for the project. LaKeesha had no problem with working overtime or collecting extra pay if doing so was necessary.

However, she was offended by the thought of purposely slowing down the pace of work to create a crisis requiring overtime.

LaKeesha kept to her normal work routine and made good progress every day. The problem was her fellow team members were producing only half as much as LaKeesha during normal working hours. If she didn't slow down, the supervisor would soon catch on to what her teammates were doing. Their scheme would be revealed if the supervisor ever asked, "How is it LaKeesha can turn out a sufficient amount of work during normal hours and the rest of you can't?" Consequently, the pressure on LaKeesha to go along with the overtime scheme was intense. But when she told her coworkers she would not go along because of her Christian beliefs, particularly the Eighth Commandment, they just looked confused. Her teammates were not Christians, so they could not understand her reluctance. LaKeesha finally realized just stating her Christian beliefs would not convince her unbelieving teammates they are wrong. She needed to take a different approach, but she wasn't sure what that should be.

The workplace cries out for the positive examples of committed Christians. As has been mentioned several times already, I encourage Christians to make quitting their jobs the last option exercised when temptation, pressure, and persecution in the workplace seem overwhelming. Christians cannot show their coworkers the way of Christ unless they are present and showing others the way of Christ is part of every Christian's job description. Setting a Christ-like example for coworkers depends on your ability to effectively translate Scripture into workplace-appropriate action. When translating Scripture into action, you must be both wise and innocent. This is the admonition contained in Matthew 10:16, which is the theme of this book.

Christians who learn how to confront sin in ways that are biblically sound (innocent) and workplace-appropriate (wise) serve Christ and benefit their employers. An important question then is this: What is a *workplace-appropriate* response? In the simplest terms, it is a response that accords with Scripture and is appropriate in a workplace setting.

"Appropriate" in the current context means a response likely to produce a positive outcome, even with unbelievers. It will probably not surprise you to learn responding to temptation, rejection, or persecution in ways that are biblically sound and workplace appropriate is one of those things easier said than done.

What qualifies as an appropriate response to sinful behavior in a church may not be appropriate in the workplace. A church is a family of generally like-minded believers. This being the case, we can respond to sin among church members in ways at least widely accepted, if not always appreciated by those being corrected. Nevertheless, those who join a church agree to submit to its rules concerning how sin among the members will be handled. The workplace, on the other hand, is a montage of believers and unbelievers, as well as different kinds of believers.

The general like-mindedness characterizing church congregations does not typically exist in the workplace. Instead, the prevailing belief system at work is secular humanism reinforced by political correctness. Unfortunately, much of what we, as Christians, believe is considered politically incorrect. As a result, the workplace is not always a friendly environment for Christians. In fact, there might even be outright hostility toward Christianity in some cases. This means what works in a church setting may not be effective, much less welcomed, in a work setting. Further, the mission of an employer is not the same as that of a church. This is one more reason why appropriate responses to sin in your church may not be appropriate on your job. Consequently, it is important to follow the admonition of Matthew 10:16 when responding to temptation, rejection, or persecution in the workplace.

The purpose of this chapter is to help you learn how to be both wise and innocent when responding to faith-related challenges in the workplace. I present specific strategies that will allow you to respond to these challenges in biblically sound and workplace-appropriate ways. Two workplace situations are presented as examples and analyzed to demonstrate how you might respond to faith-related challenges at work. Comporting yourself well in the workplace can take a lot of practice.

I encourage you to analyze all the stories presented in this book and the cases presented at the end of each chapter to help develop your skills in this critical area.

TRANSLATING SCRIPTURE INTO BIBLICALLY SOUND, WORKPLACE-APPROPRIATE ACTION

Recall from Chapter 2 the story of John, the overt Christian and CPA, who was called on the carpet for refusing to join clients in sampling the local nightlife. When confronted by his boss, an unbeliever, John was humble and respectful, but he made it clear bar-hopping violated his Christian beliefs. But he didn't stop there. He also told his boss that seeing the firm's CPAs carousing in bars like college students on spring break would not be good for the firm's image. Then he told his boss about the front-page test and how he applied it in his life. After considering the matter for a few days, John's boss not only sided with him but adopted John's front-page test as company policy. That story demonstrates how a Christian responded to a faith-related challenge at work in a way that was both wise and innocent.

Let's analyze how John responded when called on the carpet by his boss. First, John was humble and respectful, two traits harmonizing with the teachings of Scripture and therefore biblically sound. That part of John's response fell under the heading of being innocent. Further, John made no secret of the fact engaging in the types of activities his clients enjoyed after hours violated his Christian beliefs. That acknowledgment was also part of the innocent side of the equation. But John didn't stop there.

Knowing his boss was an unbeliever who was unlikely to be moved by John's Christian beliefs, the CPA also explained how the behavior in question could harm the company's image, reputation, and, ultimately, bottom line. In other words, he made his point in terms his boss, an unbeliever, could relate to and appreciate. This was the wise aspect of John's response.

John's handling of this faith-related challenge was both biblically sound and workplace appropriate. John could have simply dug in his heels and told his boss he had no right to ask him to compromise his Christian beliefs. That approach, though valid and understandable, would not have been workplace appropriate. John knew his unbelieving boss would not accept an argument that was based solely on Scripture. Consequently, John reinforced his religious qualms with a bottom-line business rationale.

Now let's analyze another situation in which a Christian responded to a faith-related challenge in a biblically sound and workplace-appropriate way. Alice was being pressured by several coworkers on her sales team to make false claims about their company's products. Her coworkers were intent on bolstering their sales numbers by making their product sound better than it was. In their defense, Alice's coworkers were forwarding recommendations for product improvements to the company's design department. But the needed improvements had yet to be made, and it was not clear if they ever would be.

The key factor driving the unethical behavior of Alice's teammates was money. If the team could increase its sales volume by 10 percent, all its members would receive a hefty cash bonus. Theirs was a good product, but not as good as they were claiming. Alice, a committed Christian, refused to give in to the pressure to make false claims to customers. As a result, her fellow sales representatives were applying every kind of pressure they could think of to bring Alice into their nefarious scheme. For example, to make her feel guilty, Alice's coworkers claimed she was going to cause them to lose money they all badly needed. One teammate went so far as to tell Alice that by refusing to go along with their scheme she was "taking food out of the mouths of my children."

This claim hit Alice, a mother, especially hard. She knew her teammates could use the extra money, but she also knew lying about their company's product was the wrong way to get it. In fact, for Scriptural guidance, Alice looked no further than the Ninth Commandment (Exodus 20:16). She needed no further guidance. The Ninth Commandment is clear in its meaning: You shall not lie. Had they been discussing this situation in a Sunday School class, a Bible study, or a prayer breakfast, Alice could simply have told her coworkers they were breaking the Ninth Commandment. Because, as Christians, they would all subscribe to the Ninth Commandment, Alice would be on solid ground in refusing to lie to customers. But Alice's situation was happening in a different setting: the workplace. Her teammates were not Christians.

Consequently, simply pointing out her fellow sales representatives were breaking the Ninth Commandment was not likely to have the desired effect. Her unbelieving coworkers would probably have said, "Who cares?" Those who were hostile to Christianity might even have become angry, or worse. Consequently, Alice needed to respond to her teammates in a way that was biblical. It took much prayer and some wise counsel from her pastor before Alice came up with a plan.

To be biblically sound, Alice had to refuse to go along with lying about their company's product during sales presentations, which she did. There was no question in her mind about refusing. She knew exactly what the Bible required concerning honesty. However, the way in which she went about refusing was important. Rather than just refuse and chastise her coworkers for lying, Alice responded in a way that was honest, patient, humble, courteous, thankful, selfless, forgiving, and steadfast. When Alice disagreed with her coworkers, she did so without being disagreeable. She also listened to what her teammates had to say and ignored their anger and other inconsiderate behavior. To be workplace appropriate, Alice presented her side of the argument from the perspective of the long-term good of the individuals involved rather than from just the perspective of the Ninth Commandment.

Alice listened patiently to the arguments of her teammates, thanked them for explaining their side to her, and humbly acknowledged she understood their desire to earn a performance bonus. She even acknowledged, like them, she could use the bonus money. Alice thought that kind of response was more likely to produce positive results than choosing to return their anger and accusations. She was comforted knowing her response exemplified what is written in Proverbs 15:1. In this verse, we read a gentle response prevents anger, but an unkind response can cause anger. Alice knew it was important to avoid putting her coworkers on the defensive by painting them into a corner.

Next Alice told her colleagues they had become so focused on earning a bonus they were overlooking the long-term consequences to them and their company. She gently asked such questions as: "What is going to happen when our product does not do the things we say it will do?" "Who is going to be blamed when it becomes apparent we oversold the product?" "Who will be blamed for making customers angry by inflating the capabilities of our product?" "What will happen to future sales when word gets around we oversell our product?" "Why not see if we can increase sales without overselling and making false claims?"

Her coworkers continued to disagree with her, often in a disagreeable manner. But Alice stuck to her convictions and refused to respond in-kind. She was determined to be biblically sound (innocent) by refusing to go along with lying and by responding in patient, humble, and courteous ways. Alice's coworkers knew her reservations were based on religious convictions. But she did not base her arguments against making false claims solely on her Christian beliefs. Instead, she presented a workplace-appropriate rationale that supplemented her personal beliefs.

Alice was being workplace appropriate (wise) when she presented her views in the context of the long-term good of the individuals involved, the sales team, and the company. Although her coworkers may have been angry and frustrated with Alice, in their hearts they knew she was right. Further, having time to consider the matter rationally, they eventually came to appreciate Alice's point of view. Once they considered the potential consequences of their actions, Alice's coworkers acknowledged she was right and just dropped the idea of inflating sales claims.

Alice's coworkers were not happy with her for a while, but they eventually came around. When this happened, they worked together as a team to help the designers of their product add some of the features customers wanted. Eventually, through this kind of collaboration, the product was improved to the point sales increased substantially. When that happened, Alice and her team were given bonuses for working with the design team to improve the product, as well as bonuses for increased sales. This situation had a positive ending because a committed Christian handled it in a way that was biblically sound and workplace appropriate. Alice's interactions with her coworkers were both wise and innocent, as we are admonished in Matthew 10:16.

This story would probably have had a different ending had Alice chosen to become righteously angry or had she simply lectured her team-mates on what the Bible says about lying. She never once tried to cover up or disguise her Christian convictions. But she did not stop there. She understood her unbelieving coworkers would probably reject an argument based solely on Scripture. Consequently, she added a practical element to her argument. By being wise and innocent, Alice turned a bad situation into something good and did it in an edifying way for her coworkers.

FORMULATING WORKPLACE-APPROPRIATE RESPONSES

For Christians, it should not be difficult to identify biblically sound actions when confronted with faith-related dilemmas. Scripture, prayer, and the wise counsel of fellow believers are always available to help us with this side of the equation. Often, when we claim to struggle with finding the biblically sound course of action, we are struggling not with understanding what the Bible tells us but with our own reluctance to accept what it tells us. However, even after factoring in our sinful nature, identifying a biblically sound course of action is not usually a major problem.

Often the more difficult challenge is to formulate responses both biblically sound and workplace appropriate. There is less help available on the workplace-appropriate side of the equation. Consequently, over the years, I have developed a list of questions to help Christians coping with faith-related dilemmas. When responding to faith-related challenges in the workplace, ask those who are tempting, rejecting, or persecuting you any or all the following questions:

- *Would the action you are recommending pass the front-page test?* In other words, if all the thoughts, facts, and motives of the individuals recommending the action in question were to be printed on the front page of their local newspaper, would those individuals be proud of themselves or ashamed?

- *Is the action in question likely to stand the test of time?* Is the recommended action going to be as beneficial in the long run as it seems to be in the moment? Is the recommended action likely to cause more problems in the long run than it solves in the short run?

- *Who will be blamed if the action in question goes awry?* Are those who recommend the action in question prepared to accept responsibility when things go wrong? Are they prepared to be held accountable?

- *Is the action in question good for the overall organization or just the few who are recommending it?* Are those recommending the action trying to benefit in ways that might be detrimental to the rest of the organization? Who will benefit and who will be hurt by the recommended action?

- *Will the action in question help or harm the professional reputations of those involved?* If others in the organization, members of the profession, or the general public learn the details of the action in question, will the reputations of those involved be enhanced or damaged?

- *Is the action in question a lawsuit waiting to happen?* In today's litigious society, there are those who profit from the poor judgment of others by filing civil lawsuits. Is the perceived benefit of the action worth finding oneself on the receiving end of a lawsuit?

- *Is the action in question unethical?* Most organizations adopt strict policies for ethical conduct. There are often stiff penalties, including termination, for violating ethics policies. Have those recommending the action in question considered the ethics of their proposed actions and the

potential consequences of violating the organization's
code of ethics?

- *Is the action in question illegal?* Are the perceived benefits
  of the action in question worth going to jail for?

In the story of Alice and her fellow sales representatives, she used
pointed questions similar to these to help her colleagues see the folly
of their proposed action. These questions frame an argument for
doing the right thing in the context of self-interest. They all really ask
the same question: What will happen if you are caught? If framing an
argument in terms of self-interest is distasteful to you as a Christian,
do not despair. Look at these questions again. Although they are purposely asked from the perspective of self-interest, each of the questions has a basis in Scripture.

The Scriptural foundation of these questions is as basic as the second
Greatest Commandment. Loving your neighbors, including your organization's stakeholders, requires selflessness. Selfless people do not know-
ingly do things that would fail the *front-page test,* fail the test of time,
result in finger pointing, benefit the few but harm the many, damage
professional reputations, result in unnecessary lawsuits, violate ethical
standards, or break the law. Because the questions I recommend for
helping you formulate workplace-appropriate responses are all grounded
in Scripture, even this side of the equation is biblically sound.

DISCUSSION CASE 5.1: "I AM REALLY STRUGGLING WITH THIS DECISION."

Randall has a decision to make causing him sleepless nights. His college's
star basketball player is flunking the course Randall teaches. If this
basketball player makes less than a C in Randall's course, he will lose
his eligibility. If this player loses his eligibility, the college's basketball
team will probably lose in the upcoming national tournament. With this
player on the floor the team is great. Without him, the team is good, but
not good enough to win the championship. The pressure on Randall

from the coach, dean, alumni, and several of Randall's colleagues is immense.

Randall, a committed Christian, has already prayed and sought help in Scripture. In fact, he knows the right thing to do is to award the student the grade he has earned and let the chips fall where they may. But that grade is not just an F; it is a low F. Counting on his basketball prowess to protect him, this student has done none of his assignments, failed every test, and skipped more than half of his classes. When Randall approached his pastor for counsel, he was tempted to simply give in and pass the basketball star. He told his pastor, "I have never felt so much pressure in my life. I am really struggling with this decision. Right is on my side, the rules are on my side, and the student's poor performance is on my side, but the entire college is against me."

Discussion Questions

1. Have you ever faced a dilemma at work in which you knew the right thing to do but were under immense pressure to do something different? How did you respond?
2. If you were Randall's pastor, what would you advise him to do? Is there a response Randall could adopt that would be both biblically sound and workplace appropriate?

DISCUSSION CASE 5.2: "THE PRESSURE FROM MY FRIENDS IS BECOMING UNBEARABLE . . ."

Page Brunson has never felt so alone or so pressured to do something she knows is wrong. The problem is magnified by the fact the pressure is coming from fellow teachers. She has worked with these teachers for more than fifteen years. They are more than just colleagues; they are friends. Page's fellow teachers have decided the only way they can pass a graduate course they are all taking is to cheat. What is worse, they all need this course to renew their teaching certificates. Consequently, they have worked out an elaborate scheme for dividing up the take-home exam. Each of them will complete one part of the test. Then all will share their work with the others. The problem is Page, a committed Christian, is refusing to go along. Consequently, her friends are applying intense pressure. One even told Page "your self-righteous attitude is going to cause me to lose my teaching certificate." Page recently told her sister, "The pressure from my friends is becoming unbearable. I don't know what to do."

Discussion Questions

1. Have you ever been pressured by coworkers to do something either illegal or unethical? How did you respond? How should you have responded?
2. How could Page respond in a biblically sound and workplace-appropriate way? You may assume her coworkers are not professing Christians.

REVIEW QUESTIONS FOR INDIVIDUALS AND GROUPS

1. What is meant by the term "biblically sound" in reference to the responses we make to workplace pressure, temptation, or persecution?
2. What is meant by the term "workplace appropriate" in reference to the responses we make to pressure, temptation, or persecution in the workplace?
3. Can our responses to faith-related trials in the workplace be biblically sound but not workplace appropriate? Explain.
4. Can our responses to faith-related trials on the job be workplace appropriate but not biblically sound? Explain.
5. What are several questions you might ask coworkers as part of your response to temptation, rejection, pressure, or persecution in the workplace?

CHAPTER 6

BUILD POSITIVE RELATIONSHIPS WITH UNBELIEVING COWORKERS

"Little children, let us not love in word or talk but in deed and in truth."

1 John 3:18

Matthew's construction crew consisted of eight unbelievers and him, so he often felt out of place. Matthew wanted to fit in, but fitting in with his fellow crew members would mean compromising his faith. They worked hard all day, but on breaks and during lunch they told ribald stories and inappropriate jokes. To Matthew, their language was embarrassing and crude. Consequently, he kept his distance. During breaks and lunch, Matthew kept to himself. He was often heard to say, "I may have to work with these guys, but I don't have to socialize with them." Matthew viewed his unbelieving coworkers as enemies of his beliefs. It wasn't until later he learned to view them as fellow sinners in need of his Christian example. In other words, Matthew had to learn to view unbelievers as opportunities.

Ironically, over the years, some of my most positive and productive working relationships have been with unbelievers. The workplace is replete with people who reject Christianity or, at the very least, are ambivalent about it. In fact, in the various organizations where I serve as a business consultant, overtly professing Christians are in the minority. This is why Christians in the workplace sometimes feel like sheep in the midst of wolves. Some Christians I counsel view their minority status in the workplace with trepidation believing it puts them at a disadvantage. But a Christian I will call Mary views her minority status in the workplace in a more positive light. Being one of the few who believe among the many who don't just means more opportunities for Mary to witness for Christ.

Mary seldom goes to lunch with the other two Christians in her department. Instead, she typically chooses to join several unbelieving coworkers for lunch. Once, when her fellow believers asked why she would go to lunch with people who reject her faith, Mary got right to the point. "Their rejection of our faith is why I go to lunch with them. The two of you are already believers. They aren't. I believe it is my duty to minister to unbelievers. I can't do that without spending time with them. It is more enjoyable and more comfortable sharing lunch with the two of you, but I feel like Christ wants me to reach out to those who don't know him. This is one of the ways I do that."

In viewing her unbelieving coworkers as opportunities, Mary put into practice what Christ said in Mark 2:17. In this verse, Christ made it clear He came to call unbelievers, not those who already believe. He explained the sick, not the healthy, need a physician. To translate this verse into contemporary language, we might say Christ does not expect us to preach only to the choir. Like the physician who treats the sick, Christ wants us to reach out to unbelievers.

When you work with people who reject your beliefs, the temptation is to imitate the tortoise and pull back into the comfort and safety of your shell. Peer pressure is a powerful force. Further, it is only human to want to fit in with your coworkers. Which is why some Christians in the workplace hide their faith and why others segregate themselves from coworkers. These approaches, though understandable, are wrong. The better approach is to invest the time and effort necessary to build positive working relationships with your unbelieving coworkers. You will never influence coworkers for Christ by segregating yourself from them or hiding your faith and going along to get along. It is important to understand, as Christians, we can work with people who reject our faith without validating their worldviews. We should view unbelievers as people who reject Christ now but may see the light at some point in the future. Remember you might be the instrument Christ uses to change the hearts of unbelieving coworkers. This is more likely to happen if you have established good working relationships with them.

SCRIPTURAL GUIDANCE FOR WORKING WITH UNBELIEVERS

Several Christians who have approached me for help with faith-related dilemmas at work have expressed concern about Paul's admonition in 2 Corinthians 6:14–18 to avoid being unequally yoked with unbelievers. These Christians were concerned that by working with unbelievers, they were allowing themselves to be unequally yoked. This is a fairly common, though misguided, concern among working Christians. The misunderstanding comes from a faulty interpretation of what it means to be "unequally yoked."

Paul's caution against being unequally yoked is a warning against entering relationships so intimate and personal the other person will have the power to adversely influence your faith. Marriage is such a relationship. Paul is not warning against professional relationships in which work is the common ground. We know this because in 1 Corinthians 5:9–10 Paul asserts it would be impossible for believers to avoid working with unbelievers. Paul claims to do that would require us to ". . . go out of the world." Indeed it would.

Guarding against being unequally yoked is a matter of being cautious about the kind of relationship you have with unbelievers. Professional relationships do not have the same kinds of intimate emotional attachments as marriage, or at least they shouldn't. Proper professional relationships should have no adverse influence on your faith. If you keep your professional relationships centered on work while maintaining your personal relationship with Christ, you won't be adversely influenced by unbelieving coworkers. It really comes down to a simple question. Whom do you want to please: God or your coworkers? If you find yourself wanting to please coworkers instead of God, it is time to step back and reassess your work relationships. You may have a problem even bigger than being unequally yoked.

It is entirely appropriate for Christians to work side-by-side with unbelievers, albeit without validating their worldviews or being adversely influenced by those views. Instead we should approach our time with unbelievers as an opportunity to show them the ways of Christ. Rather than avoid or reject unbelievers, we should pray for them. This is the message in Matthew 5:43–44 where we are told to love our enemies and pray for those who persecute us. Unbelieving coworkers are not really the enemy. The real enemy is Satan. But coworkers can be the instruments Satan uses to attack your faith. On the other hand, you can be the instrument Christ uses to turn them from Satan.

To avoid being unequally yoked to unbelieving coworkers, keep your relationships with them professional and focused on getting the job done well, on time, and within budget. What you must avoid is allowing relationships with unbelievers to develop in ways that give them the influence to undermine your faith. You will know this has happened if you find yourself being more concerned with pleasing unbelieving coworkers than with pleasing Christ. When you become sufficiently yoked to an unbeliever, you find yourself being influenced to compromise your faith, and you have become unequally yoked. This, of course, is a danger we all face as working Christians. It is why when Christ sent his Apostles out into the world He warned them to be both wise and innocent (Matthew 10:16). He knew even His Apostles had feet of clay and were, therefore, susceptible to the nefarious schemes of Satan.

If you ever become concerned that working with unbelievers is somehow a violation of your Christian beliefs, just think of the example of Christ. Had Christ limited His ministry to those who shared His beliefs, the Gospel would not have spread beyond the Apostles and a relatively small group of other followers. Rather than avoid relationships with unbelieving coworkers, it is better for you to view the workplace as a mission field and yourself as a missionary. When you do this, it is easier to build positive working relationships with unbelieving coworkers.

Remember, the best way to influence people for good is to begin by establishing the trust and respect that come from investing yourself in them. You are more likely to influence those with whom you have positive relationships than those who consider you an outsider. If you grow weary of trying to build positive relationships with unbelieving coworkers, consider the example of James Chalmers, the great missionary to the natives of Papua, New Guinea. He labored among the natives for eleven years before even one of them came to Christ. Before he could influence them for good, he had to first win their trust. It took a long time, but Chalmers persevered and eventually succeeded. After that first conversion, many more followed. His example of perseverance and patience is one we, as Christians, should emulate.

To build positive relationships with unbelieving coworkers without becoming unequally yoked to them it is necessary to consistently apply several character traits. These traits are honesty, patience, humility, courtesy, gratitude, selflessness, and forgiveness. You will find even the most ardent unbelievers like to work with teammates who exemplify these traits. Further, once unbelieving coworkers understand these traits grow out of your Christian beliefs, they will be more inclined to respect those beliefs.

HONESTY IN WORK RELATIONSHIPS

Scripture is replete with admonitions to be honest, not the least of which is the Ninth Commandment. Nobody likes to be lied to, not even a compulsive liar. If your coworkers are going to be influenced by your Christian example, they have to trust you. Those you hope to influence must know they can count on you to tell the truth, deal forthrightly with them and others, keep accurate accounts, and do your job without taking unethical shortcuts. Scripture speaks to honesty in the workplace in Proverbs 11:1, where we are told a "false balance" is an "abomination to the Lord." The broader meaning of this verse is God expects us to be honest in all of our dealings.

People who sneak out early but claim to have worked a full day, exaggerate on their expense accounts, charge personal items to company credit cards, submit false reports, take credit for the work of others, or engage in other kinds of self-serving, dishonest behavior will earn, at the very least, the silent scorn of their coworkers. Ironically, even people who commit these sins look down on others who commit them. The sinful nature of human beings makes us capable of doing the very things we condemn others for doing and then finding ways to justify our actions. This is why Christ counsels us we need to remove the logs from our own eyes before we can see clearly to remove the specks from the eyes of others (Matthew 7:5).

It is not uncommon for money to be the driving force behind the dishonesty sometimes observed in the workplace. Often people who find themselves in a financial bind will rationalize their dishonesty by claiming "need." The problem with this rationale is financial need—even when legitimate—does not justify dishonesty. Consider what Proverbs 19:1 has to say about dishonesty motivated by money. In this verse, we are told it is better to be poor and honest than wealthy and untrustworthy. Christians who are scrupulously honest earn the respect of superiors, coworkers, and subordinates. When you earn the respect of your coworkers by being honest with them, they will be more open to respecting the Christian beliefs behind your honesty. They will also be more likely to ask questions about your beliefs. When this happens, a door has opened. Make sure you are prepared to walk through it.

When dealing with faith-related challenges in the workplace, remember people do not have to endorse your beliefs to respect them. Further, just because people act in sinful ways does not mean deep down they reject your Christian values. Even as Christians, we often act in ways at odds with our professed beliefs. This is what the Apostle Paul wrote about in Romans 7:18–19. In these verses, he makes clear how difficult it can be to do what is right even when you know what is right. Like you and me, Paul wanted to do right, but often found it difficult. Of course, not all people want to do the right thing. But even those who do, including the most committed Christians, sometimes struggle.

LIARS ULTIMATELY LIE TO THEMSELVES

Amber always looked forward to her weekly business luncheons with a group of old college friends. Her friends worked for different companies but had similar jobs. During one of the lunch meetings, a friend, Margot, asked if she could have the receipts from the others after they paid for their meals. Margot explained she could claim their luncheon as a meeting with clients and submit all of the receipts for reimbursement. Her claim would make it appear she paid for all the meals. This would increase Margot's reimbursement five-fold. To Amber's surprise, she was the only member of the group who questioned Margot's plan. Apparently, the others saw nothing wrong with bilking an employer out of a few extra dollars. Margot was not happy with what she called Amber's "self-righteous attitude." Nevertheless, Amber's refusal to go along was enough to cause Margot to drop the idea.

Things were chilly between Amber and Margot for a while. Then, out of the blue one day, Margot approached Amber and offered her a job. The job would mean a promotion and a pay raise for Amber. Recently promoted to supervisor of her department, Margot needed colleagues she could trust to join her team. The good news was Margot had been promoted. The bad news was she inherited a team with a record of unethical behavior. Margot was given the specific charge to "clean up" the department. As a result, she needed a trustworthy colleague to help her.

From experience, Margot knew she could trust Amber to be honest and to tell her the truth. This example illustrates what Solomon wrote in Proverbs 16:13: Good leaders appreciate advisors who will tell them the truth. Even a supervisor whose own integrity is questionable wants his or her subordinates to be honest and trustworthy. In fact, even the most dishonest people prefer to deal with others who are honest. This is an ironic but common enough characteristic among people. When she was put in charge and told to clean up the department, Margot knew she would need honest people she could trust. So, she reached out to Amber and offered her a job.

One day, Margot asked Amber why she was so committed to being honest. Given the opening, Amber quoted Ephesians 4:25. In this verse, we read, people who lie to others end up lying to themselves. Amber went on to explain that, although dishonesty might appear advantageous in the short run, it invariably creates problems in the long run. Amber also explained that, although an employee's dishonesty certainly hurts his or her company, in the long run it hurts the liar even more.

PATIENCE IN RELATIONSHIPS WITH COWORKERS

Susan and Adam were shift supervisors for a fast-food restaurant. Susan, a committed Christian, earned the loyalty and commitment of her subordinates by being patient, caring, and kind toward them. As a result, they worked hard to repay her, giving Susan the most productive team on the restaurant's payroll. Adam, on the other hand, was stridently demanding and treated his subordinates with callous disregard and impatience. He liked to claim, "I don't suffer fools gladly."

As things turned out, the real fool was Adam. His propensity for managing by tirade undermined the commitment of his team members and, in turn, his team's performance. Not surprisingly, Adam's subordinates resented his impatient tirades. As a result, they responded by just going through the motions and doing only enough to get by. They adopted the classic passive-aggressive response to Adam's bullying. Susan's patience paid dividends in loyalty and performance, whereas Adam's impatience cost him in both areas.

Being patient means selflessly enduring the everyday exigencies of life as well as the perceived foibles of other people. Further, it means doing these things while maintaining a positive attitude. The Bible is clear in teaching we are to be patient. In Ephesians 4:1–2, we are admonished to live our lives with patience. In Colossians 3:12, we are told to put on patience. Impatience, on the other hand, is an outworking of self-centeredness. It manifests itself as an attitude of annoyance when things don't go our way, or when things take more time than we want them to. Here is rule of thumb you can use concerning being patient with your coworkers: *Impatience is about me—patience is about thee.*

God knew we would be tempted by impatience because of our tendency toward self-centeredness. This is true of unbelievers, but it is also true of believers. The temptations to be impatient in the world are magnified in the workplace because of deadlines, pressure to perform, and ambition to name just a few. This means a faith-related challenge you are certain to face is impatient coworkers and superiors. However, even when coworkers are impatient with us, we are admonished to be patient with them. It is said patience is a virtue, but it is actually more. It is a Scriptural requirement. That being the case, Christians can be presumed to be exemplars of patience, right? Not necessarily. For some Christians, being patient requires a concerted effort. If patience is a virtue, it can be an elusive virtue for some of us, myself included.

Impatience is an outgrowth of self-centeredness. Self-centeredness, in turn, is an outgrowth of one's sinful nature. Impatience is so common a sin businesses take advantage of it for commercial purposes. The business world understands its customers are impatient, which is why businesses invest so much time and energy in eliminating or reducing customer waiting. Customer service consultants teach their clients that one of the worst mistakes they can make is to force customers to wait. When customers have to wait, they spend that time thinking bad thoughts about the business making them wait. Businesses that have implemented measures to minimize waiting use those measures to gain a competitive advantage in the marketplace.

Banks provide ATMs. Fast-food restaurants provide drive-through windows. Numerous businesses allow you to order online. All these things are done for the convenience of the customer. In other words, they are done because businesses understand customers are impatient. Disneyworld has made a science of moving large crowds through its various attractions in ways that minimize waiting. As a society, we have microwave ovens, ever-faster Internet service, instant oatmeal, toaster waffles, cell phones, texting, instant messaging, and hundreds of other ways to eliminate or reduce the amount of time spent waiting. I have observed people angrily cursing computers because the devices did not respond in microseconds to their commands. Businesses take advantage of our impatience to increase sales, but in reality, all this pandering to impatience only fuels more impatience.

Unfortunately, human nature is such that the less we have to wait, the less patient we become with waiting. This ironic phenomenon has led to such problems as road rage and texting while driving. People have become so impatient they are willing to verbally abuse or even physically attack each other over minor disagreements while driving. Road-rage incidents involving shootings are now common. As I write these words, the morning news programs just reported a baby was shot in a road-rage incident. A man angered by how slowly the child's grandmother was driving, shot into the car, missing the grandmother, but killing the baby.

Then there is the problem of texting while driving. People have become so impatient they are willing to risk an automobile accident rather than wait or pull over to read a meaningless text message. Frankly, we have become a nation of impatient people who want what we want, when we want it, and how we want it. Further, if the demands of our impatience are not met, some of us become angry and act out in destructive ways. Consequently, Christians can expect to be confronted by impatient coworkers. This being the case, developing patience yourself while also learning how to deal with impatient people, is important for working Christians.

The impatience of the world at large gives you and me an opportunity to set a different and welcome example in the workplace. Waiting patiently is a fundamental aspect of Christianity. Psalms 27:14, for example, admonishes us to "wait for the Lord." As Christians, waiting patiently is supposed to be what we do. But we cannot demonstrate patience unless we are willing to develop patience. Patience is like a muscle that can be developed if you are willing to work at it. It is also like a muscle in that you will lose it if you stop working on it. As you work on developing patience, remember this: It does not mean reluctantly tolerating people while silently fuming. Rather, it means confronting your own self-centeredness and learning to wait for others in a Christ-like frame of mind.

If you want to develop muscles, go to the gym. If you want to develop patience, go to Scripture. Begin with Philippians 4:6, where it is written we are to be anxious for nothing. Rather than be impatient, we are to let our needs be known to God through "prayer and supplication with thanksgiving . . ." An effective strategy to develop patience is to memorize Philippians 4:6 and recite it over and over any time you feel impatience bubbling up within you. By the time you have silently recited this verse several times your impulse to respond impatiently will probably have passed. If it hasn't, recite the verse again along with a prayer for God's help in taming the self-centeredness at the root of your impatience.

In a work setting where impatience is the norm, your example of quiet and loving patience will be welcomed. When people fall behind in their work, being impatient with them just increases their anxiety. This, in turn, leads to errors in their work and their judgment. When deadlines loom, the worst thing you can do is become impatient with coworkers and subordinates. A better approach is to patiently chip in and help or patiently show others what is needed and how to get it done right and on time. Patiently keep coworkers focused on the work to be done, not the deadline. Any impatience on your part will just generate stress, and stress diminishes performance.

Let me be clear that exemplifying Godly patience on the job does not mean tolerating laziness, ineptitude, or lack of commitment. Remember even Christ displayed righteous impatience and indignation when He drove the moneychangers out of the temple (Matthew 21:12). But refusing to tolerate laziness, ineptitude, and lack of commitment in others does not mean responding impatiently.

When you must point out the shortcomings of others on the job, do so with patience. God is infinitely patient in dealing with us. Consequently, to reflect the image of Christ we must be patient when dealing with others, even those who fail to perform up to our expectations in their jobs. When you feel yourself becoming impatient with a low-performing coworker or a subordinate, remember you don't perform up to Christ's expectations either. If Christ can be patient with us, we can be patient with others. We just have to work at it.

HUMILITY IN RELATIONSHIPS WITH COWORKERS

Humility is a fundamental Christian trait and essential in building positive human relationships. In 1 Peter 5:5–6, we read God opposes the proud but gives grace to the humble. Back in my private-sector days, I learned a valuable lesson about humility. My boss gave me a difficult project with an unforgiving deadline. The pressure was on. There was one positive note though. The project was so important my boss allowed me to handpick my own team members. When I submitted my list of potential team members, he quickly approved every name on it; every name, that is, but one. Concerning the one he rejected, my boss told me putting an individual I will call Bill on the team was a bad idea. He suggested I choose a coworker named Melvin instead.

This surprised me. I didn't really know Bill or Melvin well, but I knew Bill's reputation for being a go-getter. I also knew Melvin to be a quiet, unassuming type. He was not someone who would generate a lot of interest from a project manager's perspective. When I explained why Bill was my first choice, my boss replied: "You are falling for Bill's self-promotion and boasting. Take Melvin. He doesn't brag, but he gets the job done." That turned out to be good advice. My boss was right. Quiet, unassuming Melvin turned out to be a humble dynamo when it came to getting the job done right, on time, and within budget. He didn't blow his own horn, but he performed, and well. Bill, as it turned out, was an empty suit. He was big on self-promotion but small on performance.

God expects us to be humble. In Matthew 18:1–4, Christ teaches to enter the Kingdom of Heaven we must first humble ourselves on earth. His disciples wanted to know who was the greatest in the Kingdom of Heaven. Christ answered that whoever humbles himself like a child is the greatest. What Christ said to His disciples should be heeded by Christians in the workplace. People at work soon learn, in spite of the boasting and bragging of self-promoters, who gets the job done right, on time, and within budget. Humility coupled with effectiveness is a power-ful combination.

As Christians, the ultimate role model for humility is Christ. Christ's entire time on earth was characterized by humility and service. In Philip-pians 2:6–8, Paul tells how Jesus humbled Himself and led the life of a selfless servant. With Christ's example so readily available to us, one might think humility would come naturally to Christians. It doesn't. In fact, humility is like patience; for many of us it comes hard. For most of us, humility, like patience, must be developed through self-evaluation and concerted effort.

Humility is the opposite of pride. Whenever workplace conflicts arise, misguided pride is usually a factor. Misguided pride is synonymous with self-centeredness, arrogance, and egoism. These traits can, in turn, be unwittingly encouraged by the competition for recognition, status, and pay present in the workplace. They can cause people to exaggerate their ability and accomplishments. People who feel compelled to trumpet and embellish their own accomplishments are often driven by insecurity, a condition that exists because they know their own weaknesses and shortcomings. Insecure people often hide their insecurity behind a mask of boasting and self-promotion. Rather than do what is necessary to improve their skills, some insecure people resort to portraying themselves as more capable than they really are. They oversell their own abilities.

Because there is always competition between individuals in the workplace for promotions, salary increases, and recognition, some people engage in self-promotion and boasting to influence decision makers in their favor. Others boast to cover shortcomings. Yet others boast out of fear of being overlooked. It does not help that the standards of society, aided and abetted by the media, have devolved to the point braggarts are often viewed as celebrities. Consequently, chest-beating and over-the-top displays of narcissism and arrogance are commonplace in our society. The hard truth, though, is deep down most people are still offended by bragging and self-promotion.

A better and more effective way to "blow your own horn" in the workplace is to let your work do it for you. Humble Christians who earn a reputation for consistently getting their work done right, on time, and within budget will stand out in the long run much better than self-promoting braggarts. People who attempt to cover up their insecurity or shortcomings by boasting are eventually found out. Further, boasting and self-promotion are the antithesis of teamwork, and teamwork is the key to productivity in the workplace. Teamwork is about *we*. Self-promotion is about *me*. Nobody likes to work with a self-promoting braggart, not even another self-promoting braggart.

COURTESY IN RELATIONSHIPS WITH COWORKERS

Good manners, though still valued, are rarely taught these days. As a result, young people who use words of common courtesy such as "ma'am," "sir," "please," and "thank you" are becoming a rare breed. What has become common behavior for young people these days would have sent a youngster of my generation to the woodshed. In fact, young people who are courteous stand out like welcome beacons in contemporary society. The lack of common courtesy has become an unfortunate characteristic of people in contemporary society. Predictably, its effects have made their way into the workplace. Even people in positions of authority in the workplace seldom hear themselves referred to as "sir" or "ma'am."

In a setting where poor manners and rudeness are common, a little courtesy can go a long way. Nobody likes to be treated rudely, but many are in today's workplace. In fact, the pressures of the workplace often encourage rudeness. As Christians, we are called to exemplify the kind of love spoken of in 1 Corinthians 13. Part of exemplifying biblical love is being courteous to others. Verses 4–6 of 1 Corinthians 13 remind us what love is and what it is not. In these verses, we read love is "patient" and "kind." We also read love is not envious, jealous, "irritable," or "resentful." When we are patient, kind, and courteous to others, it is harder for them to be rude to us, or even to others when around us. Further, when we are courteous to others, it is easier for us to influence them for good. Coworkers who respect your good manners will be more likely to respect your Christianity.

Doug is a committed Christian who may be the most unfailingly courteous person I have ever met. As a result of his commitment to treating others with kindness, patience, and courtesy, Doug rarely finds himself in conflict with coworkers. Even those who do not appreciate his Christian beliefs appreciate his courtesy. Doug opens doors for colleagues—male and female—gives up his seat when conference rooms fill beyond capacity, makes a point of remembering birthdays and anniversaries, treats people with respect, and remembers to greet people with a smile and a handshake. He even uses such words as "please," "thank you," "ma'am," and "sir" when appropriate.

Doug once overheard a teammate talking about him with another coworker. This individual said, "I am not a Christian, but if all Christians were like Doug I might change my mind. He is the most courteous and thoughtful person I have ever met. I try to make sure Doug is the first person I see every morning because he always greets me with a smile. That really gets my day started on a positive note." That was powerful testimony about Doug's Christian example from an unbeliever. By simply being courteous Doug has credibility with his coworkers. He also has influence. Courtesy is one of those rare concepts that costs nothing but returns big dividends.

GRATITUDE IN RELATIONSHIPS WITH COWORKERS

Gratitude is a powerful concept. But in a world in which entitlement is becoming the norm, gratitude is taking on even more importance. Gratitude is the opposite of the entitlement mentality. People with an attitude of entitlement believe they deserve success and the perquisites that come with it, regardless of commitment, effort, or contributions to an organization's performance. Christians with an attitude of gratitude know all good things come from God. Consequently, as Christians on the job, we should be thankful for His blessings.

The Bible is replete with admonitions to be thankful. For example, James 1:17 states everything good comes from heaven (meaning God). Consequently, being thankful for the many ways God blesses us each day is fundamental to being a Christian. This is easy to do when things are going well. Unfortunately, things don't always go well. This is where the rubber hits the road concerning gratitude. We are called to show gratitude even during times of adversity and even when we feel overwhelmed by difficulties. This challenge is what Paul alluded to in 1 Thessalonians 5:17, where he wrote we should thank God in all circumstances. When God sends us adversity, we are supposed to be mindful that He has a reason for doing so. This being the case, we can be thankful, even when we don't understand God's purpose, and even though we would rather not have to deal with the adversity he sends us.

There are going to be times when you feel anything but thankful. Count on it. In a workplace where temptation, rejection, and even persecution are common, even the most committed Christian is going to struggle with feelings of resentment, frustration, anger, bitterness, doubt, and occasionally a desire to lash out or strike back at coworkers. There are going to be times when you feel abandoned by superiors and shunned by coworkers; times when you feel overlooked, threatened, lied to, alone, and vulnerable. Summoning up an attitude of gratitude will be difficult in these times. However, it is at times like these gratitude will serve you best.

Being thankful during good times is easy. Even the most ardent unbelievers can be thankful when things are going their way. But, as Christians, one of the characteristics that should distinguish us from our unbelieving colleagues is a willingness to navigate through stormy waters with an attitude of gratitude, an attitude that thanks God for trusting us enough to send adversity our way. When God sends bad times into our lives, He is giving us an opportunity to show others how Christians respond to adversity. When you struggle to maintain an attitude of gratitude during difficult times, refer to Psalm 136:1, where we are told to be thankful because God's love never quits. When we come to understand this verse, we can be thankful even in the most difficult of times.

Mandy is a committed Christian whose example of gratitude during difficult times has bolstered the spirits of her coworkers on many occasions. Once, an economic recession was wreaking havoc on her company's bottom line. As a result, employees were being expected to work longer hours to fill the void left by vacant positions their employer could not afford to fill. A distraught teammate asked Mandy how she managed to stay positive in the negative circumstances they faced every day. Mandy replied, "I focus on what I have to be thankful for instead of the difficulties we face."

Her exasperated coworker responded, "You're kidding, right? What do we have to be thankful for? I am working ten-hour days, most weekends, and even some holidays. I hardly see my family anymore and can't remember the last time I went shopping or to a party." Mandy replied, "If you can't be thankful for anything else, be thankful you have a job. In this economy, many people don't." Mandy's example makes an important point. When facing trials in the workplace, as in life, we can usually find someone who is facing even worse difficulties. Knowing others are suffering too may not alleviate our suffering, but it will help us view it from a better perspective, perhaps even a thankful perspective.

SELFLESSNESS IN RELATIONSHIPS WITH COWORKERS

For most of us, selflessness can be a real challenge. Human beings are inclined to be selfish, not selfless. If this were not true, there would be no need for the many admonishments in the Bible against selfishness. The Bible is replete with guidance admonishing us to be selfless, to seek not our own good but the good of others. Paul wrote of this in Philippians 2:3–4, where he told us to do nothing from selfishness and to count others more important than ourselves. He goes on to say we should look not just to our own interests but also to those of others. Notice Paul does not say in these verses we are to completely neglect ourselves. Rather, he says we should not focus solely on our own interests but also on the interests of others. He is not telling us to neglect our own work, responsibilities, or interests. Rather, he encourages us to remember the needs of others while taking care of our own. Paul wants our focus to be outward, not inward.

It appears Paul understood his audience. He knew that as sinners we do not have to be admonished to look out for number one. Doing so comes naturally. To put Paul's admonition into a workplace context, we are to look to the needs of our coworkers and help them in every way we can without neglecting our own work and responsibilities. I understand this can be difficult counsel to accept, even for the most committed Christians. I have been told many times by Christian brothers and sisters they barely have time to take care of themselves, much less others. My response to this complaint is always the same: Taking care of others without neglecting yourself is a matter of the heart, not the clock.

Of course, the ultimate example of selflessness is provided by Christ. His example is described in powerful terms in Philippians 2:5–8, where Paul wrote Christ purposefully made Himself low, presenting Himself as a servant, and He humbled Himself by being obedient even to the point of going to His death on the cross. Of course, in going willingly to the cross Christ was looking out for others, not number one. He was looking out for you and me. When you consider the selflessness of Christ, the example we, as Christians, are expected to set in the workplace will seem less daunting.

Pedro is one of the most selfless people I have ever known. He works as a designer for a structural engineering firm and is good at his job. But what really sets Pedro apart from his coworkers is his selflessness. When coworkers fall behind on their projects, Pedro is always the first to come to their assistance. There have been many times when Pedro worked late, came in on weekends, and even gave up holidays to help others in his department get their work done on time. He does this without compensation.

Pedro is an overt and committed Christian who feels it is not just his duty to help others but his privilege. Having given up an evening, weekend, or holiday to help a coworker, he then thanks that individual for giving him the opportunity. This attitude of selflessness sometimes confuses coworkers who cannot grasp it. Pedro once worked all weekend for a teammate who was critical of his "Christian ways." Pedro's critic wanted to attend his son's baseball tournament. When he returned to work on Monday, he thanked Pedro profusely for standing in for him. Pedro responded, "You are welcome, but let me thank you for the opportunity to help." When his coworker asked where he got such an attitude of selflessness, Pedro used the opening to explain how he is called to sacrifice for others just as Christ sacrificed for him. Since that day, Pedro's coworker has never again belittled his Christian beliefs. In an era of me-centeredness, an example of selflessness can send a powerful message to coworkers.

FORGIVENESS IN RELATIONSHIPS WITH COWORKERS

Here is a claim I feel comfortable making: You have worked with teammates who mistreated you in some way. A coworker or supervisor may have lied to you, claimed credit for work you did, embarrassed you in front of teammates, made false claims against you, been hypercritical of your work, or even tried to bully you. Whatever form the maltreatment took, it probably caused you frustration, distress, or even anger. There may have been times you wanted to lash out at the offending party, strike back, or even seek revenge.

The possibility of being mistreated at work is a fact of life for Christians, just as it is for anyone who works. On the other hand, it is also a fact, as Christians, we are admonished to forgive others just as we are forgiven. In a sinful world, which includes the workplace, you must be willing to forgive people you have no desire to forgive and who, in your mind, don't deserve forgiveness. Never forget you and I are as undeserving of Christ's forgiveness as your coworkers may be of yours.

A willingness to forgive is not some abstract principle that sounds good in the Bible but has no application in the workplace. Rather, it is a critical concept for working Christians. Why is forgiveness so important? First, it is important because forgiveness is a Scriptural mandate. In fact, it is so important Christ included it when he gave us the Lord's Prayer to demonstrate how we should pray. In this prayer, He told us we are to forgive others as we hope to be forgiven. Another reason we should be willing to forgive is Christ forgives us. If Christ is willing to forgive you and me, we must be willing to forgive our coworkers.

In addition to being a biblical mandate, forgiveness has practical benefits. On a practical level, forgiveness is important to Christians because (1) it gives us opportunities to show our coworkers the image of Christ, and (2) it keeps us from being stressed out by festering, unrelieved anger, resentment, and frustration. Here are some things that may happen to you in the workplace that will test your willingness to forgive:

- Having your religious convictions mocked, belittled, or scorned
- Being persecuted because of your faith
- Having your good work overlooked by a boss who takes you for granted
- Seeing others take credit for your hard work
- Having your job security threatened
- Being lied to by coworkers

- Being unappreciated
- Being mistreated or bullied by a supervisor or coworker
- Suffering repercussions for doing the right thing
- Having trusted coworkers let you down or even turn against you
- Having coworkers fail to follow through on promises
- Being cheated by coworkers
- Having a promotion or raise you deserved go to someone else who is less deserving
- Having a colleague poach your clients
- Having a jealous coworker sabotage your work

In short, people in the workplace are going to disappoint, mistreat, or even abuse you. In a fallen world, this is a reality we, as Christians, must face. How we face it is important.

Priscilla may be the most forgiving person I have ever met. She refuses to hold grudges, even when people she works with are self-centered, uncaring, rude, or even dismissive of her faith. She has developed an approach to forgiveness working Christians would do well to emulate. Her approach consists of three steps: (1) pray for the individual who has mistreated you, (2) ask God to take away all feelings of anger and resentment and the desire for vengeance, and (3) if the individual seeks it, you must forgive.

When Priscilla prays for someone who has mistreated her at work, she is exemplifying what is written in Luke 6:27–28, where we are told to love our enemies and pray for those who abuse us. We are called by Christ to answer evil with good. The best way to do this is to heed the admonition in Luke 6:27–28. If we do our part and pray for those who abuse us, God will take care of the rest. Rude, inconsiderate, or abusive people have a day of reckoning coming, but it is with God, not us. God will reckon with them in His own way and in His own time.

In the second step of Priscilla's approach, she refuses to give in to anger, resentment, or the desire for revenge. As individual Christians, we are not the dispensers of justice in this world or in the workplace.

Ultimately, that task is left to God. Consequently, rather than do battle with the individual who has mistreated her, Priscilla does battle with her own inclination to strike back or hold a grudge. To help with this challenge, Priscilla relies on a verse from Scripture. James 4:12 reminds us that there is only one person who can make the laws and sit in judgment, and that individual is neither you nor I. When the urge to get even rears its ugly head, Priscilla repeats this verse over and over until the urge passes. She knows people never get even. They just continue to escalate their sinful behavior until it is out of control and something worse than the original offense occurs. When this happens, both parties to the conflict lose and, in turn, the organization employing them loses.

In the final step, which doesn't always occur, the offending person may ask for forgiveness. Priscilla forgives her offender. She understands forgiving others is the biblical mandate best expressed by Jesus in His sacrifice for us. This is not to say Priscilla forgets what was done to her. Christians are not called to be doormats or dupes for coworkers who abuse them. If someone takes credit for your work today, for example, he or she could very well do it again. Priscilla's approach is to forgive the coworker, then kindly but firmly convey the message that the offender's behavior is unacceptable and that further offenses may require a response to set the record straight, a response the offender might not like.

In conclusion, working with unbelievers is not the same as being unequally yoked in the biblical sense. However, you can become unequally yoked if you allow work relationships to develop to the point coworkers can adversely influence your faith. You will know you have started down the wrong path when it becomes more important to please your coworkers than to please God. As Christians, we are to build positive working relationships with coworkers while setting a Christ-like example of how Christians do their work, make decisions, interact with others, handle adversity, and balance their time between work and personal obligations. Always remember your Christ-like example might be the only sermon your unbelieving coworkers ever hear. Make sure it is a good one.

DISCUSSION CASE 6.1: "MAYBE I AM NAÏVE."

Alex had never worked in a situation like his new job. As a committed Christian, he was becoming increasingly frustrated with his coworkers at XYZ Corporation because he could not trust them. It seemed Alex's fellow computer programmers were willing to do or say anything that served their purpose in the moment. Lying, distorting, and misleading by omission or commission were normal and acceptable practices for his coworkers. Whenever Alex questioned the veracity of statements made by his fellow computer programmers, they simply dismissed him as being "naïve" and told him to "get real."

What worried Alex most was the behavior of his coworkers was beginning to wear him down. He had to admit there were times when the company seemed to benefit from the distortions of his fellow programmers. Recently, XYZ Corporation was awarded a major contract with an important customer because Alex's colleagues promised they could develop the required computer code by a certain deadline they knew was not just unrealistic but impossible. Because of their willingness to make a dishonest claim, the entire department received a nice bonus from higher management. Of course, no one was discussing what would happen when the programmers failed to meet the contracted deadline. When Alex raised this legitimate question, he was shouted down by disdainful colleagues. Alex had to admit there were days when he thought, "Maybe they are right. Maybe I am naïve. Maybe being dishonest is just part of how business is done."

Discussion Questions

1. Have you ever felt like the lone dissenter concerning an issue at work? Have you ever been told being honest and trustworthy are signs of naivety? If so, what was the situation and how did you handle it?
2. If Alex approached you for wise counsel, how would you advise him to deal with his doubts?

DISCUSSION CASE 6.2: ". . . I DON'T SEE HOW I CAN FORGIVE HER THIS TIME."

Savannah was angry and frustrated. In fact, she was livid. This was the second time her teammate, Marcie, took credit for her work. But this time Marcie's nefarious scheming was rewarded with more than just a pat on the back. This time she received a cash bonus and was named "Sales Professional of the Month." Savannah kept telling herself, "I forgave her once, but I don't see how I can forgive her this time."

Savannah and Marcie were sales agents for a major real estate firm. Savannah did all the legwork to secure the listing for the office complex in question, found the buyer, and closed the deal. However, while she was out of town on a business trip, Marcie inserted herself into the process, entered her name in all the right places on the paperwork, and claimed she was responsible for making the sale. Even as a committed Christian, Savannah could not help entertaining feelings of vengeance. When she approached her pastor for advice and counsel, the thing foremost in her mind was payback.

Discussion Questions

1. Have you ever had a colleague take credit for your work? If so, what was the situation and how did you handle it?
2. If Savannah approached you for advice and counsel, what would you tell her to do in this situation?

REVIEW QUESTIONS FOR INDIVIDUALS AND GROUPS

1. How can honesty help when trying to translate Scriptural guidance into action in the workplace? Who is ultimately hurt most by lying and why?
2. You may have heard someone say, "I don't suffer fools gladly." Will such an attitude help or hurt when trying to translate Scriptural guidance into action in the workplace? Why?

3. Have you ever worked with someone who boasted, bragged, and/or engaged in self-promotion? If so, was the experience positive or negative? How did the individual's boasting, bragging, or self-promotion color your attitude toward him or her?

4. Have you ever observed a situation where acts of courtesy prevented or mitigated conflict? If so, what were the circumstances? What happened?

5. How does gratitude in others affect you and your attitude toward them? How does a lack of gratitude in others affect you and your attitude toward them?

6. Why is it so difficult for people—including Christians—to be selfless? Have you ever worked with a selfless person? If so, how did this individual's selflessness affect those he or she worked with?

7. Have you ever found it difficult to forgive the acts or behavior of someone you work with? Why is forgiveness so important when working with other people?

CHAPTER 7

MAINTAIN POSITIVE RELATIONSHIPS WITH UNBELIEVING COWORKERS

"If one of the unbelievers invites you to dinner and you are disposed to go, eat whatever is set before you without raising any question on the ground of conscience."

1 Corinthians 10:27

Steven wasn't sure what to do about his friend and coworker, Brad. Outside work, Brad was a nice guy. He was smart, well-read, and interesting to talk to. Brad was not a Christian, but Steven was working on that. Ironically, although he was pleasant enough outside work, at work Brad was a bit of a terror. Steven and Brad worked together for two years. During that time, Steven learned Brad did not like to lose an argument. If he thought he was right—and Brad tended to think he was always right—he could become downright obnoxious in pressing his views.

Brad's approach to discussing issues was to state his opinion and then attack, belittle, or scorn anyone who disagreed with him. Brad could quote more passages from Shakespeare and other famous writers than anyone Steven ever knew. But what he could not do was disagree with coworkers without being disagreeable, a fact that was hurting Brad's chances for advancement. If Brad was going to make a career for himself in the publishing field, he was going to have to develop some people skills. Steven wanted to help Brad but wasn't sure how to go about it. His attempts so far served only to bring a chill to their relationship.

The previous chapter focused on how to establish positive working relationships with unbelieving coworkers. This chapter focuses on how to maintain those relationships. It is important to understand that establishing good working relationships with unbelieving coworkers is one kind of challenge, while maintaining those relationships is another. Relationships are established by building trust. Trust is earned through the consistent application of the traits explained in chapter 6: honesty, patience, humility, courtesy, gratitude, selflessness, and forgiveness. When these traits are part of the example you set for coworkers, you will eventually earn their trust. Once trust is established, relationships can flourish. However, trust is a fragile concept. It is difficult to win, but easy to lose. It is important to understand how to maintain the trust of coworkers once you have earned it.

To maintain the trust of coworkers and, in turn, your positive working relationships with them requires you consistently apply several specific people skills. These skills include the ability to disagree without being disagreeable, listen well, deal effectively with people who become difficult, overcome envy and jealousy, and converse positively with people who question or even reject your faith. If you have already developed these people skills, good. Read on. It never hurts to review what you know or to hone your skills. If you have not yet developed these essential people skills, don't be concerned. This chapter will help you.

LEARN TO DISAGREE WITHOUT BEING DISAGREEABLE

An essential skill for maintaining positive relationships is the ability to disagree without being disagreeable. The examples of Angela and Don illustrate the importance of this skill. These two people are a study in opposites. When there are disagreements during team meetings, Angela is always willing to listen to the ideas and opinions of others. Don, on the other hand, is prone to state his opinion, then cross his arms in a gesture of finality. If coworkers offer a differing opinion, Don aggressively challenges them as if his opinion, once given, is the final word.

Angela handles these types of situations much differently. It isn't that Angela never disagrees with others. She does. The difference between Angela and Don is reflected in how she goes about disagreeing. Angela is a committed Christian who personifies the type of love described in 1 Corinthians 13. Consequently, she is able to disagree without being disagreeable, even when the subject of disagreement is her faith. She can be as firm in defending her positions as Don. But unlike Don, Angela's steadfastness would never be confused with stubbornness.

When Angela disagrees, rather than attacking, as Don does, she keeps an open mind and gives others a chance to state their case. Rather than criticize opinions she disagrees with, Angela tries to point out where the opinions of others have merit. Angela has a talent for pointing out where apparently differing opinions share common ground, even when that common ground is minimal. Angela is effective at stating her ideas and defending them, but she makes a point of doing so in a kind, caring, and respectful manner. Not Don. If anyone disagrees, he immediately goes on the attack. He begins his attacks by belittling the logic and reasoning of those who differ with him. Then, if this approach fails, Don quickly shifts gears and adopts the ad hominem approach. First, he attacks their motives, and if that approach fails, their character.

Don's responses to people who disagree with him are often personal in nature. Angela, on the other hand, never strays beyond the bounds of propriety. Because she can disagree without being disagreeable, Angela is a welcome addition in discussions of ideas and problems. She is especially effective at brainstorming and at encouraging others to voice their ideas and opinions. Her participation in meetings encourages discussion and creative thinking. This, in turn, often results in better ideas and solutions. Don's approach, on the other hand, tends to shut down discussion and discourage idea sharing. Consequently, nobody wants to involve Don in team meetings or brainstorming sessions.

Angela is an example of an individual who has learned how to disagree without being disagreeable, a fact that endears her to coworkers, including those who do not share her faith. Because she is able to disagree with others without belittling them or their opinions, Angela's Christian views are respected, even by those who reject them. To develop your ability to disagree without being disagreeable, practice the following strategies:

- *Listen nonjudgmentally without preconceived notions or negative assumptions.* Proverbs 17:28 provides sound guidance for Christians who need to learn how to listen nonjudgmentally. This verse tells us even a fool may be considered wise if he remains silent. It is when fools stop listening and start talking they reveal who they really are. Learn to use silence wisely. Give others a chance to state their opinions and offer their ideas. As they make their cases, listen carefully. Put aside any preconceived notions or negative assumptions you may have concerning the speaker or the individual's ideas or opinions. Don't jump to conclusions. Listen attentively and give others a chance to state their case, make their points, and have their say. Do not let your disagreement register on your face or through other nonverbal gestures. When others are stating their opinions, keep your facial expressions and other nonverbal cues in neutral. Remember what is written in Proverbs 18:17. This verse makes the point that people who speak first may seem right for the time being. But their point of view often falls apart upon questioning by others. You will get your chance to question the opinions and ideas of others. Let others state their opinions and make their cases before the examination begins. When it is your turn to comment, remember a little courtesy, patience, and humility go a long way toward helping others see your point of view.

- *Listen for common ground.* As you listen to others, avoid focusing solely on areas of disagreement. Note them, but don't focus solely on them. Rather, look for areas of common ground. Listening for common ground is a sign of the kind of wisdom written about in Proverbs 2:2. In this verse, we are told to make our hearts attentive to wisdom and understanding. Even the smallest items of agreement can become building blocks for establishing broader agreement. Are there parts of the individual's argument that have merit? Is the speaker making any points that with a little tweaking might make them acceptable? People who find common ground in apparently divergent points of view can use it to build bridges spanning differences of opinion. When this happens, seemingly divergent views sometimes begin to merge or, at least, overlap around the edges. Granted, there might not be enough common ground between your opinion and others to render further discussion unnecessary. However, the more common ground you can find, the less there is to disagree about.

- *Give others time to state their case—do not interrupt.* Many people have a tendency to interrupt speakers the minute they say something questionable. Another tendency is to speak up the minute a thought comes to mind, even if someone else is speaking. Avoid both these mistakes. Instead, heed the admonition in Proverbs 18:13, where we are warned that giving an answer before listening is foolish. Give people time to state their opinions and present their ideas without interruption. Even if you disagree with what is being said, wait until you have heard the entire argument. There may be information not yet presented that could change your mind. One of the keys to disagreeing without being disagreeable is to respect speakers and to be courteous to them. Interrupting a speaker is disrespectful and discourteous. Further, it puts the speaker on the defensive and singles you out as an opponent rather than someone who is open to listening.

- *Use questions rather than statements of disagreement.* Disagreeing without being disagreeable requires a certain amount of wisdom. Rather than saying things such as, "That will never work, we've tried it before," or "You haven't thought this through well enough," use questions to help speakers come to their own realization of where they might be off course. For example, assume a coworker has just proposed the team adopt a four-day work week. Rather than just claiming a four-day work week could be a bad idea, you might say: "John, there are days when I would really like a four-day week. But have you thought about how starting work an hour early and staying an hour later might affect working parents whose schedules revolve around getting their children to and from daycare and school?" Using inoffensive but thought-provoking questions rather than just dismissing someone's suggestions out of hand is a kinder and gentler way to point out weaknesses in another person's argument. Ecclesiastes 9:17 applies here. In this verse, we are told the words of wise people heard in quiet will be more effective than those of a ruler who shouts. Thought-provoking questions asked quietly will be more effective in winning converts to your opinions than loudly stated disagreement.

- *Look for common goals. People can share the same goal but disagree on how to accomplish it.* It is much less disagreeable to be told, "I like where you are going with that idea but would like to discuss how you plan to get there," than to be told, "Nope, bad idea, won't work." When people realize they have the same goal, it is less difficult for them to discuss different ways of accomplishing it. Further, people can have worthy goals but less worthy ideas for accomplishing them. For example, assume a coworker is moved to help the homeless in the community. This is a worthy goal. But what if his idea is to rob wealthy citizens and give his ill-gotten gains to the homeless. That would be an unworthy approach to accomplishing his worthy goal. A man I once worked with used to call this phenomenon, "Having the right string, but the wrong yo-yo." It is not uncommon for people to be so convinced of the viability of their goal they give less thought than they should to the means of achieving it. It's as if they think because their goal is worthy any means used to achieve it must also be worthy. By gently pointing out to coworkers you agree with their goal but would like to discuss their plans for achieving it, you can have more influence on what ultimately happens.

Practice these steps and you can develop a powerful human relations skill solidly based in Scripture: the ability to disagree without being disagreeable.

LEARN TO LISTEN PATIENTLY TO YOUR COWORKERS

Proverbs 18:13 warns against giving an answer without first listening carefully and completely. Becoming a good listener is an effective way to gain positive influence with your coworkers. One of the most often heard complaints from adults in the United States is "Nobody listens to me." We have become such a fast-paced, impatient society, and people who are willing to listen to others are in short supply. To make a difference for good in the workplace, become one of those rare individuals. If you want others to heed your Christian example, try listening when they need to talk. In an era when people are prone to tell others, "Just text me," your willingness to listen will earn the appreciation of coworkers.

To become a good listener, it is necessary to do battle with your human tendency toward self-centeredness. Effective listening is about focusing outward on others instead of inward. The key to effective listening is found in Philippians 2:3–4, where we are told to humbly count others as more important than self and, in turn, to take care of others. Part of taking care of others is listening to them. Being a good listener is more attitudinal than physical. Once you have adopted an outwardly focused attitude, learning to be a good listener is a matter of practicing the listening techniques explained herein. When someone needs to talk, apply the following techniques:

- *Remove all distractions.* Give the speaker your undivided attention. Turn off your cell phone, do not allow interruptions, do not look at the clock or continue to do paperwork, and do not fidget. Distractions will shut down communication and undermine effective listening.
- *Look directly at the speaker.* Show speakers a reassuring, empathetic countenance; look them in the eyes; and assume a posture that says, "I am listening." Looking off into the distance, at your hands, or anywhere else except directly at the speaker may cause you to tune out and let your mind wander. Looking directly at the speaker sends a message that says, "I am listening."
- *Concentrate on what is being said.* Avoid thinking ahead to where you assume the speaker is going. Avoid making assumptions or giving in to preconceived notions. Listen

carefully and concentrate on what the speaker is saying (or not saying). No matter how convinced you are beforehand of what the speaker is going to say, give the speaker the opportunity to state his or her case. Then pay attention. People will sometimes surprise you.

- *Watch for nonverbal cues.* Facial expressions, tone of voice, volume of speech, willingness to make eye contact, and posture are all nonverbal cues. Don't be concerned you haven't had formal training in the interpretation of nonverbal communication. You don't need it. You have been able to interpret nonverbal messages since you were a baby. Even a baby yet to speak knows when its mother is angry, tense, agitated, or sad. The baby knows because of the nonverbal cues its mother gives. You recognize boredom, nervousness, fear, anger, and other human emotions from the nonverbal cues people present, even when they don't mean to. The key is to watch and listen for agreement or disagreement between what is said verbally and what is said nonverbally. Do not assume any given gesture means any specific thing. Rather, look for agreement or disagreement between the verbal and the nonverbal. If the two do not match, something is amiss, and you should ask questions to determine what it is.

- *Be patient and wait.* Some people have trouble getting out what they want to say. The connection between brain and mouth doesn't always work properly in some people. We have all experienced the phenomenon of struggling to cogently put our thoughts into words. When this happens to speakers, do not rush in to rescue them. Just wait. Give the speaker a reassuring facial expression and the time needed to formulate his or her words. If you jump in to rescue a hesitant speaker, your interruption might have the opposite effect. It might do more harm than good. Be patient and wait. Sometimes major pauses in a conversation indicate the speaker is trying to decide not just what to say but if he or she is going to say it. Interrupting at this crucial point in a conversation can shut down communication.

- *Ask clarifying questions.* When what is being said does not make sense, does not square with the facts, is illogical, does not match the nonverbal cues, or is unclear, ask clarifying questions. Be tactful and kind, but make sure you are getting the full and accurate picture of what is being said. For example, assume a coworker complains, "Jane is always late for work," but you have never known Jane to be late. Obviously, something is amiss. You might comment: "Help me out here. You say Jane is always late for work, yet I have never known her to arrive late for work. She has always been punctual and reliable. What am I missing?" Clarifying questions can reveal a hidden agenda. At the very least, clarifying questions will help elicit accurate information, so if a decision must be made or action must be taken, you will have the benefit of a complete and accurate picture of the situation in question.

Few things will help you become more influential with coworkers, subordinates, and even superiors than being a good listener. All people, regardless of position or status, need to know someone who will listen to them with patience and empathy. You can be that person and, by doing so, gain the respect of your coworkers. Even the most ardent unbeliever will find it difficult to sustain a negative attitude toward a Christian who is a good listener.

LEARN TO DEAL EFFECTIVELY WITH DIFFICULT PEOPLE

People tended to avoid Adam. To be blunt, Adam was a challenge to deal with. He was the most difficult person to be around most of his coworkers ever met. Adam was grouchy, short-tempered, opinionated, and demanding. Frankly, had he not been so good at his job, Adam would have been fired long ago. But he was good at his job—exceptionally good. Adam was an asset to his employer, but trying to talk to him was like trying to talk to an angry pit bull. The only person who seemed able to cope with Adam was Darren.

Darren, a committed Christian, was able to work well with the most difficult people including, to the surprise of his coworkers, even Adam. Darren's ability to work with Adam and other difficult people made him a valued asset to his employer and among his coworkers. Darren's secret, if it can be called that, was his willingness to patiently suffer the foibles of his fellow man. Darren simply did not take personally the rudeness, impatience, or lack of civility exhibited by difficult people. Once when asked by a coworker how he could endure working with people like Adam, Darren replied, "If Christ can put up with me, I can put up with Adam."

Because of the sinful nature of human beings, people can be difficult to deal with, and often are. People can be ill-tempered, rude, or inconsiderate. Some people can be all these things, and more. There is no end to the ways people in the workplace can be difficult. Consequently, as Christians, we must become adept at dealing with difficult people. This is a challenge that can test your Christian patience. Consequently, when you find your patience wearing thin because of the inconsiderate behavior of others take a moment to step back from the situation and regain your composure.

Don't respond immediately or in-kind. Take a moment to pray for God's help in taming the desire welling up inside you to lash out or strike back. If you need more help, consult Scripture. A good place to start is 2 Timothy 2:2–3, where we are admonished to be strengthened by the grace of Christ and suffer as good soldiers in Christ Jesus. Dealing effectively and positively with difficult people is often a matter of doing just that: suffering as good soldiers in Christ. Learning to ignore or overlook the ill manners of inconsiderate people is a must if you are going to become adept at dealing with difficult people.

People are the most complex entities in God's creation. Compared with people, rocket science is easy. My daughter is a math professor at the same college where I teach business and management courses. She teaches calculus. One semester, my daughter taught a calculus class on Monday evenings. The class ended at 6:15 p.m. That same semester, I taught a management class on Monday nights immediately after my daughter's class and in the same room.

When my management students walked into the room and saw all the complicated calculus equations still on the board, they commented, "I am sure glad I don't have to take that class." "I could never figure out those equations." I just laughed at their naivety and told them by the time they have been managers for a few months they would probably wish they majored in math. "Calculus equations may look complicated to you, but unlike people, they don't have personalities, agendas, ambitions, quirks, biases, debts, problems at home, frustrations, fears, and unmet dreams. Trying to inspire people to give their best to an organization is going to be a more challenging endeavor than solving calculus equations. At least with calculus, there is an answer book."

I wrote the previous paragraph while having lunch in a favorite restaurant. The owner, a friend of mine, plopped down beside me and with a big sigh said, "I feel like quitting." When I asked what was bothering him, he answered in one word: "people." It had been a particularly busy week for him, and in addition to the normal challenges of running a popular restaurant, my friend lost four experienced employees in just two days. One was arrested for drug use and another for domestic violence. The other two left town together when their adulterous affair was discovered by their spouses.

People are individuals. As such they have their own worldviews, personalities, agendas, foibles, biases, attitudes, dreams, fears, frustrations, motivations, and beliefs. Jesus knew this about people when He sent the Apostles out into the world to spread the Gospel. He prepared them for what they might encounter by telling them to be both wise and innocent (Matthew 10:16). Jesus made it clear to the Apostles He was sending them into the "midst of wolves." Christ's advice to His Apostles all those years ago is good advice for us today. The "wolves" we encounter in the workplace can be difficult. However, the strategies presented in this and other chapters will help you deal with them in ways both wise and innocent. These strategies will help you work among wolves without being devoured.

Much has changed since the days when Christ walked the earth, but people haven't. They can be just as sinful today as they were in Christ's time and just as prone to view the world and others in it from the perspective of self or some other sinful motive. What is different today is all the high-tech gadgets wolves can use to undermine and attack Christians in the workplace. The Apostles faced some difficult and even ugly situations because of their faith, but they didn't have to cope with cyberbullying, hurtful postings on social media, or doctored photographs on the Internet. You probably will. Unfortunately, the workplace often unintentionally encourages the more disagreeable aspects of human nature, those aspects run counter to the beliefs we, as Christians, hold dear.

When dealing with difficult people, particularly those who reject Christianity, you will have to become proficient at applying all the strategies explained in this chapter, as well as in the other chapters in this book. It will be necessary to be honest, patient, humble, courteous, grateful, selfless, forgiving, and steadfast. It will also be necessary to apply your skills at listening, calming your own anger, coping with the anger of others, and dealing with envy and jealousy.

Admittedly, doing all explained in this chapter and the other chapters in this book can be a tall order. In fact, applying the strategies presented in this book might, at times, seem overwhelming. When that happens, remember what is said in Colossians 3:12–14, where we are told to be kind, humble, meek, patient, and forgiving as the Lord has been forgiving toward us. Finally, in Verse 14 we are told to show others biblical love. In short, we are to follow the example Christ set for us. Notice nothing in these verses suggests following His example will be easy. The key is to remember, although we are undeserving, Christ is kind, humble, meek, patient, forgiving, and loving to us. Consequently, there is no reason why we, as followers of Christ, should object to demonstrating these same characteristics when interacting with coworkers, even those who are undeserving.

INTERPERSONAL TECHNIQUES FOR DEALING WITH DIFFICULT PEOPLE

Dealing with difficult people takes effort, practice, and a willingness to endure some frustration. For Christians willing to put forth the effort, practice regularly, and persevere, the following interpersonal techniques will help.

Refuse to respond in-kind to anger, rudeness, and other forms of inconsiderate behavior

We have become an angry society. You see it everywhere. Road rage is a national scourge, people attack each other over meaningless disagreements, providing anger-management classes is now a growth industry, and workplace violence has become a regular feature on the nightly news. At its heart, anger is the child of self-centeredness and immaturity. The exception to this is righteous anger, the kind Christ displayed when he threw the money changers out of the temple.

Christians in the workplace should avoid the temptation to become angry and then claim theirs is righteous anger. This is especially the case when you have simply failed to exercise self-control. When it comes to anger, you are wise to heed the admonition in James 1:20, where it is written anger does not encourage a righteous life. Better to leave righteous anger to Christ and do what is necessary to control your temper. Anger in the workplace, yours and others', is typically the result of self-centeredness coupled with poor self-control, not righteousness.

Rudeness and other forms of inconsiderate behavior are also caused by self-centeredness, immaturity, or both. Often self-centered people become angry, rude, or inconsiderate when they don't get what they want, when they want it, and how they want it. They want the world to revolve around them. When this does not happen, they sometimes respond with inconsiderate behavior. Although it can be tempting to respond in-kind, doing so is a bad idea. Anger is like a fire, it requires fuel. Responding to anger with anger is just adding fuel to the fire. Consequently, as Christians, we should avoid stoking the flames of another person's anger by responding to it with anger.

Refusing to respond in-kind to anger is spoken to in Psalm 37:8, where we are told to refrain from anger, wrath, and fretful emotions because they lead us straight to evil. Regardless whether people are angry at you or just angry at the world in general, when they aim their venom at you, do not respond in-kind. Instead, take a deep breath, bite your tongue, and be patient. Look past the outward anger and other forms of bad behavior and stand your ground patiently. Be firm but be kind. This is an example of what is meant in Romans 12:20, where it is written we are to heap hot coals on the heads of our enemies by treating them kindly.

It was amazing to me how a former colleague I will call Charlotte could defuse another person's anger. She was so adept at maintaining her equilibrium in the face of anger, one of her coworkers once made a bet he could "get her goat." He lost. Charlotte never backed down from angry coworkers, nor was she cowed by them. Rather, she patiently and kindly used words to hold a mirror up to them. Her favorite technique was to give an angry coworker an empathetic look and say, "You must really be angry about this. I'm sorry to hear it. I know how that feels. Would you like to talk about it?" It was amazing to me how effective these simple statements could be in helping a coworker who lost control regain it.

Even self-centered, immature people will find it difficult to continue being angry, rude, or inconsiderate to someone who responds with patience and kindness. Often difficult people, given time to vent or reflect, will feel remorse over their inconsiderate behavior. But even if this does not happen, as Christians, we are responsible in the eyes of God for our response. We cannot control how people choose to behave, but we can control how we respond to their behavior. Regardless of how they behave, our response to coworkers should reflect the image of Christ, not their poor behavior.

Help difficult people transition from problem mode to solution mode

Many different factors can trigger inconsiderate behavior in people. Here are just a few of them: having to wait, feeling overwhelmed or confused, pressure from superiors or coworkers, difficulty in communicating, frustration over problems unrelated to work, fatigue, job insecurity, feeling rushed, feeling powerless, missing deadlines, and feeling no one will listen. In addition to these, there is always the issue of self-centeredness.

Regardless what factors trigger inconsiderate behavior in coworkers, the problem in question will not be solved until the individual in question stops emoting and starts focusing on solutions. People who are so focused on a problem they respond rudely or angrily are not in the proper frame of mind to solve the problem. Before they can begin to make progress in dealing with the problem in question, inconsiderate people must first make the transition from problem mode to solution mode.

You can help difficult people make this transition by responding to their tirades with kindness, patience, and empathy. The key to helping a difficult person make the transition from problem mode to solution mode is found in Proverbs 15:1, where it is written a gentle answer can defuse anger, but a harsh answer just inflames it. To translate this verse into action, it will be necessary to look past the emotional turbulence of angry or otherwise difficult people. Do not allow yourself to get caught up in their anger, rudeness, or inconsiderate behavior. Instead, ignore these things and start building a bridge between problem mode and solution mode.

Statements patiently acknowledging the individual's inflamed emotions and offering hope for a solution are the best way to help difficult people make the necessary transition. A manager I will call Bill is a master at bridging this gap. Whenever he is confronted by someone who is angry, frustrated, or otherwise behaving badly, Bill says something like this: "These situations are frustrating aren't they? I don't blame you for being angry. It would frustrate me too. But I have seen you handle worse problems than this. Tell me what's bothering you and let's see if we can't find a solution." He never says things like "get a grip," "grow up," or "why don't you calm down." Such statements would probably just make the angry person angrier.

Confrontational or demeaning comments such as "get a grip" or "grow up" tend to make difficult people defensive, which in turn, is likely to make them even angrier or more frustrated. By validating their emotions, Bill lays the foundation for the bridge he needs to build. By telling them they have solved worse problems, Bill bolsters their confidence and soothes their ego. By offering to listen and help devise a solution, Bill gives difficult people two important things: an ally and hope. Bill is the personification of Proverbs 17:27, where it is written a man who is wise and understanding uses words with restraint and maintains an even temper.

Listen past anger, frustration, and rudeness for the real message

Often people who are upset will say things they don't really mean or, at least, would not say if they were in control of their emotions. Proverbs 14:16 touches on this subject when it refers to fools who are "reckless" and "careless." When people are being reckless with their words, give them the benefit of the doubt. Listen past the anger, frustration, and rudeness, and try to identify the real problem. Ask yourself: "What could be bothering this individual so much that he or she would behave in this manner?"

For example, a colleague once yelled at me, "Where have you been. I've tried to call you a hundred times!" From his words and corresponding body language, I could see my colleague was bubbling over with anger. My initial thought was to push back and say: "Stop exaggerating. You haven't called me a hundred times. My cell phone buzzed just twice." But that would have been responding to the wrong message: the anger instead of the problem causing it. Instead I said, "I am sorry I couldn't answer. I was in a meeting. This must be important to you. Tell me how I can help."

It turned out my colleague was being pressed by our boss for some information he did not have but knew I did. The only way for him to get the information for our boss, who was not a patient individual, was to get in touch with me. Once I told him what he needed to know, he settled down immediately and even apologized. Had I chosen to fight fire with fire in this case, the situation might have turned out badly. Instead, after some initial bluster, my colleague settled down and the situation turned out well.

Be aware of your own body language—keep it in neutral

When someone has spoken to you in anger or behaved rudely toward you, a natural response is to ball up your fists, at least metaphorically if not actually. When this happens, your body language is likely to show it. You might adopt an aggressive stance, show anger on your face, or speak in an indignant tone of voice. Any of these nonverbal responses will probably just make matters worse. Instead, make a point of keeping your nonverbal messages either positive or, at least, neutral. Assuming a chin-to-chin stance, raising your voice, or using sarcasm is the interpersonal equivalent of pouring fuel on a burning fire. It is just as ill-advised to express anger nonverbally as it is to express it verbally. Don't give in to your emotions and start venting when someone is being inconsiderate or rude. Instead, follow the guidance found in Proverbs 29:11. In this verse, we are told a fool gives in to his anger, but the wise exert self-control. When you feel yourself becoming angry, repeat the lesson in this verse over and over until you gain control of your emotions.

You are a child of God—make sure there is a family resemblance

Often the natural reaction to anger, rudeness, or other kinds of inconsiderate behavior is to say, even silently, "I don't have to put up with this." That is true. You are a Christian, not a punching bag. Accepting with bovine docility the abuse of inconsiderate coworkers is neither recommended nor smart. However, as a Christian, your response should reflect the image of Christ. When you feel like lashing out at a difficult person, remember who you are. You are a child of God. This being the case, there should be a family resemblance, and that resemblance should show in your response. Stand up for yourself but do so in a manner pleasing to Christ.

An old maxim says, *Tell me who you walk with and I will tell you who you are.* As a Christian, you walk with Christ. Because you walk with Christ, you are different from people who don't. This means your response to inconsiderate behavior must be different. People who mistreat others are accustomed to having their inconsiderate behavior returned in kind or seeing the other person wilt in the face of it. As Christians, neither of these responses is acceptable. Rather, we are called to stand our ground resolutely but with patience, kindness, and Christian love.

When you are forced to deal with the inconsiderate behavior of difficult coworkers, think of the words in Romans 12:21. In this verse, we are admonished to overcome evil with good. Evil is never overcome by evil, but it can be overcome by good. Remember this: The outcome of an inconsiderate exchange is not even about you. Rather, it's about showing your difficult coworker a better way, Christ's way. Always remember your example of forbearance may open a door for talking frankly about the good news of Jesus Christ to a coworker who needs to hear it. Sometimes you have to *earn* access to an unbeliever's heart. Persevering in setting a Christ-like example is an effective way to do this.

LEARN TO DEAL WITH ENVY AND JEALOUSY—YOURS AND THAT OF OTHERS

The human ego often causes problems in the workplace. Some of the worst problems occur when ego manifests itself as envy and jealousy. God knew we would struggle with envy and jealousy, which is why He gave us the Tenth Commandment. In addition to the Tenth Commandment, the Bible is replete with examples of people ruining their lives, as well as the lives of others, by giving in to envy and jealousy.

In Genesis 3, we see Satan was envious of God. His envy and jealousy drove him to approach Eve in the form of a serpent. You know how that story ended. You also know what happened when Cain became jealous of his brother Abel. Perhaps the most tragic example of what envy and jealousy can do is seen in how the Pharisees responded when they became jealous of Jesus. Other examples of the destructive power of envy and jealousy abound in the Bible and in everyday life. Envy and jealousy have been part of the human condition since the Fall in the Garden of Eden. A word of caution is in order here. Although the fallen nature of human beings is a fact, it should never be used as an excuse. "I am only human" is no excuse when we choose to sin. The Bible clearly defines right and wrong. God gives us volition in the form of free will. Therefore, when we sin we choose to sin.

A project manager I will call Janice had a problem with envy and jealousy. In fact, the *green monster* was so deeply embedded in her psyche Janice would sabotage the work of coworkers rather than see them receive recognition for a job well done. Even worse, Janice perfected the art of elbowing her way into projects that were going well and then taking credit for their successful completion. On one occasion, she schemed, plotted, and connived for more than a year to have a highly successful program taken from a coworker and turned over to her. Correspondingly, if one of her projects was progressing poorly, Janice would plot and scheme until she found a way to hand the project off to someone else. She once went so far as to take unwarranted sick leave so she could turn a failing project over to a coworker.

Janice was caught up in the poisonous tentacles of envy and jealousy. If someone else had something of value, Janice coveted it, even if she had no need for it. When coworkers earned recognition for their work, Janice's response was to spread malicious gossip to undermine their credibility. She even refused to attend recognition ceremonies unless she was the person being recognized. Janice's envy and jealousy finally caught up with her and, when it did, her career took a nosedive. It was at this point she asked for my advice.

In spite of her envious and jealous behavior, Janice professed to be a Christian. Although her claim would have been difficult for some of her former coworkers to accept, it did give me a starting point for counseling her. Fortunately, Janice required little counseling. When I asked who her envy and jealousy hurt most, she quickly got the picture. As it turned out, what a lot of people did not realize was Janice was tremendously talented. She had the know-how to become a top performer in her field, but for various reasons she had no confidence and her self-esteem was low. Had Janice not been entangled in a web of negativity because of her envy and jealousy, she could have been a real asset to her company. In fact, after she eventually was hired by another firm, Janice put envy and jealousy aside and became a highly valued, well-respected professional.

When you feel yourself being pulled in the wrong direction by envy and jealousy, step back, go to your Bible, and read about how destructive these sins were in the cases of Cain and Abel, Saul and David, Joseph and his brothers, and the Pharisees and Jesus. Look up James 3:15, where jealousy and selfish ambition are called "unspiritual" and "demonic." Read James 3:14–16 over and over until the urge to be envious or jealous passes. Pray about the Scriptural guidance provided in these verses. Remind yourself when someone else excels it does not mean you have done poorly. Then replace your envy and jealousy with sincere gratitude for the achievements of others.

Even when others do not deserve or have not earned their good fortune, envy and jealousy are inappropriate responses for Christians. Any reckoning that comes to people over unwarranted success is between them and God, not them and you. As Christians, we are told to be content in whatever circumstance God places us (Philippians 4:11). Christian contentment is the opposite of envy and jealousy. When you allow your Christian contentment to be undermined by envy and jealousy, the person hurt most is you.

If you find yourself dealing with people who are prone to fits of envy and jealousy, people like Janice in the earlier example, remember their behavior is driven by insecurity and self-centeredness. When people become distraught, it is usually because bad things are happening to them. But when envious and jealous people become distraught, it is because good things are happening to others. This is a sad state of mind because good things are going to happen to others, as well as bad things. Those who are wounded by the good fortune of others will be wounded often.

It is easy to become angry at envious and jealous coworkers, but anger is the wrong response. Rather than becoming angry, pray for your coworkers. Pray they will overcome their insecurity and self-centeredness and mature to the point where they can enjoy the success of others. People who can delight in the success of others are often more successful themselves. Further, they earn the appreciation of their coworkers. Think about it. It will be difficult for unbelieving coworkers to reject your Christianity when you are so supportive of their success.

LEARN TO CONVERSE LOVINGLY WITH PEOPLE WHO REJECT YOUR FAITH

When in church, you and I can enjoy the convenience and comfort of interacting with fellow believers. But on the job, we must be prepared to work closely with people who don't share our faith. Therefore, learning to converse with unbelievers in a way that reflects the love of Christ is essential. In 1 Corinthians 10:31, Paul writes that, as we interact with unbelievers, we are to do so for the glory of God. Learning to converse lovingly with people who reject our faith is yet another way to honor God through our work.

It is tempting to just avoid unbelievers. Don't give in to this temptation. Instead, remember we are called to interact with them in ways that bring glory to God. This is important because you will probably work with people who go beyond just questioning your faith to rejecting it. Although working with people who reject our faith can be challenging and even frustrating, as Christians, we need to view such people as opportunities, not the enemy. Their presence on the job is why you, as a Christian, should view the workplace as a mission field. Like anyone else on the mission field, learning to converse lovingly with those you want to reach for Christ is critical. Coworkers will not be receptive if your message is contradicted by your example.

Christians who choose a life on the mission field do vital work for the Kingdom of God. But you do not have to serve in a foreign country to be a missionary. When at work you need look no farther than your coworkers to find people who need to hear the Gospel. This fact means the workplace is a mission field. Anywhere unrighteous people exist is a mission field, and the unrighteous are everywhere, including in the workplace. The Bible confirms this fact. For example, in Ecclesiastes 7:20, we read there is not a righteous man anywhere on earth who never sins. That includes you, me, and our coworkers. If you are willing to train yourself to converse lovingly with unbelieving coworkers, your organization, your career, and your coworkers will benefit.

There are plenty of people in the workplace who reject Christianity, and you will probably work with some of them. The key to working effectively with teammates who reject your beliefs is to view them as people in need of your Christ-like example rather than as enemies to be verbally smitten. Rather than be offended by their lack of faith, demonstrate for them why faith in Christ is a better way than the one they have chosen. When you learn to converse in a patient, loving manner with those who reject your faith, they will eventually realize there is something different about you, something special. Further, they may come to admire the ways in which you are different from others and be drawn to you because you are different.

It is not appropriate to spend your time on the job handing out tracts and verbally evangelizing. This is not what you are being paid to do. However, it is always appropriate to pray for coworkers and to set a Christ-like example that demonstrates the desirability, benefits, and soul-saving power of Christianity. Part of that example should be conversing lovingly with unbelievers. Evangelizing by example is always workplace appropriate, no matter where you work. Further, it is what Christ expects of you and me. In Ephesians 4:1–3, Paul exhorted believers to evangelize by example when he wrote we are to walk in a manner worthy of our calling. In these verses, he admonishes us to make humility, gentleness, patience, and bearing with one another in love part of the example we set for others.

When dealing with coworkers who reject Christianity, conversing lovingly with them is an effective way to build bridges between you and them. When unbelievers come to the point where they respect your faith, even if they don't accept it, they will be less likely to tempt or pressure you to compromise it. Further, when unbelievers question you about your faith, they have just opened a door and invited you in. When this happens, you may augment your example with words. Always be prepared for such opportunities.

When a door is opened by a coworker, by all means enter and share the Gospel. Remember what is written in Romans 10:15. In this verse, we read God considers the feet of those who preach the Gospel to be beautiful. This verse applies to more than ordained ministers. It also applies to you and me. In the workplace, we share the Gospel through our Christ-like example until that example opens doors. When it does, we should be prepared to share the Gospel with our words. However, a note of caution is in order here. When we share the Gospel with coworkers, we should do so during breaks, at lunch, or after work. Neglecting your work and taking others away from theirs, even to share the Gospel, will undermine the example you are trying to set for them.

A college professor I will call Gary is particularly effective at drawing unbelievers to him by dint of his conversational skills. When interacting with people—including unbelieving skeptics and critics—Gary is always kind, considerate, patient, and a good listener. When unbelieving colleagues challenge his faith, Gary never becomes angry. Rather, he makes a point of disagreeing without being disagreeable. He welcomes questions about his faith and is happy to answer them. He views skeptics and critics as uninformed people to be prayed for, not enemies to be bested in arguments. Gary uses his conversational skills to draw people to Christ. He does not use them to score debating points against hapless opponents of Christianity.

Gary knows the Bible well and is not intimidated by those who question his faith or even the inconsiderate comments they sometimes make about it. He refuses to fight fire with fire, makes a point of remaining calm and courteous, and never tries to verbally smite unbelievers or skewer them with the sword of his superior knowledge. He uses the Bible as a tool, not a weapon. Gary sees his duty as answering the questions of unbelievers as best he can, praying for them, and letting God do the rest. He knows his duty is to set the kind of example Christ expects of him and, then, to share the Gospel when opportunities present themselves.

One of the reasons Gary is so well-respected by his faculty colleagues is he makes a point of listening more than talking. If asked for advice about matters of faith, he gives it forthrightly. For the most part, Gary lets his example do the talking for him. When a colleague, no matter how hostile to Christianity, falls on hard times or suffers from grief, Gary is quick to offer assistance, words of comfort, and encouragement. Gary makes sure his interactions with others, including unbelievers, are characterized by the kind of love described in 1 Corinthians 13. When interacting with colleagues, Gary is positive, helpful, and kind.

Over the years, Gary's example, particularly during times of adversity, has won him the respect of his colleagues and even helped a few make the decision to put Christ at the center of their lives. What is particularly gratifying for Gary is to have unbelieving colleagues defend him when politically correct colleagues tell him to keep his Christianity to himself. Because of his willingness to converse with unbelievers in a kind and loving way, Gary is respected and even occasionally protected by his colleagues, including some who still reject his faith. His approach to dealing with colleagues who reject Christianity is one you and I would do well to emulate.

DISCUSSION CASE 7.1: "I AM STRUGGLING WITH FEELINGS OF ENVY AND JEALOUSY . . ."

Lee Bailey is struggling. Several of his coworkers have jumped ahead of him on the career ladder after receiving well-deserved promotions. Whereas most of his coworkers are sincerely happy for the good fortune of those who were recently promoted, Lee is not. In fact, he is angry and frustrated. Lee is consumed by envy and jealousy. As a Christian, Lee knows his reaction to the good fortune of his coworkers is wrong. He knows envy and jealousy are the opposite of what he should feel, but he is honest enough with himself to admit his sinful feelings. In desperation, Lee finally approached a friend from church and told him, "I am struggling with feelings of envy and jealousy and don't seem to be able to get past them. What can I do?"

Discussion Questions

1. Have you ever struggled with feelings of envy or jealousy because of the good fortune of others? How did you handle this situation?
2. If you were the friend Lee came to for help, what would you tell him?

DISCUSSION CASE 7.2: "HOW CAN I CONTINUE TO SAY NO WITHOUT BEING DISAGREEABLE?"

Deanna Johnson has never felt so alone or so pressured to do something she knows is wrong. Frankly, she is fed up with the pressure and is becoming angry. The problem is the pressure is coming from friends she has worked with for years. Deanna's coworkers have decided the only way they will be able to pass an online professional recertification exam is to cheat. They have worked out an elaborate plan in which they will use books with pages earmarked and notes during the test. They have been told by other coworkers who have already taken the test that online security is not just lax but nil. The problem is her coworkers want to copy Deanna's notes. She is the best note-taker among them and has cross-referenced her notes to the different sections of the practice test provided for them. According to coworkers who have taken the exam, the practice test is structured just like the real thing. The problem is Deanna, a committed Christian, is refusing to go along. However, her friends are applying pressure in every way they can. Deanna is becoming angry. Lately she has been asking herself, "How can I continue to say 'no' without being disagreeable?"

Discussion Questions

1. Have you ever been pressured by coworkers to do something either illegal or unethical? Did the pressure make you angry? Did the pressure cause you to respond in a disagreeable manner?

2. How might Deanna go about disagreeing without being disagreeable in this case? You may assume her colleagues are not professing Christians.

REVIEW QUESTIONS FOR INDIVIDUALS AND GROUPS

1. Can you disagree with others without being disagreeable? Why do you think this is such a challenge for some people? Have you ever worked with someone who could do this well? How did that individual's ability to disagree without being disagreeable affect others?

2. Are you a good listener? Why is listening so difficult for some people? How does it affect you when someone is willing to listen patiently to your opinions, concerns, or point of view?

3. Can you deal effectively with difficult people (e.g., rude, angry, inconsiderate)? Have you ever known someone who was good at dealing effectively with difficult people? If so, what were some of this person's techniques?

4. Have you ever felt envy or jealousy over the good fortune of others (whether the good fortune was deserved or not)? Why are envy and jealousy so destructive in human relations? What can you do to overcome these emotions if you start to feel them?

5. Are you able to converse lovingly with people who reject Christianity? What skills do you still need to develop to be able to do this?

6. At this point, do you have the skills needed to maintain positive relationships with unbelieving coworkers? What skills do you still need to work on to be effective in this endeavor?

CHAPTER 8

APPROACH YOUR JOB AS A MINISTRY— LET YOUR EXAMPLE BE A DAILY SERMON

". . . and keep the charge of the Lord your God, walking in His ways and keeping his statutes, his commandments, his rules, and his testimonies, as it is written in the Law of Moses, that you may prosper in all that you do . . ."

1 Kings 2:3

Michelle and Savannah liked to spend their lunch breaks together. As the only two Christians in their work team, they made a point of supporting each other and being mutual accountability partners. On this day, Michelle surprised Savannah by asking, "Do you ever get tired of working hard when you know other members of the team are loafing?" She went on to tell Savannah she knew setting an example of applying a positive work ethic and being a good team player were important. But, it was getting hard for her to keep setting this kind of example when others were coasting. "They get paid as much as we do but work only half as hard. What's worse is they know they can get away with loafing because we will take up their slack."

Savannah acknowledged feeling the same way at times but then reminded Michelle that in addition to setting the right kind of example they should also be critical thinkers and creative problem solvers. "If our teammates are taking advantage of us rather than following our example, maybe we need to think more critically about the situation and see if we can find a creative solution." Then Savannah smiled and asked, "When do you plan to take your vacation this year? I wonder what will happen with our team's productivity if we take our vacations at the same time?"

Savannah and Michelle hit upon a solution to a serious problem that put Christ's admonition in Matthew 10:16 into practice. They were innocent in that they continued to set a good example of working hard even though their teammates were taking advantage of them. However, they were also wise in finding a way to show their supervisor what was happening in the team. Their plan worked. By the time they got back from vacation, changes were already made. Neither Michelle nor Savannah was willing to back off from demonstrating their Christian work ethic in spite of the behavior of their teammates because both viewed their job as a ministry and their work ethic as a daily sermon.

An excellent way to reflect the image of Christ in the workplace is to approach your job as a ministry. Think about what ordained pastors and priests do. Among other things, they minister to their flocks and deliver sermons expounding on the Word of God for their congregants. The previous chapters in this book have demonstrated how you can minister to your coworkers by setting a Christ-like example of how to work, make decisions, interact with others, and solve problems. This chapter focuses on how your Christ-like example can be a daily sermon for coworkers.

As a sermon, your example should reflect the image of Christ for others in practical terms applicable in the workplace. This means your example should exemplify, among other things, leadership, a positive work ethic, team skills, openness to diversity, and the ability to think critically and creatively. Pastors teach their congregants the ways of Christ through their words. You can teach coworkers the ways of Christ by your example. Then, when your example opens doors, you can share the Gospel in words.

EFFECTIVE SUCCESS STRATEGIES ARE GROUNDED IN SCRIPTURE

One of the facts I always stress with Christians who are pursuing careers is this: The most effective strategies for building a successful career are also strategies that will help you honor God through your work. Go to any secular bookstore and browse through the section on professional and career success. You will find books advocating leadership, a positive work ethic, integrity, teamwork, effective communication, critical thinking, working in a diverse environment, and other similar strategies. Those concepts are widely advocated as success strategies in secular literature.

This may surprise you, but the common ground among all these success strategies is they are all solidly grounded in Scripture. That's right. In spite of the challenges to your faith occurring in the workplace, the success strategies most likely to enhance your career come directly from Scripture. Ironic isn't it? When espoused in secular literature, those success strategies are stated in nonbiblical language to appeal to a broader audience, but their origins are, nonetheless, Scriptural. What are these strategies? There are many, but some of the most widely advocated are these:

- Exemplify a positive work ethic
- Be a good team player
- Think critically and act creatively
- Communicate often and well
- Work with integrity and honesty
- Be a leader among your coworkers

Because the final three strategies on this list—communication, integrity, and leadership—are covered in other chapters, they are not explained here. Instead, this chapter focuses on work ethic, teamwork, thinking critically, and acting creatively. The emphasis is on how these strategies can be applied to help maintain positive working relationships with unbelieving coworkers while also advancing your career.

PUT YOUR WORK ETHIC TO WORK

Organizations operating in a competitive environment need personnel who will work hard, smart, and, when necessary, long. In other words, organizations need their personnel to have a positive work ethic. As Christians, we know God expects us to have a positive work ethic. We are to honor God by how we do our work. You cannot honor God by doing your work poorly. Consider the words of Ecclesiastes 9:9–10, where we are told no matter what our job happens to be we should do it with all of our might. These verses leave little room for misinterpretation. How you do your job is an indicator of your work ethic. Your work ethic can, in turn, be a daily sermon for your coworkers.

The Christian work ethic is a belief that Christians have an obligation to be diligent, self-disciplined, and hard-working because the work we do, no matter what it is, is a gift from God. Consequently, we are to show our appreciation by how we do our work. In all cases, Christians work first for God and second for their employer, a fact verified in Colossians 3:23–24. In these verses, we are told to do everything we undertake with our whole hearts because we are working for the Lord. This being the case, it is important for Christians to honor God by the quality and quantity of their work. When you do your work well, you are giving a sermon by example on the value of the Christian work ethic.

The Bible is clear God expects us to show our thanks for the work He provides us by doing it well. For example, in Proverbs 10:4–5, we read a "slack hand" will make us poor, but diligence will make us rich. These verses also make clear those who work hard are wise, whereas the slothful come to shame. As Christians, we are to be "wise" sons and daughters which means, in part, doing our work well. Doing our work well is an effective way to reflect the image of Christ for our coworkers.

Unfortunately, American society has been beset by an entitlement mentality, a self-centered attitude the polar opposite of the Christian work ethic. People who have adopted an entitlement mentality think the world owes them a living and they are entitled to success without having to work for it. Their worldview can be summarized in these four words: "It's all about me." This kind of attitude is a far cry from the sacrificial outlook we, as Christians, strive to adopt.

Those with an entitlement mentality seek to honor no one through their work, except perhaps themselves. Working hard, working smart, and working long are not part of their make-up. Self-centeredness and narcissism are common characteristics of the entitled. People with this kind of attitude are referred to as "sluggards" in the Bible, and the Bible is replete with verses condemning them. Proverbs 21:25 summarizes what God thinks about sluggards when it states the sluggard's ways put him to death because he refuses to work. This is a powerful statement. This verse doesn't say the wages of sloth are limited to just poverty and privation. It says sloth will result in death.

Frankly, employers, regardless their religious convictions or lack thereof, do not like sluggards any more than the author of Proverbs 21:25. This fact can be helpful to Christians who consistently exhibit a positive work ethic. Because the entitlement mentality has become ubiquitous in America, it is easier for employers to find people who want a paycheck than people who want to work. That is why people with a positive work ethic are such assets to organizations. When you work for the Lord and commit your efforts to Him as commanded in Proverbs 16:3, a positive work ethic will be part of the example you set for coworkers.

Even Unbelievers Want to Work with People Who Have a Positive Work Ethic

Just because someone rejects Christianity does not mean he or she rejects the Christian work ethic. I have seen this fact borne out in my own career many times. When working in the private sector early in my career, one of my company's project managers was an ardent atheist. I will call him Jake. Jake was vocal about his disdain for Christianity. In fact, he belittled Christians for being "illogical and susceptible to emotionalism." I often heard Jake state unequivocally ". . . any educated person who professes to believe in God should be stripped of his college degree." For obvious reasons, those of us in the engineering department who were believers tried to avoid being assigned to Jake's projects. We knew from experience Jake made a point of being hypercritical of the work of believers.

But Jake had an interesting quirk. He also made a point of assigning those of us who were believers to his most difficult, important, and time-sensitive projects. We thought this was because he wanted to set us up to fail. But as things turned out, we were misinterpreting his motives. Jake did lord it over us at every opportunity, but he had a much different reason for assigning us to his difficult projects: He needed our work ethic. There is no question Jake disliked Christians, but he liked our work ethic more than he disliked our beliefs.

When I confronted him one day about the irony of criticizing Christians for being "emotional dummies" while insisting we be assigned to his most challenging projects, he admitted forthrightly he liked our work ethic. When I asked him why he refused to acknowledge the source of our work ethic; he simply brushed me off. When I asked, "Who is being illogical now?" he scowled and told me to get back to work. However, we did notice after that confrontation Jake's criticism of Christianity became less frequent and less vocal. It did not go away by any means, but it was toned down. By exemplifying the Christian work ethic, we were able to influence our boss, an atheist, for good.

BE A GOOD TEAM PLAYER

Most of the work done in organizations is done by teams rather than individuals. Because effective teamwork enhances competitiveness, organizations need their personnel to be good team players rather than self-serving individualists who focus solely on their personal agendas. To succeed in a competitive marketplace, organizations need personnel who can make their work teams perform better. In other words, they need good team players. An unchanging rule of thumb about organizational performance is this: The better an organization's work teams perform, the better the organization performs. This is important because the better the performance of an organization, the more competitive it will be. The more competitive the organization, the better the chances for job security and career advancement for employees.

Teamwork is fundamental to an organization's success in a competitive marketplace, but it is also a Christian imperative. The Bible describes teamwork as an effective approach for people who are trying to accomplish the same purpose. In the case of Scripture, that purpose is spreading the Word of God. In the case of employers, the purpose is competitiveness. By being a good team player, you can set an example that is a daily sermon for your coworkers. Your example will spread the Word of God and at the same time help improve your organization's competitiveness. This, in turn, will enhance your potential for advancement.

1 Corinthians 12:17–20 provides an analogy that describes how teams are composed of people with different talents, but each contributes in some way to achieving a common purpose. The analogy used in these verses is the human body. The human body is composed of many parts. Each individual part serves a specific purpose, but all of them, working together, serve a common purpose. This is the best description of the team concept I have ever seen. Like the body, work teams are composed of different parts (people) who contribute in different ways to achieving a common purpose.

Consequently, an effective way to earn the respect of your coworkers and enhance your career is to help your work team achieve its purpose. In other words, be a good team player. As a Christian, it should be easy for you to grasp the significance of being a good team player. This is because effective teamwork is built on the most fundamental Christian principle: sacrifice. Your example of sacrificing on behalf of the team rather than selfishly pursuing your own ends can be a daily sermon for your coworkers.

Because teamwork is based on the concept of sacrifice—a willingness to put the team's mission ahead of personal agendas—it is one of the most Scriptural of all secular success strategies. Romans 5:8 reminds us Christ made the ultimate sacrifice when He went willingly to the cross for our sins. Because of Christ's example, Christians should understand the concept of sacrifice better than anyone they work with. This understanding can make you a better team player. Being a better team player can, in turn, do much to advance your career.

Sacrificing to Achieve the Team's Purpose: Christ's Apostles

It would be hard to find a better example of individuals sacrificing on behalf of a team than the example of Christ's Apostles. The Apostles were a diverse group of men with different backgrounds and different talents who became a team when they committed to the common purpose of spreading the Gospel of Christ. For example, Peter was a fisherman, and Matthew a tax collector. However, they eventually committed to their common purpose and became a team in spite of their individual differences. In fact, one could argue they became the most important team in human history.

To succeed in carrying out the team's purpose, the Apostles had to be willing to sacrifice for that purpose. As we know, the lives and deaths of the Apostles illustrate in stark terms just how much they ultimately sacrificed for their team. The Apostles gave up their creature comforts, economic security, and careers to pursue the purpose Christ gave them. We see in Mark 5:8,9, Christ instructed the Apostles to take nothing on their journeys except the clothes on their backs, the sandals on their feet, and a walking staff. They were to take no money, food, or extra clothing. Christ instructed the Apostles to leave their old lives behind and devote themselves to spreading His Word. He also told them to be both wise and innocent because they would soon find themselves in the midst of wolves of the human variety (Matthew 10:16).

Leaving behind all they knew up to that point was, of course, just the beginning of the sacrifices the Apostles would be called on to make.

Putting aside Judas Iscariot, all the Apostles except John eventually sacrificed their lives for the team's purpose. Peter was crucified upside down in Rome. James, son of Zebedee, was beheaded. Andrew, Bartholomew, Philip, Jude, and Simon were crucified. Matthew was killed with a halberd and Thomas with a spear. James was beaten to death with a club after being stoned and crucified. Matthias, Judas Iscariot's replacement, was stoned and beheaded. Only John, also a son of Zebedee, died a natural death in his old age. John escaped the gruesome deaths of his fellow Apostles, but he did not escape unscathed. He was forced to suffer in exile for trying to carry out the mission Christ gave the Apostles. It was while in exile John wrote some of the most edifying words in the New Testament.

The stories of the Apostles' lives and deaths illustrate in stark terms that sacrifice is the foundation of effective teamwork. Of course, the sacrifices you may be called on to make for your work team are not likely to be so costly as those made by the Apostles. You may have to sacrifice some of your free time to get the job done for the team, or you might have to sacrifice personal recognition in favor of team recognition. You might have to sacrifice an individual award or a personal bonus in favor of a team award or team bonus. I do not mean to characterize these kinds of sacrifices as minor, but when you find yourself resenting the sacrifices required of good team players, remember those made by the Apostles in carrying out their mission to spread the Gospel. Doing this will put your sacrifices in the workplace in proper perspective.

People in the workplace, regardless their views on Christianity, will appreciate fellow team members who make their team perform better. By being a good team player—meaning one who is willing to sacrifice for the good of the team—you can be the team's *Most Valuable Player*. When you are perceived by teammates as an asset to the team, you will be respected by your fellow team members regardless their views on Christianity. In fact, when they come to understand your views on being a good team player come from Scripture, unbelievers on your team might be more open to hearing what Scripture has to say about teamwork, as well as other workplace issues.

Think Critically and Act Creatively

To accomplish the complementary goals of succeeding in a secular career and reflecting the image of Christ for your coworkers, it is necessary to follow the advice Christ gave His Apostles in Matthew 10:16. This fact is restated and emphasized throughout this book. When Christ told His Apostles to be "wise," He was warning them to think critically and act creatively, or they would suffer at the hands of the very people they were trying to reach with His message. Sheep who find themselves in the midst of wolves will not survive long if they are foolish or naïve, nor will Christians who work among people who behave like wolves. Therefore, critical thinking and creative action are essential if you are going to shine your light in the workplace.

Critical thinking involves objectively evaluating information, situations, directions, problems, opinions, arguments, and recommendations rather than accepting them at face value. Critical thinkers never assume the input they receive from others is correct. Rather, they are wise evaluators of the world around them. They make decisions and form opinions based on critical analysis of the information available to them, coupled with their own experience, intuition, and common sense. Critical thinking is the opposite of naively accepting things at face value.

Creative action is a logical extension of critical thinking. It means taking imaginative, original, and innovative action, based on critical thinking. It is the opposite of continuing to do things the way they have always been done for no reason other than habit. It is also the antidote to doing things the way people with nefarious agendas would tempt, trick, or pressure you to do them. One of the most illustrative examples of what can happen when people in the workplace refuse to think critically and act creatively is the quartz-powered digital watch.

For decades, the wristwatch was a mechanical analog timepiece. The undisputed leaders in watchmaking were the Swiss. A Swiss watch was more than just a symbol of quality; it was a symbol of status. Consequently, when a forward-looking inventor developed the quartz-powered digital watch, his only thought was to approach Swiss watchmakers with his invention. He wanted his prototype to be manufactured by the best. To him, the quartz prototype coupled with Swiss quality seemed like an obvious and mutually beneficial match. However, to his surprise and chagrin, the staid, conventional Swiss turned their noses up at his invention.

According to Swiss watchmakers, nobody would want a quartz-powered digital watch when they could have the old reliable timepieces produced in Switzerland for hundreds of years. Disappointed but undeterred, the inventor took his quartz-powered prototype to the Japanese who were, at the time, intent on becoming the world's leader in digital technologies. The rest is history. Digital watches powered by batteries are now the norm worldwide. Mechanical Swiss watches, on the other hand, are museum pieces.

Critical Thinking and Creative Action in the Bible

Perhaps the most compelling example of critical thinking and creative action is one found in 1 Kings. It is the story of the two harlots who brought their dispute over a child before King Solomon. Each woman claimed to be the mother of the baby. Christians are familiar with the story. First, King Solomon had to think critically because the harlots presented him with two different stories, only one of which could be true. Second, Solomon had to act creatively to ensure the indisputable truth came out.

As shown in 1 Kings 3:24–26, King Solomon—thinking critically and acting creatively—ordered the child to be cut in half, with half going to each of the claimants. Of course, King Solomon, being a wise ruler, knew the real mother would never consent to having her baby cut in half. She would give up her child rather than see it die in such a gruesome manner. This is exactly what happened. Recall that on being crowned, Solomon asked God to grant him wisdom. His request was granted. Wisdom allowed Solomon to think critically and act creatively. By doing so, King Solomon was able to discern the truth and, in turn, make the right decision. Christians in the workplace will do well to emulate the example of King Solomon. When faced with temptation, rejection, pressure, persecution, or other trials in the workplace, ask God for wisdom, then think critically and act creatively.

People who think critically and act creatively exemplify the Scriptural concept of wisdom. Proverbs 3:13 tells us those who find wisdom will be happy and will also gain understanding. This verse contains a pertinent and powerful message for working Christians. Gaining understanding before making decisions is fundamental to success. People who make decisions or take action without first gaining a thorough understanding of the problem are likely to make bad decisions. Bad decisions, in turn, lead to ineffective solutions, which often make the original problem worse. This is why wisdom and understanding are so important to working Christians: They lead to better decisions, and better decisions lead to better solutions. Better solutions, in turn, lead to better performance.

Gaining understanding before making decisions or taking action is important, but it can be difficult at times. People in the workplace have their own ambitions, egos, agendas, biases, attitudes, and worldviews. Consequently, to gain understanding when dealing with people, we must be wise enough to think critically rather than accepting at face value the things they tell us. This is because the information conveyed by others can be colored by their individual ambitions, egos, agendas, biases, attitudes, and worldviews, as well as such factors as inexperience and habit. It is also wise, having thought critically, to act creatively because when solving problems, the best result will not necessarily come from continuing to do things the way they have always been done. Some of the best solutions to problems come as the result of thinking outside the box and finding creative new approaches to old problems.

Successful people are always looking for ways to do their jobs better. By better I mean more efficiently and effectively. This is one of the reasons they are successful. The need to get better all the time grows out of the concept of competition, which is the driving force behind the push for continual improvement. Critical thinking coupled with creative action will not only help you avoid being led astray by coworkers with nefarious agendas, when practiced together, they will promote continual improvement on your part. This is important because continual improvement is fundamental to success in a competitive environment.

I once received a call from a Christian who worked as a CPA who was chewed up by a wolf in his organization because he failed to think critically. I will call him Nhieu Vo. One of Vo's professional goals was to become a partner in his CPA firm. After years of working long, hard, and smart, his goal was finally in reach when failing to think critically set him back. He eventually became a partner, but not without enduring a heartbreaking detour that could have been avoided. At a point in time when Vo was making good progress climbing the career ladder, he got knocked off it—at least temporarily—by a wolf disguised as a colleague and friend.

The wolf, Vo's colleague Samantha, also wanted to become a partner in the firm. For a time, Samantha viewed working long, hard, and smart as the keys to becoming a partner. However, in recent months she changed her approach. Now, rather than working long, hard, and smart to succeed, Samantha began to use guile and office politics as her preferred strategies. Unaware Samantha had become a wolf, Vo became her prey, an unfortunate turn of events critical thinking and creative action could have prevented.

Aware Vo was her competition for the firm's next partnership, Samantha began to covertly undermine his credibility. She was careful and subtle in her efforts. On the surface, she seemed to be supportive of Vo and even helpful, but Samantha was a wolf in sheep's clothing. For example, to *help* him Samantha told Vo the firm's senior partner welcomed advice and constructive criticism directly from associates and no one ever became a partner in the firm without taking the initiative to frankly and honestly share his or her opinions with the CEO, even to the point of disagreeing with him.

According to Samantha, "This is how our CEO determines if an associate has the gumption to challenge the boss and speak truth to power." Had he thought critically about Samantha's assertion, Vo could have asked several pertinent questions including (1) How do you know our CEO welcomes constructive criticism? (2) Have you ever given him constructive criticism yourself? (3) Is there anyone I can talk to who has been rewarded for giving the CEO constructive feedback? and (4) Why are you telling me this? But Vo asked none of those questions.

Unfortunately, Vo failed to think critically in this situation. Rather, he accepted his colleague's input at face value and began emailing unsolicited advice to the CEO. He also began to offer constructive criticism on company policies, corporate decisions, and other executive-level issues. Determined to win the competition for the next partnership, Vo set about showing the CEO he had gumption and initiative. This went on for several months before Vo and his supervisor were summoned to a meeting with the CEO. During the meeting, Vo learned that not only was the CEO loath to receive advice directly from associates, he didn't want to hear from them period. Anything Vo had to say was supposed to come through the established chain of command. Not only did Vo receive a severe scolding, his unwitting supervisor received one too because of Vo's "impertinence."

Finally, aware he was duped by Samantha, Vo tried to defend himself, but this just made matters worse. The CEO told him pointedly, "If you are so naïve as to allow yourself to be deluded in this way, you will never become a partner in this firm." Vo learned a hard lesson, but it was a lesson that after much prayer and reflection he took to heart. When Vo read in Ephesians 5:15 he was to be circumspect and wise, he knew he had been a fool. Vo also realized he would have to become a critical thinker and a creative action taker if he was going to work with wolves without being devoured.

It took two long and often frustrating years of working hard, working smart, thinking critically, and acting creatively to rebuild his credibility in the firm, but eventually, Vo's efforts paid off. He became a partner. He was offered the partnership when Samantha, who secured her partnership by deluding Vo, was forced to leave the firm under a cloud. It took some time, but eventually, Vo gained a thankful perspective on the bad episode Samantha put him through. He came to view it as a growth experience. Samantha meant it for bad, but God meant it for good. As a result, Vo never again made the mistake of failing to think critically and act creatively.

DISCUSSION CASE 8.1: "DO AS I SAY, NOT AS I DO."

Sam was a nurse for ten years when he was named the head of nursing for the hospital where he worked. His record as a nurse was excellent and his work ethic legendary. Sam thought he was ready to lead. His first thought upon taking over as the hospital's head nurse was, "I am going to whip this team into shape." His first act as head nurse was to call a meeting of all nurses and give his new charges a lecture titled "No Excuses." The gist of his lecture was, "I don't want to hear about why you can't get the job done. I want you to show me how you are going to do get it done in spite of the obstacles. No excuses. If you will work as hard as I do, we will be the highest performing unit in the hospital." The problem was once Sam became the head nurse, he stopped working. He viewed his job as giving orders and making sure others followed them. His example of a positive work ethic went out the window. Sam's unstated motto became, "Do as I say, not as I do." Within a couple of months, the morale and performance of the nursing staff took a nose dive. Absenteeism was up, complaints from patients skyrocketed, and recordable errors in patient care increased.

Discussion Questions

1. Have you ever had a supervisor whose example said, "Do as I say not as I do?" If so, how was this approach received?
2. If Sam were a friend and asked for your help, what advice would you give him about a better approach to leading people?

DISCUSSION CASE 8.2: "I DON'T UNDERSTAND WHY I AM ALWAYS PASSED OVER . . ."

Marie was ambitious. She wanted to make it to the top in her profession. A mentor told her doing good work wasn't enough. She needed to make sure her superiors knew she did good work. Her mentor told her to "blow your own horn and make sure your boss hears it." She also told Marie,

"If you don't take care of yourself, nobody else will." Unfortunately, Marie interpreted this advice to mean she was alone in her efforts to succeed and needed to adopt an *it's-all-about-me* attitude toward her work. Consequently, Marie was not a good team player, a fact that caused her teammates to resent her. What they really disliked about Marie was her tendency to take credit for the work of the team as if she were solely responsible for its success. As time went by, Marie did not receive the promotions she desired, although other members of her team did. In a talk with her mentor, Marie said, "I don't understand why I am always passed over. I blow my own horn just like you taught me, and I make sure my boss hears it."

Discussion Questions

1. Have you ever worked with an individual who was so focused on climbing the career ladder he or she was willing to step on others to advance? If so, how did the individual's coworkers respond?
2. What advice would you give Marie concerning the approach she is taking to promote herself in the eyes of her boss? Is there a better way?

REVIEW QUESTIONS FOR INDIVIDUALS AND GROUPS

1. What is the ultimate measuring stick for defining what is "good" or "better" concerning the work and behavior of people in an organization?
2. What is meant by "influencing people for good" in the workplace?
3. What is meant by the term *Christian work ethic*?
4. Why is having a positive work ethic so important for Christians on the job?
5. What is the most important element of being a good team player?

6. What does it mean to think critically?
7. What does it mean to act creatively?
8. Why is it important for Christians in the workplace to think critically and act creatively?

CHAPTER 9

APPROACH DIVERSITY IN A CHRIST-LIKE MANNER

"And He made from one man every nation of mankind to live on all the face of the earth . . ."

Acts 17:26

As a gay man, Alajandro was not happy when his boss asked him to team up with his coworker Luther on an important work project. He knew Luther was a committed Christian and feared they would clash over the issue of homosexuality. Although Luther always treated him with respect and courtesy, Alajandro knew Luther was a church deacon. Further, he heard Luther once participated in a protest march against same-sex marriage. Consequently, Alajandro was surprised to find his fears about working with Luther were unfounded.

When the supervisor brought them together, Luther shook Alajandro's hand and said he was pleased to be working with him. Luther also told Alajandro he admired his work. Once they completed their assigned project—ahead of schedule and under budget—Alajandro asked Luther if they could talk for a few minutes after work. They met in the break room, and Alajandro came right to the point. "I appreciate your acceptance of my sexual preference. Because you are a Christian, I was sure you wouldn't want to work with me or would go along only begrudgingly." Luther smiled and responded, "Actually, I don't accept your worldview, but I do accept you, and I am proud to work with you. If you would like to discuss my views on homosexuality, I will be happy to share them with you. Like me, you are part of God's creation. That means you deserve my respect regardless of your worldview. We can disagree on homosexuality without rejecting each other as coworkers. There are a time and a place for debating this issue, but it is not at work."

People of every race, religion, nationality, worldview, and culture come to America seeking a better life. As a result, the United States is the most diverse country in the world, and this diversity is reflected in the workplace. If handled well, human diversity can be an asset to an organization. But if handled poorly, diversity can divide an organization into feuding factions based on race, sex, age, education, culture, religion, politics, worldviews, and other factors. Unfortunately, diversity is not always handled well in the workplace. Ironically, this fact represents an opportunity for you and other Christians who are pursuing careers.

As a Christian, approaching diversity in ways that bring people together can be part of the Christ-like example you set for coworkers. With this said, a caveat is in order. When the diversity issue in question is sexual preference, remember you do not have to accept or validate the views of other people in order to work with them. Working with someone who holds a different worldview and validating that individual's worldview are two different things. In fact, when you work with people whose views run afoul of Scripture, remember to view them as opportunities not enemies. Even Christ refused to condemn a woman who was guilty of adultery. But in defending her, Christ did not validate her sin. Rather, he sent her away with the admonition to go and sin no more (John 8:1–11).

Christianity is a big tent that accommodates any and all who put their faith and trust in Christ and subscribe to what is taught in His

Word. There is always room for more in the tent. People whose world-views go against the teachings of Scripture today may repent and be welcomed into Christianity's big tent tomorrow. Further, you might be the instrument Christ uses to make this happen. In this sense, the workplace is a mission field, and you are a missionary.

Political correctness pervades the modern workplace, and it demands Christians tolerate the views of people who believe they can choose a sex other than the one God gave them. But, as Christians, we must be biblically correct, not politically correct. That means, although we are called to show lesbian, gay, bisexual, transgendered, and queer or LGBTQ coworkers the image of Christ in how we treat them, we are not called to validate their worldview. The bulk of this chapter deals with traditional diversity issues such as race, gender, culture, politics, and age. But the final section is devoted specifically to working with members of the LGBTQ community.

One can find Christians scattered around the globe in every nation, race, culture, and circumstance. Christians differ from each other in many ways. We are a diverse group. But we are the same in the one way that matters most: We trust in Christ as our Lord and Savior and seek His grace and mercy. As a Christian, you can show coworkers how to approach diversity in a positive manner by setting an example for them that reflects the image of Christ. Doing this will help your organization benefit from diversity rather than suffer because of it. People who can contribute to making diversity the asset it can be in organizations will be valued by those organizations as well as by their coworkers.

"TOLERANCE" OF DIVERSITY IS A MISNOMER

The watchword of secular humanists when it comes to diversity is "tolerance." But tolerance is a misnomer, at least for Christians. Christ did not tell us to tolerate our neighbors. He told us to love them, and He made no exceptions for race, gender, or other diversity factors. In fact, one could argue you have not really given Christian love until you have given it to someone who differs from you in ways that make it difficult.

Loving your neighbors as yourself involves more than just tolerating them. I will get to Christ's admonition in the Second Greatest Commandment shortly, but first some background.

The government attempts to promote diversity in the workplace by enforcing regulations that protect defined groups of people from discrimination. Those who are protected fall into several categories that include race, age, sex, and national origin, among others. *Tolerance* is the watchword among advocates of this approach. Tolerance is to a secular humanist what Christian love is to you and me. To a secular humanist, being tolerant makes you a better person. It is ironic, then, that humanists are willing to tolerate almost anything, except, of course, Christianity.

Although there is certainly nothing wrong with being tolerant of others, there is a problem with the concept. The government has become a major player in the diversity arena. As often happens when the government gets involved in an issue, the issue becomes a political hot potato. This is certainly the case with tolerance. Predictably, the concept has taken on different meanings for different people. To some people, tolerance means being open to human differences. To others, it means complying with the government's Equal Employment Opportunity regulations. To yet others, it is a politically correct code word for giving preferential treatment to selected people.

The best way to cut through the fog created by the different meanings associated with tolerance is to take a Christ-like approach to diversity in the workplace. As a Christian, you will find the kind of love set forth in I Corinthians 13 will trump government regulations and political correctness every time. To approach diversity in the workplace in a Christ-like manner, it is necessary to first understand what the concept of tolerance really means or, at least, what it meant before the concept was politicized.

Before tolerance became a political hot potato, tolerating something meant *putting up with* it. In a workplace context, the things being put up with are human differences. Note, tolerance did not originally mean accepting or embracing human differences, just putting up with them.

As a Christian, I suspect you sometimes wonder when the concept of tolerance is going to be extended to you. Many of the believers I counsel feel as if their Christianity is the only thing not tolerated in today's society, including the workplace.

The government expects people in the workplace to be sufficiently tolerant that they refrain from discriminating against coworkers on the basis of diversity factors. This may be the best a government agency can expect, but from a Christian perspective, it is setting the bar too low. Frankly, Christians should not be satisfied with this view of tolerance. We are called to do better. Christ expects us to not just tolerate our neighbors but to love them as He loves us. When you begin to feel certain coworkers do not deserve your love because of their worldviews or other diversity-related factors, remember you and I don't deserve Christ's love either. He died on the cross for us not because we deserved His sacrifice but precisely because we do not.

Loving Your Neighbors Requires More than Just Tolerating Them

Government regulations have certainly made a difference in diversifying the workplace. But as progress has been made, circumstances have changed, whereas government regulations have not. As a result, government regulations sometimes result in unintended consequences that undermine the acceptance of diversity in the workplace. When we merely tolerate each other to comply with government regulations, an undercurrent of resentment and mistrust is introduced into coworker relationships. Those who do the tolerating, as well as those being tolerated, begin to resent the concept. People can sense intuitively when they are being tolerated to comply with government regulations rather than accepted. The sense of artificiality inherent in tolerance can undermine coworker relationships.

A Hispanic friend I once worked with got a rough start to his career because of the artificiality of politically correct tolerance. Orlando was a committed Christian and a highly qualified engineer, but at the beginning of his career, he felt like an outsider among his colleagues. There was nothing specific in their behavior he could put his finger on, but Orlando felt tolerated not accepted. Orlando once told me he felt certain his colleagues thought he got his job because of the government's equal employment opportunity regulations rather than his qualifications.

In the beginning, nobody wanted Orlando to be assigned to their projects, nor did they include him in social gatherings. When he asked for my counsel, I suggested he take a two-pronged approach to deal with the situation. First, he was to ignore the attitudes of his *tolerant* colleagues and make a point of treating them the way he would like them to treat him. Second, he was to prove them wrong in their perception of why he got his job by doing outstanding work. Orlando did both. It took time for things to get better, but after less than a year, Orlando was the most frequently requested engineer by all our project managers. Further, the begrudging tolerance of his colleagues was replaced by respect.

The government can ensure a measure of diversity in the workplace by enforcing regulations, but it cannot change the human heart. Only Christ can do that. This distinction is important because *reluctant compliance* with government regulations will never make diversity the asset it can be in organizations. Only when the hearts of people in the workplace are changed will diversity be the asset it can be. This is where you come in. You can be the instrument Christ uses for changing the hearts of coworkers concerning diversity.

Long before the federal government enacted its alphabet soup of diversity-related policies, a much higher authority told us we are to love our neighbors as ourselves. When Christ delivered this message, he made no exceptions for age, education, race, culture, sex, religion, politics, worldviews, or any other factors. The Second Greatest Commandment does not say we should love those neighbors who are like us. Rather, it says we are to love our neighbors, period. Doing this is a much higher calling than merely tolerating them. With this point made, let me be quick to add the Second Greatest Commandment does not say we are to validate the worldviews, actions, or behavior of our neighbors. It says we are to love them. Christians should never confuse the two concepts. Loving and validating are two different things.

To obey the admonition in the Second Greatest Commandment, it is necessary to understand the concept of the unity of the human race in Christ. God created all of us. Further, no matter how we may appear to be different, we are all sinners in need of God's grace. If everyone in the workplace heeded Christ's admonition concerning diversity, there would be no need for federal government regulations. Further, diversity would soon become the asset organizations need it to be. Let me repeat here what was written earlier: The federal government can pass and enforce regulations concerning diversity, but it cannot change hearts. Only Christ can do this, and Christ often works through His children. This means the example you set for coworkers could be the instrument Christ uses for changing their hearts.

Because of the sinful nature of people, making workplace diversity an asset can be a challenge. This is the challenge the federal government attempts to deal with by enacting and enforcing regulations. But dealing with diversity in a positive manner requires more than government enforcement. It requires people undergoing a change of heart and government regulations rarely change the heart. In fact, when it comes to diversity in the workplace, government regulations sometimes make matters worse. They can cause resentment rather than genuine acceptance. This is why learning to deal with diversity in a Christ-like manner is so important for you and me.

Christ can change the hearts of people who resist diversity, but it is important to remember Christ might choose to employ you in this enterprise. The contribution you can make to help change the hearts of coworkers who resist diversity is to show them a Christ-like example in how you approach the issue. Christians who deal with diversity in the workplace in a Christ-like manner are peacemakers and team builders. Being a peacemaker can make you a valuable asset to your employer. Organizations need people who can bring their coworkers together. When people with different talents, perspectives, points of view, experience, and backgrounds come together and focus on a common goal, the results can be powerful. Your example of approaching diversity in a Christ-like manner can help bring diverse people together and get them focused on a common goal. It can also help lead them to Christ.

CHRISTIAN LOVE IN THE WORKPLACE

Showing coworkers the kind of love Christ spoke of in Matthew 22:39 can be difficult. After all, by "love" Christ meant putting the needs of others ahead of your own. This is not something that comes naturally. As sinful people, we tend to practice what I call *ice cream love*. We *love* the way ice cream tastes, looks, and makes us feel, so we claim to *love* ice cream. The truth is we *love* ice cream for what it does for us. We don't do anything for the ice cream. Hence, ice cream love is not love at all. Rather, it is a manifestation of self-centeredness. Ice cream love is not about the good of others. Christ's view of love is described in detail in 1 Corinthians 13. This chapter in Scripture describes a kind of love that is the polar opposite of ice cream love. It describes a kind of love in which you put the good of others ahead of self.

Ice cream love is worldly love, not biblical love. Worldly love is clearly proscribed in Scripture. In Romans12:2, it is written we are not to conform ourselves to the world. Rather, we are supposed to be changed for the better by God. Those who conform themselves to the world practice ice cream love. They *love* others for what others can do for them and how others make them feel. But as Christians, we are called on to "be transformed" and to practice Christ-like love. We are to love our neighbors as ourselves. This requires putting aside our normal human biases and interacting positively with people who appear to be different.

Christians who come to me for counseling sometimes ask about the emotional aspect of love. Those who raise the question of the emotion seem to think love is just a feeling. You either feel love or you don't. But Christian love is not just an emotion. It is Christ's admonition in the Second Greatest Commandment put into action. This is what people mean when they say love is a verb. You demonstrate your love for others by what you do, not by what you feel.

When we display Christian love, we act in ways that show genuine obedience to Christ's command to love our neighbor as our self. In showing biblical love to our neighbors, we do not ask whether they can satisfy our needs or if they look, talk, dress, eat, or think like we do. In fact, our commitment to Christian love has not been tested until we are called on to love those who do nothing for us or those who do not return our love. Biblical love requires we love our neighbors because, regardless of their race, culture, sex, politics, national origin, or worldview, Christ commands us to do so. There is a vast difference between tolerating diverse people because it is the politically correct thing to do and loving them because it is the Christ-like thing to do.

Christian Love Is better than Political Correctness

Obeying Christ's admonition to love our neighbors as ourselves can be a difficult challenge, even for the most committed Christians. However, doing so will help you make greater inroads with diverse people than political correctness ever will. In Ephesians 4:1–3, we are told to walk in a manner worthy a follower of Christ and to treat others with "humility," "gentleness," and "patience." Obeying the words contained in these verses will be more effective in promoting positive relations with coworkers than will the artificial, legalistic, and fickle tenets of political correctness. People will respond more positively to sincere kindness and caring than to politically correct platitudes.

Political correctness was probably one of those well-intended concepts at some point, but it has since morphed into something unintended. It has been transformed in meaning by advocates with an agenda. If its intent was really to discourage words or practices that might be perceived as offensive to others, political correctness would not be the controversial topic it has become. After all, as Christians, we should make every effort to avoid unnecessarily offending people. But what makes political correctness controversial is its proponents often take the concept to absurd extremes. In too many cases, the concept is used to control what is said and by whom. It has become an inhibitor of speech, particularly Christian speech. Vocal proponents of political correctness have been known to label Christ's words of love from Scripture as "hate speech."

A further problem with political correctness is it can make people reluctant to speak their minds and tell the truth. As Christians, we are commanded to speak the truth. We are to do so with tact and kindness, but we are to communicate with others without distortion, adornment, or artifice. For example, a male supervisor once told me he was reluctant to give even the most constructive criticism to female subordinates. He was once accused of bias by a female subordinate who did not like to receive constructive criticism. When his weakling of a boss refused to support him, this supervisor saw the writing on the wall. From that point on, he gave constructive criticism to male subordinates only. The irony in this situation is his male subordinates became better at their jobs than their female coworkers because they were the only ones receiving constructive criticism, a necessary ingredient in continual improvement.

The artificiality of political correctness is the Achilles heel of the concept. People have an innate ability to sense when others are less than genuine in their relationships. They can tell when people are going along to be politically correct rather than getting along out of mutual respect. People can sense hypocrisy in others. Political correctness can suppress some of the external manifestations of human bias, but all this usually accomplishes is the creation of a simmering resentment in the hearts of people who feel coerced. Unless the hearts of people are changed concerning diversity, tension in human relations will still exist. The tension and resentment might be driven underground, but they do not go away. Further, under certain circumstances, suppressed tension and resentment can bubble up to the surface and explode. When this happens, human conflict is the usual result. To make matters worse, when diversity is involved, human conflict can quickly get ugly.

People in the workplace, regardless their age, race, sex, nationality, or other diversity factors, will appreciate Christians who are genuinely compassionate, kind, and caring in their human relations. They will also appreciate those who set positive examples of treating people with dignity and respect regardless of perceived differences. Those who approach diversity from the perspective that all people are part of God's creation can be invaluable assets to organizations. People whose human interactions are guided by sincere Christian love can make workplace diversity an asset in their organizations.

John 16:33 reminds us to take courage because Christ has overcome the world. Because of Christ's victory, His love applied consistently in the workplace can overcome the bias, prejudice, stereotyping, labeling, and discrimination so prevalent in today's society. The government seeks to do this through the enforcement of regulations. Christian love, on the other hand, does this by changing hearts. Christians who demonstrate the heart of Christ in their human relations will be assets to their organizations. They will also be better able to influence their coworkers for Christ.

Christian Love Can Keep You from Stumbling Over Diversity Issues

The stumbling blocks relating to diversity manifest themselves in such practices as bias, prejudice, stereotyping, labeling, and discrimination. Christian love can help you maneuver over, around, or through these stumbling blocks without tripping. Christ does not want us to limit our Christian love to those who look like us, think like us, and believe like us. Further, *different* should not be taken to mean bad or inferior. It is important to grasp this simple fact because people can be different in so many ways. Even members of the same family can be vastly different in terms of such attributes as age, gender, physical ability, intelligence, religious beliefs, education level, personality, skills, experience, personal preferences, appearance, attitude, political orientation, and so on. If there can be this many differences between family members, imagine how many differences there can be among people in the workplace.

It is so important for Christians who are trying to reflect the image of Christ in the workplace to internalize the Scriptural imperative contained in 1 John 2:10. In this verse, we are told if we love our brother we abide in the light and have no cause for stumbling. When you consider how diverse the workplace has become and then factor in your sinful nature, there will be plenty of potholes that might cause you to stumble. The best preventive measure available to you is the kind of Christian love described in 1 John 2:10 and 1 Corinthians 13, not political correctness. Showing your coworkers true Christian love will do more to build positive relationships than politically correct platitudes ever will.

One thing is certain concerning your career. You are going to work with people who do not look, talk, dress, eat, think, interact, socialize, believe, or vote like you. In fact, with some of your coworkers, the only thing you will have in common, at least on the surface, will be your work. Fortunately, when you show people compassion, caring, kindness, and respect, the hallmarks of Christian love, human diversity factors become less an issue. Christian love will help you bridge the gap created by perceived differences between you and your coworkers. This, in turn, will help you take advantage of the job-related factors you have in common with coworkers and use them to build better relationships.

When coworkers who appear to be different experience the genuine compassion and caring of Christian love, the walls of suspicion separating you from them will begin to crumble. As the walls of suspicion come down, they can be replaced with bonds of trust. As trust grows, people typically find they have more in common than they might have originally thought. In fact, people who plant the seeds of trust in common ground are often surprised to learn, when those seeds begin to sprout, how much they have in common. It is also common for them to find their shared interests outweigh their supposed differences. One more thing to remember is this: When the love of Christ is what we have in common with coworkers, other differences become insignificant.

RESISTANCE TO DIVERSITY IS A LEARNED BEHAVIOR

Matthew 12:25 warns against what can happen when divisive issues—such as those rooted in diversity—go unresolved. In this verse, we learn a house divided against itself will not stand. Organizations that mishandle diversity can quickly become houses divided against themselves. When this happens, organizational performance suffers. An organization's personnel can put their energy into continually improving performance, or they can put it into feuding over diversity issues. People have sufficient energy for one or the other but not both. Consequently, organizations trying to compete in the global marketplace cannot afford to ignore resistance to diversity. These organizations need people who can help make diversity an asset. Because you understand the Scriptural imperative concerning Christian love and how it applies to diversity, you can be such a person. Helping diverse coworkers learn to work well together can help propel you up the career ladder.

People who are uncomfortable with diversity are not necessarily bad, but they have learned some bad attitudes which, in turn, can result in bad behaviors. The term "learned" is important here because most of the negative behaviors associated with resistance to diversity are learned behaviors (e.g. bias, prejudice, stereotyping, labeling, and discrimination). To understand why people resist accepting those who appear to be different, consider the example of young children. Left to themselves, little children will happily play with each other with no thought of race, gender, or other differences. They are just happy to have playmates. It is only as they grow older some *learn* to adopt negative attitudes toward people who appear to be different. As they grow older, some children learn from their parents, peers, or society in general to adopt negative attitudes toward those who appear to be different.

The reason it is important to understand that negative attitudes about diversity are learned is that what can be learned can be unlearned. People who have learned negative behaviors can learn to replace them with positive behaviors. Your Christ-like example can be a catalyst for the learning process. Showing coworkers a Christ-like attitude toward all people you work with must be part of the example you set for them.

Two young men I served with in the Marine Corps—Steve and Ron—were textbook examples of how learned biases can be overcome. Steve was African American, northern, and urban. Ron was white, southern, and rural. Steve grew up in the inner city of South Philadelphia. Ron grew up on a farm in a small town in Mississippi. During their formative years, they both learned from peers and their respective slices of American society to distrust people of other races. Both developed some serious racial biases. Consequently, when they became bunkmates in our barracks sparks began to fly. But then a strange thing happened.

With the not-too-gentle encouragement of our drill instructors, Steve and Ron learned they actually had much in common. Both were abandoned by their fathers at a young age, both experienced run-ins with the law, both dropped out of high school to help their mothers support the family, and both hoped to change their lives for the better by joining the Marine Corps. As things turned out they were also both well-suited for life as Marines. They were tough, in top physical condition, good with firearms, and natural leaders. After a rough start, they became as close as two people can be. In fact, they were inseparable. The bad attitudes about race they brought to boot camp were soon replaced by a newfound love that transcended race. They began to see each other as people rather than faceless members of racial groups.

OVERCOMING LEARNED RESISTANCE TO DIVERSITY

This section provides specific strategies you can use to overcome learned resistance to diversity. These strategies are workplace appropriate and biblically sound. Your example of applying these strategies might do more than just help you overcome learned resistance to diversity, it might also help coworkers overcome prejudiced attitudes they have learned. The strategies I recommend to Christians I counsel are explained in the following paragraphs.

Focus on Character Rather than Race, Gender, Culture, or Other Differences

The Scriptural imperative to love your neighbor as yourself leaves no room for creative interpretations that distort Christ's meaning. Nor does it allow for discriminating on the basis of factors over which an individual has no control; factors such as race, gender, and culture. People do not choose their race, gender, or culture, nor are these things achieved through personal effort. Rather, they are determined by God. This being the case, when interacting with people, it is wise to focus on factors they can control rather than those they cannot.

The one factor people can control—a factor not determined by birth or life's circumstances—is character. People choose whether or not to live with integrity and whether they will be honest, dependable, and trustworthy. These traits are not determined at birth. Rather, they are developed on the basis of individual decisions made by people of every race, both genders, and all cultures. Individual circumstances can certainly make it more difficult to live a life of integrity, but circumstances do not determine an individual's character.

As for Christians, we are commanded by Scripture to live righteously. For example, in Ephesians 6:14, we read that having put on the belt of truth and the breastplate of righteousness, we are to stand firm in our faith. Righteousness encompasses all the individual traits comprising a person's character. Consequently, when interacting with people in the workplace, it makes sense to focus on character rather than diversity factors not character related. As Christians, our focus should be on those traits that define people, the traits that make them who they are. The defining traits of human beings are character traits as set forth in Scripture. They include the following:

- Honesty and integrity
- Selflessness
- Dependability
- Trustworthiness
- Initiative/responsibility/accountability
- Kindness/sensitivity
- Perseverance

Remember this when you form opinions of people: race, gender, culture, and the other ways they can appear different are not character traits. They do not make people who they are. There are people of every race, both genders, and all cultures who have the kinds of character traits just listed. There are also those who do not. It is a person's character, not his or her race, gender, or culture that matters.

Look for Common Ground between People

There is almost always more common ground between people than differences. Even people who speak different languages, are of different races, and have different cultural backgrounds share more similarities than differences. People of all races, nationalities, and cultures as well as both genders tend to share similar desires, ambitions, hopes, fears, and needs. Even more important than these similarities, at least to you and me, is people of all races, nationalities, and cultures as well as both genders are part of God's creation.

The key to bridging gaps created by outward differences is to find common ground with people who appear to be different. In the workplace, this should be easy to do because people at work already have something important in common: the need to support themselves and their families. Add to this the need to excel to advance one's career and the things working people have in common begin to multiply. Finally, consider that, like you, people in the workplace need the love of Christ in their lives, even if they refuse to acknowledge the fact. The common needs of people in the workplace give them plenty of common ground.

I saw the value of finding common ground between people demonstrated in a powerful way when going through Marine Corps boot camp at Parris Island, South Carolina. Our recruit platoon was made up of African Americans, Latinos, Caucasians, and Asians. We hailed from North and South as well as urban and rural. We were mostly poor and middle class but with a few sons of wealth sprinkled in. In short, we were a quintessentially American group. Our recruit platoon was easily the most diverse group of people any of us were ever exposed to, and this exposure came with no preparation. We were simply thrown together in a barracks and expected to work things out.

At first, the recruits in my platoon eyed each other with suspicion and wariness. This was 1971, a time of great social upheaval in America. Dr. Martin Luther King, Jr., was assassinated just three years earlier, there were major race riots in several of America's largest cities, and bussing to achieve integration of public schools in the South was still a political hot potato. These factors just multiplied the suspicions and mistrust most of us harbored toward each other.

Acting out of ignorance and stereotypical thinking, my fellow recruits and I quickly arranged ourselves into groups of race. We did this to gain a modicum of comfort and familiarity in an uncomfortable and unfamiliar environment. Having never spent much time in close quarters with such a diverse group of people, we naturally gravitated toward others with whom we felt comfortable. Fortunately for all of us, this self-segregation by race did not last long. Our drill instructors saw to that in their own inimitable way.

On our first day of training, the entire platoon was required to stand at attention as three drill instructors demonstrated the Marine Corps' policy on race. One drill instructor was Hispanic, one was African American, and one was Caucasian. This alone spoke volumes about the Marine Corps' attitude toward diversity. After explaining in stark terms the only color that mattered from that point forward was Marine Corps green, each of the three drill instructors took out a combat knife known as a K-Bar and pricked a finger with it; not much, just enough to draw a little blood. Then the drill instructors made a great show of letting us see their blood. Of course, the blood of the Hispanic, Caucasian, and African American drill instructors was the same color.

These three drill instructors gave our diverse platoon of raw recruits a lesson that can be traced back to Christ's admonition in Matthew 22:39 about loving your neighbor as yourself. From the Marine Corps' perspective, we were all "neighbors" who, like good neighbors, had to be able to trust, respect, and count on each other. It was a memorable way to drive home the point that under the skin we are all the same. The drill instructors also let us know from that day forward we would be judged on the basis of character and performance, not race, culture, national origin, or any other feature over which we had no control. Said another way, we would be judged by what really mattered: the factors that would make us good Marines.

Our drill instructors emphasized this point from the first day of training and never stopped emphasizing it. As Marine recruits and individuals, we had no control over what race we were born into or what part of the country we came from. However, we did have control over our character and performance. Their point was in the Marine Corps we would be judged on the basis of character and performance—things we controlled—rather than race, culture, or national origin—things we did not control. This is a good principle to apply in the workplace.

Focus on What Really Matters

When a group of people must work together as a team to accomplish goals, what really matters quickly becomes apparent. When your job security and career advancement depend on getting the job done right, on time, and within budget, it becomes apparent what really matters about team members is not their race, gender, culture, or any other factor that has nothing to do with performance. Rather, what matters are such characteristics as talent, motivation, attitude, and work ethic. And the undeniable truth is these characteristics are not a function of race, culture, gender, or politics. To illustrate this point, I will return to my Parris Island example.

There was a great deal of competition between recruit platoons on Parris Island in such activities as push-ups, pull-ups, sit-ups, running, climbing ropes, shooting, pugil-stick fighting, marching, maneuvering through the confidence course, running the obstacle course, and classroom studies. People who join the Marine Corps tend to be competitive by nature, and boot camp has a way of bringing that trait out and magnifying it. Competition among recruits and between recruit platoons is purposely built into the training regimen in Marine Corps boot camp. It is used to enhance performance and to make the point that excellence is expected, and anything less is unacceptable.

For example, a platoon that won any kind of competition on a given day might be rewarded with a little downtime to relax for a few minutes before lights-out that night. This was a much-coveted reward in an environment where every second of every day was controlled by fire-breathing drill instructors who used it for some aspect of training. On the other hand, a losing platoon on a given day might have to relinquish some of its *sack time* to undergo what our drill instructors called, with tongue in cheek, "remedial instruction."

As a result, recruits quickly learned what mattered in the Marine Corps was not race, culture, or other diversity factors. Rather, what mattered was the talent, motivation, attitude, performance, commitment, and work ethic of the recruits. Those who helped the platoon perform better and win competitions were valued by their fellow recruits, regardless of diversity factors. Those whose ineptitude undermined performance were resented, again regardless of the diversity factors.

Because of this, we were not in boot camp long before old prejudices and stereotypes were replaced by a new outlook that focused on what really mattered. The recruits we wanted in our squads were those who could get the job done so we could earn the rewards and recognition that went with outstanding performance rather than suffering the consequences of mediocrity. Even the unbelievers among us learned to obey the admonition in Ecclesiastes 9:10 that, no matter what kind of work we do, we are to do it with all our might.

Your workplace may not be as intense as Marine Corps boot camp, but it is similar in that rewards and recognition go to those who get the job done right, on time, and within budget. People who help their team perform well are the *winners* in the workplace, and winning has everything to do with motivation, talent, attitude, and work ethic. It has nothing to do with race, gender, culture, or politics. Organizations need individuals who can convey this message to their coworkers, by example and when given the opportunity by words. Consequently, focusing on what really matters rather than on things that don't must be part of the example you set for coworkers.

Relate to People as Individuals

One of the challenges you will face in trying to help coworkers overcome prejudice, stereotyping, and labeling is if you look hard enough it is easy to find members of all races, both sexes, and every culture who validate the preconceived notions of prejudiced people. There are bound to be some individuals in every group who will display the characteristics attributed by prejudiced people to the whole group. How people become prejudiced is by learning to attribute certain characteristics of individual members of a group to all members of that group. Ironically, the negative characteristics they learn to associate with a given group can be found in any other group, including the one they belong to.

Viewing people as members of groups is an illogical approach to human relations that will guarantee you are wrong most of the time. The more dependable, logical, and Scriptural way to deal with people is as individuals created by God, not as members of racial, gender, cultural, political, or even religious groups. The minute you attribute a given characteristic to an entire group of people, you are going to be wrong much of the time. God not only created every person who ever lived, He created them as individuals. This is the message of Psalms 139:13–14. God created us as individuals, not as members of groups defined by diversity-related traits. Consequently, it is incumbent on us to treat each other as individuals rather than as members of groups. The only group God singles out is the group comprising His children.

In the workplace, there will be people of different races, genders, cultures, religious beliefs, and political persuasions who are positive, talented, and motivated. Correspondingly, there will be people who are just the opposite. In both cases—good and bad—their work-related traits are the result of their individual character or lack thereof, not diversity factors. Consequently, treating people as individuals created by God rather than as members of groups defined by diversity factors must be part of the example you set for coworkers.

WORKING WITH MEMBERS OF THE LGBTQ COMMUNITY

The acronym *LGBTQ* stands for lesbian, gay, bisexual, transgendered, and queer. As LGBTQ advocates have become more assertive in pursuing what its members believe are their rights, they have begun to clash with defenders of religious freedom. American society is deeply divided in this battle. Predictably, the battle has spilled over into the workplace. The controversy over sexual identity has left many Christians confused concerning what their attitudes toward LGBTQ coworkers should be.

The battle between LGBTQ proponents and religious freedom advocates will be fought in churches, the courts, and the town square, as it should be. Further, as a Christian, you have a part to play in that battle. However, where the battle should not be fought is in the workplace. Consequently, this section is provided to help Christians, regardless their views concerning matters of sexual identity, learn to work well with LGBTQ teammates. If you struggle with working alongside LGBTQ teammates, remember Christ's words from John 3:17. In this verse, Christ made it clear he came not to condemn the world but to save it. You, in turn, will never influence people for Christ by condemning them. That said you do not have to accept or affirm the views of LGBTQ teammates to work with them.

Andrew and Steve are supervisors on opposite sides of the same dilemma. Their company has hired a new employee who is openly gay. Andrew and Steve are concerned about working with this new employee but for different reasons. Convinced society is headed over a cliff, morally speaking, Andrew has become deeply involved in politics. He has marched in protests against same-sex marriage and is a vocal opponent of the LGBTQ movement. Andrew has made it known to coworkers he is opposed to having the new employee assigned to his team. He has discussed this situation with members of his church, and most of them agree with him.

Steve, on the other hand, accepts and affirms the LGBTQ worldview. In his eyes, members of the LGBTQ community should be treated with dignity and respect. To Steve, their sexual identity is their business and theirs alone. His church conducts same-sex marriages and has a trans-gendered pastoral assistant. Members of his church often march in parades carrying banners proclaiming, "I am gay and Christian." Steve is not homosexual, but he has marched in parades to support LGBTQ friends. Steve wants the new employee assigned to his team, so he can make him feel welcome and accepted.

Steve and Andrew personify the divide that exists in society and in some cases even the church over the issue of sexual identity. It is beyond the scope of this book to debate the issue of sexual identity. The Bible is clear on the issue. Those who wish to debate the morality of the issue should begin with a careful examination of Scripture. This book was written to help Christians in the workplace excel without compromising their faith. Part of being employed in today's workplace is likely to involve working with LGBTQ team members. Everything set forth in this chapter concerning diversity in the workplace applies when working with LGBTQ teammates. In addition, this section provides specific strategies relating to LGBTQ coworkers to help Christians who struggle with this ssue.

Working with LGBTQ Teammates without Compromising Your Faith

In today's workplace, there will probably be members of the LGBTQ community in your work team or department. In fact, at some point you will probably work closely with people whose views on sexual identity differ significantly from yours. If doing so makes you uncomfortable, remember the second Greatest Commandment and be guided by it. You are called to work in a positive manner with diverse teammates, not by the dictates of political correctness, but by the Word of God. Admittedly, loving your neighbors as yourself can be a difficult Scriptural imperative to obey. But then Christ never said following Him would be easy. What follows in the remainder of this section are specific strategies that will help you interact positively with LGBTQ coworkers without compromising your faith or validating their worldviews.

Base Your Attitude toward LGBTQ Coworkers on Scripture, Not Politics

With battles raging over religious freedom versus affirmation of the LGBTQ agenda, it is easy to get caught up in the controversy and begin viewing it strictly through the lens of politics. It is also easy to begin viewing LGBTQ advocates as the enemy. This is a mistake. Satan is the enemy. LGBTQ advocates are opportunities. Although I encourage Christians to engage in the political process as part of their civic responsibility, in the final analysis we fight Satan with Scripture first and the ballot box second. Politicians can pass laws, but they cannot change hearts. Consequently, they cannot defeat Satan. Ultimately, the battle fought by Christians in the workplace is the same one raging since the Garden of Eden: the battle between the evil of Satan and the righteousness of God.

As a Christian, I encourage you to participate in the political process. However, having said this let me be clear: It is a mistake to expect moral issues to be resolved by ballot. For example, even if everyone in the country votes to approve a ballot initiative, that initiative is still wrong if it violates the teachings of Scripture. Also, never forget all people who cast ballots are sinners, including you and me. This means the political process is corrupted from the outset. In fact, politics is sometimes referred to as the art and science of self-interest, and self-interest is the antithesis of the Christian worldview. Engage in the political process. Be an activist for what is good and right. But never make the mistake of relying solely on politics to uphold the morals of a nation.

Although Christians and LGBTQ advocates are often on opposite sides of the political fence, they can share the same pasture when it comes to working and making a living. When working with LGBTQ teammates, our job is to show them a consistent Christ-like example, not to reject them on the basis of sexual identity. Our interactions with them should be based on the kind of love described in 1 Corinthians 13, not politics. No matter how we vote on political issues, outside of the voting booth our best weapons in the culture war are the Bible and an example that reflects its teaching.

A cautionary note is in order here. Although, as Christians, we are called to treat LGBTQ coworkers with biblical love, we are not called to shrink from standing our ground should they demand we affirm their worldviews. Working in harmony with LGBTQ teammates and validating their views are two different things. The former is required of Christians in the workplace. The latter is not. How to handle pressure to give affirmation to LGBTQ coworkers is covered in Chapter 12 where I discuss how to handle persecution on the job.

Avoid Being Pulled into Discussions of Sexual Identity during Work

When at work, talk about work-related topics, not sexual identity. Just as it is inappropriate for employees to spend their time at work talking about politics, sports, television programs, or their personal problems, it is inappropriate to spend time debating the issue of sexual identity. Part of setting a Christ-like example is staying focused on what you are paid to do rather than cheating your employer by wasting time in discussions that do nothing to enhance competitiveness. At work, your relationship with LGBTQ team members should be based on getting the job done as efficiently and effectively as possible, not the issue of sexual identity.

Without warning, Ruth, a committed Christian, found herself working with several colleagues who were members of the LGBTQ community. These individuals had only recently revealed their sexual identities after having worked for years with Ruth and their other teammates. The revelations of these individuals caused quite a stir. Fortunately for everyone involved, including their employer, Ruth's approach to dealing with the situation had a much-needed calming effect. When shocked coworkers wanted to gossip about their LGBTQ teammates during breaks and side conversations, Ruth was quick to suggest they talk about their work, not sexual identity, at least not during the workday. Ruth's favorite line was, "Gossiping about teammates does not improve productivity."

When her LGBTQ colleagues interpreted Ruth's tolerance as affirmation, she was quick to respond: "I love you in the way Christ commanded, but I am not affirming your sexual identities or commenting on them one way or the other. I am simply encouraging you and everyone else to stick to talking about work-related matters during the workday. We are not paid to discuss religion, sports, politics, worldviews, or even grandchildren. Whether we agree or disagree on matters of sexual identity is not a work-related issue and should not be allowed to affect our work. I will be happy to discuss my views on sexual identity with you after work." Within a short period of time, Ruth's approach became the accepted approach among all her coworkers.

Make Decisions Based on Merit, Not Sexual Identity

When you are in a position to make decisions affecting personnel, including LGBTQ teammates, make them on the basis of merit. Do not allow your views on sexual identity—regardless what they are—to bias your decisions or cloud your judgment. When choosing team members, completing performance appraisals, awarding incentive bonuses, giving recognition awards, and recommending people for promotions, base your decisions on merit. Do not allow your beliefs concerning sexual identity or any other factors unrelated to performance to influence your decisions.

Pam was the leader in her church of a group who regularly conducted protests against such issues as transgender restrooms and same-sex marriage. Consequently, several of her coworkers were surprised when she gave a transgendered subordinate an excellent performance rating and nominated that subordinate for a recognition award. The transgendered employee was also surprised. When questioned about the performance appraisal and nomination, Pam made it clear her actions were based on the quality of her subordinate's work. Sexual identity was not a factor. Pam said, "I am opposed to the LGBTQ agenda and everyone here knows it. However, my opposition to the LGBTQ worldview has nothing to do with my attitude toward the work of my subordinates. If they do quality work for me, they will be rewarded and recognized regardless their views on sexual identity. The obverse is also true."

Be Compassionate to Coworkers Who Appear to Be Different

Part of showing your coworkers a Christ-like example is being compassionate toward them. Compassion is a combination of kindness, caring, empathy, and consideration. It is just as important to treat an LGBTQ team member with compassion as it is any other coworker. You do not have to affirm the sexual identity of people to be compassionate toward them. This distinction between compassion and affirmation is important. When Christ showed compassion to prostitutes and thieves, he did not affirm their behavior. You are not approving, affirming, or accepting a person's sexual identity when you show compassion to that individual.

Think about Christians who work in prison ministries. They work with individuals who have been convicted of serious crimes, some of them violent. In spite of this, they are taught to show the inmates compassion. But they are also taught to avoid showing even the appearance of approval. It is the same when dealing with LGBTQ coworkers. Work relationships should not be based on or defined by sexual identity. People who have nothing in common except the jobs they do together can still build effective work relationships.

Do Not Participate in Gossip or Negativity Directed at LGBTQ Coworkers

Alma felt odd defending her coworker, Heather. After all, until six months ago, Heather was Harry. Then, one day, Harry showed up at work dressed as Heather. At some point in his life, Harry decided he identified as a woman and was no longer going to, in his words, "pretend to be a man." When Harry showed up at work as Heather, it caused quite a stir. Gossip, snickering, and snide remarks about Heather abounded. Heather, who had been a popular coworker as Harry, found "herself" treated like a curiosity by some and a leper by others. Heather's former golfing buddies from work no longer invited "her" to play. Worse yet, they began excluding Heather from their traditional TGIF luncheon outings. Some even complained to the department manager they were not comfortable working with Heather.

Alma, a committed Christian, was as upset by Harry's sudden change of identity as were her coworkers. However, she was even more upset about how they were treating Heather. Alma did not approve of Harry's decision to choose a sexual identity different from the one God gave him. At the same time, she did not think treating Heather like a leper was an appropriate response and knew it was not a biblical response. Alma made a point of continuing to work with Heather as she had when Heather was Harry. She treated Heather with respect and focused on the work they did together, not the new sexual identity. As a result, Heather approached Alma one day and asked if they could talk about a personal issue. Alma agreed but insisted they talk after work.

They met at a local coffee shop and Heather got right to the point. "Alma, since I revealed my sexual identity my former friends at work have shunned me. Everybody but you, that is. You still treat me like you always have. I want to thank you for making this situation less difficult for me. You have been kind, compassionate, and empathetic. I want you to know I appreciate it." Then Heather asked Alma if her positive attitude meant she approved of his new sexual identity.

Alma explained she did not agree with choosing a sexual identity different from the one God provided in the womb. She went on to say her understanding was the Bible proscribed making such choices. On the other hand, she refused to countenance the kind of treatment Heather was receiving from coworkers. Alma told Heather her religion required she love her neighbor as herself, and that admonition applied even if she did not agree with her neighbor's sexual identity. At this, Heather thanked Alma for her forthrightness.

Heather stated her belief people should be able to work together effectively in spite of disagreeing over nonwork-related issues. Alma agreed. On issues relating to sexual identity, the two long-time coworkers agreed to disagree but without being disagreeable. On work-related issues, they continued to be the effective team they had always been. Alma's is an excellent example of how Christians in the workplace can approach working with LGBTQ teammates.

DISCUSSION CASE 9.1: "I AM POLITICALLY CORRECT, BUT MY COWORKERS STILL DON'T RESPECT ME."

Frank went out of his way to be politically correct when interacting with coworkers. He used only the latest socially acceptable terms in conversations and always ensured ad hoc committees he convened were balanced by race, sex, and culture. He even hung posters throughout his department that read, "Diversity is our strength." In spite of all this, Frank was not well respected by his coworkers and subordinates, particularly those who were of a different race, sex, or culture than his. To be blunt, Frank had an air of artificiality about him that was off-putting to people. His political correctness always seemed to be forced, condescending, and insincere.

Amaya, on the other hand, was well respected by her coworkers even though she did not go out of her way to be politically correct. Rather, she made a point of setting an example of Christian love in her interactions with coworkers. Frank and Amaya were both professing Christians. Frustrated, Frank approached Amaya for help. He told her, "I go out of my way to be politically correct, but my coworkers still don't respect me. I don't know what I am doing wrong."

Discussion Questions

1. Have you ever worked with people who seemed to try too hard to be politically correct? If so, how were their efforts received?

2. Put yourself in Amaya's place. What would you tell Frank? Is there a better way for him to go about interacting with coworkers?

DISCUSSION CASE 9.2: "YOU ARE NOT A BAD PERSON, BUT YOU HAVE LEARNED SOME BAD ATTITUDES."

This morning was the first time Mort ever counseled a friend on his attitude toward diversity in the workplace. When his colleague, Andreas, asked him to go to breakfast for an important talk before work, Mort had no idea what the subject would be. During breakfast, Andreas poured out his heart. "In the last two weeks, my boss has corrected me three times for things I have said. In fact, just yesterday he called me aside and chewed me out for a comment I made during a meeting. He told me my attitude toward race was making several of my teammates uncomfortable. It seems like nobody can take a joke anymore."

Mort and Andreas attended the same church and had known each other for years. Consequently, Mort felt comfortable talking openly with his friend. "Andreas, you are not comfortable around people of a different race and it shows. I have known this for as long as I have known you. You make jokes about it, but it is obvious you are just trying to cover up your discomfort. People can sense your attitude toward them. You are not a bad person, but you have learned some bad attitudes. If you are willing to unlearn your prejudice toward people of other races, I will be happy to help you."

Discussion Questions

1. Have you ever worked with a fellow believer who was uncomfortable in a diverse environment? If so, how did your coworkers react to this individual?
2. Put yourself in Mort's place. What would you tell Andreas about interacting with coworkers out of sincere Christian love?

DISCUSSION CASE 9.3: "HOW CAN I BE TOLERANT WITHOUT AFFIRMING . . .?"

Rashaad wanted to be tolerant of his coworker's sexual identity. After all, as an African American, he was subjected to his share of intolerant behavior. But working closely with a transgendered individual was not something he ever anticipated doing. To make matters worse, his new teammate had an in-your-face attitude about sexual identity. While discussing the matter with his pastor, Rashaad asked, "How can I be tolerant without affirming my coworker's sexual identity?"

Discussion Questions

1. Have you ever worked with a member of the LGBTQ community? If so, did your coworker's sexual identity cause any problems at work?
2. If you were Rashaad's pastor, how would you answer his question about tolerating without affirming?

DISCUSSION CASE 9.4: "I WANT TO WORK WELL WITH MY LGBTQ TEAMMATES, BUT . . ."

Felicia understands she should work well with her LGBTQ colleagues. Two of her coworkers recently made it known they are lesbians, an announcement that did not surprise Felicia or any of her teammates. She had worked with both of them for more than a year and harbored suspicions about their relationship. Her suspicions had not affected Felicia's attitude toward her coworkers or her ability to work with them. But now that they made the nature of their relationship public, she felt a little uneasy. It seemed her coworkers not only wanted everyone to know about their sexual identity, they wanted their teammates to affirm it. In a conversation with a fellow Christian, Felicia said, "I want to work well with my LGBTQ teammates, but don't want them to think I affirm their worldview. My problem is how to go about this. I don't know how to do the former without appearing to do the latter."

Discussion Questions

1. Have you ever worked with colleagues who later revealed themselves to be members of the LGBTQ community? If so, how was their revelation received by their coworkers?
2. If you were the friend Felicia approached with her dilemma, what strategies would you recommend she apply to embrace without affirming?

REVIEW QUESTIONS FOR INDIVIDUALS AND GROUPS

1. How should the term "tolerance" be defined as it relates to diversity in the workplace?
2. Why is tolerance not enough when it comes to interacting with diverse coworkers?
3. What is meant by the concept of "ice cream love"?
4. How is Christian love different from ice cream love?
5. What is political correctness?
6. How is Christian love superior to political correctness as the basis for interacting with diverse colleagues?
7. How can Christian love keep you from stumbling over diversity issues in the workplace?
8. Is resistance to diversity inherited or learned? Explain.
9. How can an individual overcome his or her resistance to diversity?
10. How does the term "character" relate to the term "righteousness"?
11. What is the difference between tolerance and affirmation?
12. Why is it important to avoid the urge to reject people who do not share our Christian beliefs?
13. As Christians, should we base our attitudes toward LGBTQ coworkers on Scripture or politics? Explain.
14. What is the difference between being compassionate and affirming when it comes to LGBTQ coworkers?

15. Why is it important to avoid joining in gossip and other forms of negativity aimed at LGBTQ coworkers?

16. When you are in a position of authority, what is the proper way to make decisions about raises and promotions for LGBTQ personnel?

17. How should you respond if an LGBTQ coworker tries to engage you during the work day in conversation about the subject of sexual identity?

CHAPTER 10

LEARN TO COPE WITH FRUSTRATION AND DISCOURAGEMENT IN A BIBLICAL MANNER

"When the righteous cry for help, the Lord hears and delivers them out of all their troubles. The Lord is near to the brokenhearted and saves the crushed in spirit."

Psalm 34:17–18

D an's situation at work was taking a toll on him emotionally and physically. Lately, he dreaded even going to work. For Dan, going to work felt like waking up and going to the same funeral day after day. As a police officer, Dan saw the worst side of people. Rape, murder, robbery, and child abuse were common occurrences in his line of work.

But it wasn't the nature of the work that was getting Dan down. It was the rejection and criticism of his colleagues, more experienced officers who were jaded by their work.

Dan worked with a team of old-school police officers who not only questioned his faith but rejected, belittled, and criticized it. Dan's fellow officers spent years responding to crimes that revealed the worst in people. This kind of experience took a toll on their view of mankind. Consequently, they could be brutal in their attacks on Christianity. One of their favorite questions for Dan was, "How can you believe in God when you see the kinds of things we see every day?" They also liked to ask, "If there is a God, why does he allow little children to be abused?"

Just the day before, Dan and another officer responded to a domestic disturbance only to find the woman who called 911 lying on the floor dead. Before taking his own life, her husband beat her to death. Surveying the tragic scene, Dan's partner asked, "Where was your God when this happened?" Dan didn't have an answer, a fact that was taking a toll on his emotional and physical well-being.

The challenges associated with working with unbelievers day in and day out without compromising your faith can become so overwhelming you can develop feelings of acute frustration and discouragement. You might even think you have fallen into depression. Because I have counseled Christians who think they are suffering from depression, an important clarification must be made at the outset of this chapter. When people begin to despair over faith-related challenges at work, they sometimes say they are "depressed." The term "depressed" is often used in day-to-day conversation to describe feelings of frustration and discouragement. But it is important to understand *depression* in the clinical sense is more than just a response to feeling overwhelmed by the frustrations of working "in the midst of wolves."

Depression, in the clinical sense, is a feeling of deep, debilitating, and unrelenting sadness, a sadness so unshakable it renders one incapable of functioning normally. Clinical depression has a very specific medical definition that encompasses frustration, discouragement, and sadness but is much more. Clinical depression is not usually what people are referring to when they claim to "feel depressed," nor is it what this chapter is designed to help you cope with.

FEELING "DEPRESSED" VERSUS SUFFERING FROM CLINICAL DEPRESSION

Over the years, I have counseled Christians who claimed to "feel depressed" because they were worn out from confronting the daily challenges of working with unbelievers. Only a few of these Christians were suffering from clinical depression. The majority were just responding to feeling tired, over-stressed, beaten down, and fed up. Because people who fit into this category make up the overwhelming majority of Christians who have sought my help, they are the audience for whom this chapter is provided. Although Christian counseling should, and I believe must, be a major part of the treatment for people suffering from clinical depression, this chapter is aimed at people who feel discouraged but do not meet the criteria for clinical depression.

This, of course, raises an important question: How can you tell if you are just frustrated and discouraged or are suffering from clinical depression? The answer can be found in the symptoms of the latter. People suffering from clinical depression typically experience at least half of the following symptoms for longer than a two-week period, all or most of the day, every day:

- Unrelenting sadness and feelings of emptiness
- Significantly reduced interest in everything, coupled with an inability to take pleasure in any type of activity
- Noticeable changes in eating patterns (significant weight loss, weight gain, or a noticeable increase or decrease in appetite)
- Noticeable changes in sleep patterns (insomnia or a desire to sleep all the time)
- Noticeable changes in behavior others observe
- Extreme fatigue
- Feelings of worthlessness and guilt

- Inability to concentrate
- Inability to make decisions
- Thoughts of suicide

If you persistently experience half or more of these symptoms most of the day every day for at least two weeks, medical treatment is advisable. Medical specialists are trained to diagnose and treat clinical depression. People suffering from clinical depression may need to be treated medically to get their emotions under control before they can benefit from Christian counseling. With this caveat understood, it is important to realize you can feel unusually frustrated and discouraged without meeting the criteria for clinical depression. When this happens, medical help may not be called for, but biblical help is. This chapter focuses on helping you learn how to cope with the feelings of despair sometimes experienced by Christians who struggle to stand firm in the faith when working "in the midst of wolves."

FRUSTRATION AND DISCOURAGEMENT: AN EXAMPLE FROM THE BIBLE

There is nothing new about God's children becoming discouraged from having to constantly swim upstream against the current of social opposition and rejection. For example, in 1 Kings, we read about Elijah, one of the most prominent biblical prophets, losing sight of God's promises and falling into a state of deep frustration. His story begins with King Solomon. Recall in his later life King Solomon became unfaithful. His unfaithfulness led to a scourge of apostasy among the people. Later, the harsh policies of his son, Rehoboam, led to a revolt among the people of the northern tribes, which resulted in the division of Israel. It was at this point the southern tribes became known as "Judah," whereas the northern tribes retained the name of "Israel."

After the division of the Kingdom, God sent prophets out among the people to warn them against worshipping other gods. All were killed, except one: Elijah. Elijah obeyed the Lord and persevered against powerful, persistent opposition to turn the people away from false Gods. In doing so, he endured drought and famine; he had to confront Ahab, the wickedest King to ever rule Israel; and he had to stand alone against 450 prophets of Baal. But with the help of God, Elijah persevered. He even slew Baal's false prophets. But when the enraged Jezebel sent word to Elijah he would be killed within twenty-four hours (I Kings 19:2), he was forced to flee for his life, a trek lasting more than three years.

Finally, the frustrations of trying to do God's will against such hate-filled opposition took a toll on Elijah and wore him down. Elijah became so discouraged he sat down under a tree and prayed to die. He cried out to the Lord to take his life (1 Kings 19:4). As sometimes happens to Christians in the workplace, Elijah became overwhelmed by the challenges of remaining faithful in the face of unrelenting opposition, and he forgot the promises God made. He also forgot God is sovereign, and He and those who are faithful to Him will ultimately prevail.

Forgetting God has a plan and He is sovereign led Elijah to commit the sin of self-reliance. Elijah tried to carry his burden alone. He forgot that alone he was powerless against the forces of evil, but with God by his side, he could not be defeated. Christians in the workplace often make this same mistake. Forgetting God is sovereign and He has a plan for us can lead to frustration. Discouragement can set in when Christians lose sight of God's promises and begin asking self-absorbed questions such as: Why is this happening to me? Why does everything have to be so hard? Why can't things go my way once in a while? What can't anyone see I am right?

If discouragement can overwhelm one of God's most effective prophets, it can certainly overwhelm you and me. All that is necessary for a Christian to fall into a destructive state of mind is to forget God is sovereign and He has a plan. Thankfully, there is a way to overcome such a state of mind. It requires putting your trust in a sovereign God and knowing that He is working His plan for you out day by day. This approach also involves acknowledging when things do not seem to be going your way, God is still in charge, He knows what He is doing and why, and He expects you and me to simply trust, obey, and press on. We are just like Elijah in that discouragement can beset us when we become so wrapped up in ourselves we ignore the fact God is sovereign, He loves us, He has a plan for us, and His plan will prevail.

FRUSTRATION AND DISCOURAGEMENT: AN EXAMPLE FROM THE WORKPLACE

A friend I will call Pablo was struggling with faith-related adversity in his job. He had a boss who constantly pressured him to "join in the fun and stop being such a self-righteous snob." Because Pablo was reluctant to join his coworkers and boss for happy hour and other after-work activities, he was openly criticized for not being a team player. The problem was, what his boss considered fun violated Pablo's Christian beliefs. Further, it also detracted from the time Pablo reserved for his family and church activities. When Pablo approached me for advice, his boss had begun to comment that he did not think Pablo fit in, maybe he needed to look for another job elsewhere. This and other not-so-subtle hints that Pablo's job might be on the line began to eat at him emotionally.

The constant snide remarks and subtle threats at work eventually sent Pablo into an emotional tailspin. He liked his job and was good at it. Pablo's job was in financial management, a rewarding field. But the rewards in this field come only after one has built up a client list, something that can take a long time. If Pablo lost his job and had to start over, it would take a long time to build up a new client list. In the meantime, there would be no way he could pay his bills. At this point in his life, Pablo was paying a home mortgage, notes on two cars, college tuition for his twin daughters, medical bills for his ailing wife, plus the normal expenses associated with running a household. The idea of losing his job and having to start over filled him with dread. Eventually, the unrelieved anxiety began to wear him down.

Pablo told me he came to dread nighttime. He would lie awake with panicked thoughts flooding his mind and painful ulcers churning his stomach. Unable to sleep, Pablo openly wept as he pleaded with God for help. This went on for weeks and, according to Pablo, God did not hear his prayers. His emotional thrashing became so pronounced he was forced to sleep on the couch to avoid upsetting his ailing wife. Because of her illness, Pablo did not want to add the burden of his problems at work to her problems. Before long, Pablo became so emotionally distraught he had trouble focusing on his work. He began to view each new workday as an ordeal. He could still do his job, but he had no peace of mind.

When we talked, Pablo was asking himself such questions as "Why is this happening to me?" and "Why is life so unfair?" Pablo told me he came to dread every new day. He was holding onto his faith and functioning at work, but doing so was becoming more and more difficult. The prayer and Bible verses we shared seemed to help, but only temporarily. As soon as he was back in the toxic environment of his job, feelings of anxiety, frustration, and discouragement reemerged. Pablo was convinced God was not listening to his prayers and did not care about his troubles. I asked Pablo to commit Psalm 43:5 to memory and repeat it over and over to himself when caught up in the grip of anxiety and frustration. The message of Psalm 43:5 is we are to hope in God when we feel discouraged.

After a couple weeks of no observable progress with Pablo, I was beginning to fret myself. Pablo's response to his situation was just making matters worse. It appeared to me he was on the verge of losing his faith, and my counsel did not seem to be helping much. Then, out of the blue one day, he called me. I will never forget this telephone call. The Pablo on the telephone was a different man from the one I had been talking with for several weeks. He was offered a new job working for a man who shared his faith. He told me a local branch of a large national bank was diversifying its services into investments. The bank's local CEO asked Pablo to come on board as vice president for wealth management. The new job would mean an immediate salary increase with the possibility of regular performance bonuses. It also meant on his first day at work Pablo would have an established client list.

Before hanging up Pablo told me from the outset he adopted a faulty perspective on the problems he experienced with his former boss. He forgot God has a plan for those who love Him, even if we do not yet understand the plan. Pablo said, "All of the problems in my former job were God's way of preparing me to leave that job and accept a new one. I should have had faith in God rather than allow myself to become discouraged. I forgot who is in charge and wanted to blame God for my troubles instead of asking for guidance concerning the plan he had for me." Pablo's telephone call was a seminar on how Christians should respond when they become frustrated and discouraged over problems on the job.

Biblical Responses for Overcoming Frustration and Discouragement

Pablo learned a valuable lesson from his experience, and so did I. When Christians begin to feel discouraged over faith-related trials and tribulations, their feelings may be rooted in an unbiblical perspective on their problems. Pablo became discouraged because life was not working out according to his plan. When, as Christians, we feel overwhelmed by faith-related problems in the workplace, rather than become discouraged because things are not going according to our plans, we should pray for guidance concerning God's plan. Rather than ask God "Why is this happening to me?" we should ask "What is your plan for me and how are these troubles part of that plan?"

The Bible is replete with examples of people who became frustrated and discouraged because things were not working out the way they planned. In Jeremiah 20:7–9, we read the words of the "weeping prophet." Jeremiah became so discouraged over his inability to get God's message across he wanted to give up and quit. In 1 Kings 19:4, Elijah was so discouraged he wanted to die. In Numbers 11:14–15, we read Moses became so discouraged over the burden God placed on him he asked God to kill him. In Job 3:11, Job was so discouraged over the torment being inflicted on him he regretted the day he was born.

Clearly, there is nothing new about God's children feeling discouraged when things are not going their way. We are, after all, human, which means we are sinners. But what should separate us from others who become discouraged over problems is the perspective we adopt in coping with these problems. What we have others don't is the grace of God. To deal with discouragement, focus on God's plan for your life, not your plan. Instead of giving way to frustration, anxiety, or sorrow over what is happening to you at the moment, ask yourself what God is doing in your life and why. Better yet, ask Him.

Although it is difficult to accept God has a plan when you are mired in a swamp of adversity, be assured there is a reason for the problems He has sent or allowed to come your way. The key to warding off frustration and discouragement is to understand this fact. Once you accept that the adversity behind your discouragement is part of God's plan for you, the next step becomes easier. This step involves praying for discernment concerning what God is trying to teach you, what He is preparing you for, and what awaits you in the future. This is the perspective Paul recommends in Romans 8:18, where he writes the sufferings he is undergoing at the moment are not even worth comparing with the glory awaiting him and other believers. No matter how difficult or discouraging things may seem to you right now, your future will be glorious beyond imagining if you remain faithful to God.

If you are discouraged because of problems at work, you might find it helpful to study some of the biblical characters who endured their own bouts of frustration and discouragement. There are a number of people in the Bible who became so discouraged they wanted to give up. A few wanted to die. Go to Psalm 73 and read the words of Asaph. He was deeply discouraged by how things were going in his life. But God brought him through. After Asaph, read about how David despaired as Absalom pursued him unrelentingly (2 Samuel 15:23). As He did with Asaph, God raised David out of the depths of despair because He had a plan for him. Consider how Paul despaired in 2 Corinthians 1:8, yet he did not give up. Had he given in to the frustration and discouragement, some the most edifying chapters in the New Testament would not have been written.

You may feel isolated and alone in your despair, but you are not. As He did in all the examples just cited, God will lift you. Cling to Him in your suffering and wait patiently for him to reveal His plan. In every case God's plan for your life, even when you do not yet understand it, is better than your plan. Admittedly, this advice is easier to give than take. I understand. But this is often the case with good advice. It worked for Asaph, it worked for David, and it worked for Paul. It will work for you too.

DISCUSSION CASE 10.1: "I DON'T KNOW HOW MUCH MORE OF THIS I CAN TAKE."

Rosita Gonzalez loves Sundays. Her life revolves around church and her church family. But lately, some of the joy she experienced from her weekly day of worship and fellowship was tinged with sadness because the next day was Monday. Mondays became the cause of much anxiety and stress in Rosita's life. Lately, she dreaded getting out of bed on Monday morning and going to work. Rosita is a devout Christian who works in an office full of unbelievers. In fact, several of her fellow real estate agents are not just unbelievers, they are downright hostile to her convictions.

For more than three years, Rosita bore the snide comments, subtle putdowns, and outright insults of several coworkers, and she did so with admirable forbearance. But lately one of her coworkers has started being openly belligerent toward her, referring to Rosita as "intolerant" and "narrow-minded." As a result, the environment at work was toxic, at least for Rosita. Rosita functions well in her job. In fact, she is a top sales agent. But lately, she was feeling so frustrated and discouraged going to work was a chore. When she approached her pastor for counsel, Rosita said, "I don't know how much more of this I can take."

Discussion Questions

1. Has the challenge of working among unbelievers ever become so overwhelming you became discouraged? If so, how did you pull yourself out of that emotional state?
2. If Rosita came to you seeking the wise counsel of a fellow believer, what advice would you give her?

DISCUSSION CASE 10.2: "I THINK I AM SUFFERING FROM DEPRESSION."

Alexander Skorinsky came to Christianity late in life, but once he gave his life to Christ, he did not veer from the course. The problem was, although he was reborn into a new life, he still worked with friends from his old life, and they liked the old Alexander better. In fact, his old friends were intent on getting the old Alexander back. The pressure on Alexander to revert to his old ways was intense. Relations with his old friends soured to the point he hated going to work. Some days he felt so frustrated with his situation he wanted to do nothing but sit in a dark room by himself and keep the world at bay. He was still productive at work but was becoming short-tempered with people, including family members. Eventually, Alexander began to worry he was suffering from clinical depression.

Discussion Questions

1. If Alexander approached you seeking the wise counsel of a fellow believer, what would you tell him concerning how to determine if he was suffering from clinical depression?
2. What advice would you give Alexander concerning how he might cope with his feelings of frustration?

REVIEW QUESTIONS FOR INDIVIDUALS AND GROUPS

1. Distinguish between being discouraged and suffering from depression.
2. What evidence would suggest an individual is suffering from clinical depression?
3. In this chapter, the story of Pablo suggests an effective approach for coping with feelings of discouragement and despair. Summarize that approach.
4. Briefly summarize the stories of several biblical characters who felt discouraged over their circumstances in life. Include how their stories turned out. Discuss the lessons we can learn from these examples.

CHAPTER 11

PERSEVERE IN THE FAITH WHEN FACING ADVERSITY

*"More than that, we rejoice in our sufferings,
knowing that suffering produces endurance,
and endurance produces character, and character
produces hope . . ."*

Romans 5:3–4

Janet didn't know how much more she could take. Things were going badly at work and worse at home. Her new supervisor was a workaholic tyrant who was happy working twelve-hour days, seven days a week. He expected the same kind of "dedication" from his employees. Not surprisingly, he no longer had a family, nor did he care about employees who did. He was fond of saying, "You'd better decide if you want to have a career or a family." What really bothered Janet was her supervisor's response when she raised the issue of work interfering with her family life. He said, "I made my choice between career and family and you need to make yours."

Because of her supervisor's attitude, Janet often worked late. But the later she worked, the worse things became at home. As a single mother, Janet needed her job. It was her only means of support. But working twelve-hour days and weekends was taking her away from her sons at a time when they really needed the guidance of a parent. It seemed to Janet the more she worked, the more trouble her boys got into. Her oldest son was suspended from school for fighting. To her horror, the principal referred to her son as a "bully." Janet was at the end of her rope.

Most working Christians have endured times when job-related adversity seemed overwhelming. I know I have, and you probably have too. There may have been times when just getting through the workday seemed a burden. Standing firm in the faith while navigating the stormy seas of the workplace can be a daunting challenge at times. Consequently, knowing how to persevere when in the grips of adversity is critical for Christians who work with people who reject their faith. As Christians, you and I need to know how to keep going when we feel like giving up. In other words, we need to know how to persevere in the face of adversity.

Unfortunately, there are Christian brothers and sisters who tire of the daily struggle, succumb to the weariness, and give up. They respond to temptation, pressure, rejection, or persecution by hiding their faith. Before long, they find themselves going along to get along. I have counseled several Christians who became so overwhelmed by the faith-related challenges of working "in the midst of wolves" they eventually went beyond just hiding their faith to renouncing it. Some were guilty of backsliding, whereas others may not have been born again in the first place. Sadly, I know of Christians who renounced their faith in these circumstances and eventually ruined their careers and lives as a result. One individual in particular stands out in my mind because he was a friend.

Without his faith to guide and strengthen him, this individual succumbed to the sins of ego and greed. Shortly after renouncing his faith, he began to make unethical choices in his work, choices that brought him adulation, money, and status in the short run. However, his bad choices eventually caught up with him. When this happened, his career and his life came crashing down around him. By the time the dust settled, this once-committed Christian lost his job, his marriage, and his health.

TEMPTATION IS A FREQUENT SOURCE OF ADVERSITY

The workplace presents you with temptations every day, temptations that will challenge your faith. In fact, temptation often causes adversity for Christians. To make matters worse, while fighting against temptation, we must also deal with the other sources of adversity ever-present in the workplace. Terminations, layoffs, lost promotions, missed raises, difficult relationships, stress, pressure to perform, competition, plant closings, buyouts, mergers, downsizing, strikes, and economic uncertainty are just a few of the factors that can cause adversity in the workplace. Increasingly, Christians can add persecution to this list.

Standing up to temptation as well as other sources of adversity is essential if you are going to maintain your faith while working among people who reject it. As in all things, Christ is our role model for meeting this challenge. Matthew 4:1–11 tells the well-known story of Christ being tempted by Satan. Having fasted for forty days and forty nights, Christ was ravenously hungry. Seeing this as an opportunity, Satan approached Christ and told Him to prove He was the son of God by turning stones into bread (Matthew 4:3). Because he took on the form of man, Christ felt the pangs of hunger just as you and I would fasting that long. But rather than give in to Satan's temptation, Christ provided an unambiguous reason for refusing to do so. He told Satan man "shall not live by bread alone" (Matthew 4:4). Christ ignored His physical hunger and said "no" to temptation.

Unwilling to give up, the devil took Christ up to the holy city and then to a high mountain. In both settings, he tempted Christ again and both times Christ said "no." Having grown weary of Satan's schemes, Christ finally ordered the devil from His presence (Matthew 4:10). In dismissing Satan, Christ gave a biblical reason for standing up to temptation. This is important because there is always a biblical reason for remaining firm in the face of temptation. Remembering you are supported by the Bible when tempted to sin will help you maintain your resolve.

Christ provided a memorable example of rejecting temptation, an example working Christians should follow. Knowing Scripture is on our side will give us added incentive to persevere when temptation rears its ugly head. Temptation will never go away in the workplace or the world at large. This is the bad news. The good news is the Scriptural guidance needed for fending off temptation never goes away either. It is always there, always available. As Christians, we should lean on the Word of God for support rather than trying to resist temptation alone.

PUTTING TEMPTATION IN PROPER PERSPECTIVE

Temptation is Satan's way of appealing to our sinful nature. He is always lurking in the shadows trying to entice us to do things we should not do. This is why, when Satan tempted Him in the wilderness, Christ did more than just say "no." He also gave us a Scriptural foundation for following His example. In doing so, Christ illustrated two important points:

- God's way, as set forth in Scripture, is the right way.
- Although we are weak, God is strong. Hence, with the help of God—through His Word and prayer—we can stand up to temptation in any of its many forms.

Temptation in the workplace can lead to such sins as office romances among married people, fraud, abuse of power and position, unauthorized use of the employer's resources, lying, claiming credit for work someone else did, customer abuse, failing to give credit where it is due, stealing, selling faulty merchandise, and a host of other unethical behaviors. Consequently, as Christians, we must be prepared to stand up to temptation in all its manifestations and to use the Bible as the basis for saying "no."

Temptation is Not Sin, but Giving in to Temptation Is

Over the years, I have seen Christians become discouraged because they are tempted to do things they know are wrong. One Christian told me on business trips he will not go to his hotel room until he is ready to go to sleep because he is always tempted to watch pornography on television. Another told me his biggest challenge when traveling is to stay out of nightclubs and bars. Several have told me of being powerfully pulled in the direction of illicit office romances. All the Christians in these examples felt intense remorse about being tempted. In fact, so many Christians I know have expressed self-contempt over feeling the allure of temptation, that it is necessary to draw a distinction between temptation and giving in to temptation.

We are all tempted. Even the most devout Christians feel tempted to do things they know they should not do. This is why we were given the warning in Matthew 26:41 to watch and pray because we may be too weak to do what we know is right. Temptation is an urge to do something you know is wrong. It is a manifestation of our sinful nature but is not in and of itself sin. Temptation can certainly lead to sin if you do not learn to persevere in standing up to it, but temptation itself is not sin. When the businessman mentioned earlier was tempted by pornography on television, he was not sinning. In fact, his refusal to put himself in a situation where he might give in to the temptation was a positive response on his part. Sin, in this case, would be for him to covertly closet himself in his hotel room, yield to temptation, and watch a pornographic movie.

It is when you stop fighting it, give in, and submit to its seductive power, temptation becomes sin. 1 Timothy 6:9 contains a prescient warning that giving in to temptation is a self-destructive choice. All Christians are tempted, and temptation can lead to death (James 1:14–15). Not everyone is tempted in the same way or by the same things, but we are all tempted. This is why in 1 Peter 5:8 the Apostle warned we should be alert because the devil is always prowling around hoping to seduce God's children. Consistent Christians are not immune to the tug of temptation. Rather, they are tempted every day but refuse to give in to temptation.

STANDING UP TO TEMPTATION

You will not have to look far to find Christians who have ruined their careers and lives by giving in to temptation. Luke 17:1 warns of this phenomenon. In this verse, Christ told His disciples they should expect to confront stumbling blocks. Of course, some of those stumbling blocks would be temptations placed in their paths. Unfortunately, Christians do give in to sin. It happens all the time, but it does not have to happen to you. You can stand up to temptation by following the example of Christ in the wilderness, in the holy city, and on the mountain when He turned away Satan's efforts to tempt Him. What follows are some strategies that will help you stand up to temptation.

Observe Others and Learn from Their Mistakes and Successes

Smart people learn from their mistakes, but wise people learn from the mistakes of others. They also learn from the successes of others. In standing up to temptation, be wise and learn from others. Paul advocated this strategy in 1 Corinthians 10:6. When you see someone in the workplace give in to temptation, ask yourself, "In the same situation, what could I have done to avoid his or her mistake?" Correspondingly, when you see someone successfully turn away from temptation make a mental note of how that individual did it. Then file your observations away for future use.

Use the Word of God as Your Armor Against Temptation

When you find yourself being pulled in the wrong direction by temptation, put on the brakes long enough to open your Bible. Find a quiet place and start reading. Focus on the many verses dealing with temptation. Ephesians 6:11 is a good place to start. It tells us the armor of God will protect us from the slings and arrows of the devil. By yourself you have no chance of defeating Satan. Satan is infinitely more powerful than mortal man. But with God on your side, Satan is rendered powerless.

A friend I once worked with kept a copy of Ephesians 6:11 printed on the back of a business card he kept in his pocket. Whenever he found himself being tempted in the workplace, my friend pulled the card out of his pocket and read the verse from Ephesians over and over until the urge to give in passed. He told me on more than one occasion using the business card pulled him back from the precipice many times.

Fortify Your Heart Against Temptation with Prayer

Few things will stop Satan in his tracks so quickly and effectively as the prayers of a believer. If you feel pulled in the wrong direction by temptation, fortify your heart with prayer and Satan will flee from you. This is the message found in James 4:7. If you don't know what to say in your prayers, pray the Lord's Prayer. Christ gave us this prayer to teach us how to pray. Part of this most revered of prayers says: ". . . and lead us not into temptation but deliver us from evil . . ." (Matthew 6:13).

Do Not Try to Fight Temptation Alone

As a Christian, you are never alone. Remember this fact when struggling with temptation and be encouraged by it. The Holy Spirit is in you, and He will strengthen you. Another strategy is to have an accountability partner, a fellow believer you can meet with or call on the telephone when temptation seems to be getting the better of you. A Christian businessman I met some years ago told me how having an accountability partner once helped him through a difficult struggle with temptation.

On the occasion in question, this businessman called his accountability partner and talked for more than an hour to avoid giving in to the temptation to meet an old girlfriend in the bar of the hotel where they were staying. They bumped into each other unexpectedly while on a business trip. She invited him to join her for drinks. Originally agreeing to meet her at a given time, he came to his senses but still felt a powerful urge to give in. Reasoning she would not wait for more than thirty minutes or so, he called a friend from church—his accountability partner—and talked for an hour. Having an accountability partner grows out of the Scriptural imperative for Christians to bear each other's burdens (Galatians 6:1–2). Christians who work among wolves are well-advised to have accountability partners. It is also good to be one for other Christians.

STANDING UP TO OTHER SOURCES OF ADVERSITY

Christians are not immune to adversity. We are just like anyone who works, at least in this regard. Giving your life to Christ changed it for the better but did not make you immune to trials, challenges, frustrations, and dilemmas. Rain falls on sinners and saints alike. This fact should be understood by Christians who work "in the midst of wolves." Persevering in the face of adversity is an important part of standing firm when facing challenges in the workplace.

God tells us we can persevere when facing adversity because He is with us, and He will bear us up (Isaiah 41:10). Those who lose faith whenever Satan puts roadblocks in their way will also lose the struggle to persevere against adversity. Adversity is an ever-present fact of life in the workplace where man's sinful nature can manifest itself in so many ways. The question we, as Christians, must face up to is not whether there will be adversity but how we will deal with the adversity we are certain to face.

Standing up to adversity is an integral part of the Christian walk as spoken of in Hebrews 12:3. In this verse, we are reminded to consider the hostility Christ endured whenever we feel beaten down and broken by adversity. Talk with Christians who have built successful careers without compromising their faith and you will find they had to endure through much adversity. You will also find they succeeded in spite of adversity because they refused to quit when they grew weary of the battle. They stood up to adversity and persevered. In fact, facing up to adversity can bring us closer to Christ if we respond to it by running to Him for support rather than running from Him in frustration.

Expect adversity to be part of what you will deal with in the workplace. Only the naïve are surprised when adversity rears its ugly head. Part of being "wise" as stated in Matthew 10:16 is not being naïve. Use Scripture and prayer to help you remain steadfast when the job gets difficult and relationships with coworkers become strained because of your faith. To stand firm in your faith when working with people who reject it, you must learn how to persevere in the face of adversity. The following strategies will help.

Remember God has a purpose for your suffering

God uses adversity to strengthen His saints, as is shown in Romans 5:3–5. These well-known verses explain how trials give us opportunities to learn perseverance. Perseverance, in turn, develops "character" and character provides "hope." These verses give Christians hope by reminding us we can stand up to the adversity we face in the workplace knowing it is part of God's plan to strengthen us for even bigger challenges in the future. God gives us challenges, trials, and tribulations, but He does not give us more than we can endure. Further, He knows better than we do how much we can endure.

Use Adversity to Bring You Closer to God

As Christians, we sometimes make the mistake of letting adversity drive a wedge between us and God. This is an unfortunate response because just the opposite is what is needed in times of adversity. Let the adversity you face in the workplace drive you closer to God. As humans we are frail, but with God we can gain the strength to persevere. We are told in Psalm 55:22 the Lord will support us and bear us up if we bring our problems to Him. Sunny-day Christians are not likely to survive when faced with constant adversity. The workplace is like life: rain is going to fall, sometimes unexpectedly. When rain comes, it falls on sinners and saints alike. However, unlike those who reject Him, you can seek shelter and comfort in the protective arms of Christ.

Marjorie had more adversity in her life than anyone I have ever known. At work, she had a supervisor—Jan—who was married to Marjorie's former husband. Jan was also Marjorie's former best friend. Marjorie's husband left her after he and Jan were caught in an adulterous affair. Jan never even held a job before she married Marjorie's husband. But after the divorce, she was installed as Marjorie's supervisor by the husband who was also CEO of the company. Work relations were understandably tense between Marjorie and her supervisor. At home things weren't much better.

Marjorie's former husband was a dead-beat dad. Although well off financially, he reluctantly paid the required child support for his three children only when forced by the court. Jan had her own children. As a result, she pressured her husband to ignore the children from his marriage to Marjorie. Every time the court made her husband pay past due child support, Jan responded by making Marjorie's work life even more difficult. Trapped in a low-level position and receiving only sporadic child support payments, Marjorie struggled to make ends meet. To make matters worse, her husband's company was the only employer in their one-horse town offering benefits such as health insurance. Consequently, Marjorie could not just resign and pursue a new job elsewhere.

Accustomed to being materially well off before their parents divorced, Marjorie's kids chafed at the perceived indignities of their new status on the lower rungs of the socioeconomic ladder. They particularly resented Marjorie transferring them from the Christian school they all attended since first grade to a local public school. Their life-long friends all attended the Christian school they left behind. Marjorie understood their feelings about school, but she could no longer afford tuition.

To make matters worse, their father vocally blamed Marjorie for the break-up of their marriage, and their kids apparently believed him. Added to this was Marjorie's need to remain in her hometown because she was also taking care of her elderly parents who, although ailing, insisted on living in their home. Marjorie had to shop, make meals, run errands, and do household chores for them. The more infirm her parents became, the more Marjorie had to do for them.

For many people, the adversity Marjorie faced would be overwhelming. But Marjorie was able to persevere because she chose to run to God for support rather than run from Him in frustration. The unrelenting adversity drove Marjorie closer to God. What sustained Marjorie was her unshakeable faith in God. Eventually, things began to get better for Marjorie. Not surprisingly, her husband's marriage to Jan ran aground when he was unfaithful to her too. Predictably, he treated Jan no better than he treated Marjorie.

After filing for divorce, Jan resigned her position with the company and moved to another town. When his unfaithfulness to two wives became an issue in their small community, her now former husband left the company too. With Jan and her former husband both gone, Marjorie's work life improved. She was promoted to supervisor to take Jan's place. This meant a substantial increase in pay for her. In addition, the court finally tired of her former husband's refusing to pay required child support. When the judge made it clear he could either pay what he owed and pay on time from that day forward or go to jail, Marjorie's financial status improved even more. Things, in turn, got better at home. Her kids returned to their Christian school, and Marjorie was able to hire a home healthcare company to help with her parents.

Remember You Are Not Alone in Your Adversity

2 Timothy 3:12 warns that all who live Godly lives will be persecuted. Persecution is just one more form of adversity you might face as a Christian in the workplace. When you suffer adversity at work, remember you are not the first Christian who has done so. Seek out fellow Christians who have suffered but persevered, learn from their experience, and grow from their wisdom. If you don't know any fellow Christians who have suffered in the workplace because of their faith, go to Scripture to find some role models there. Begin with Job.

In the previous example of Marjorie, one of the things that sustained her was the help of friends from church. Several fellow believers made sure Marjorie was always surrounded by love, and she got the help needed to persevere. Having each faced her own bouts of adversity, Marjorie's friends understood what she was going through. They made sure Marjorie knew she wasn't alone; God was right there with her and always would be. Marjorie, in turn, reached out to her friends eagerly. They listened when she needed to talk, gave her a shoulder when she needed to cry, helped with her children and parents, and prayed with her. Marjorie knew she was never alone and God was with her because He sent his children from church to help her. In fact, Marjorie thought of her friends from church as the angels God sent to sustain her.

Know There Will Be Times When Your Perseverance Will Not Be Rewarded in Human Terms

In a fallen world, life is seldom fair. Christians who honor God are always rewarded, but the reward may not come in human terms or in human time. When this happens, take comfort in knowing your reward will come, and when it comes nothing on earth will compare to it. This is the promise contained in the words of Matthew 5:11–12. The message in this verse is we are to be happy and thankful when our faith is challenged because our reward will come in heaven. This is not to say you will never be rewarded on earth. This can and does happen. But how you are rewarded and when it will happen are in God's hands.

Melissa learned this lesson the hard way when she was fired for refusing to go along with the demands of her company's CEO to file false reports with OSHA. OSHA is the federal government's agency for monitoring workplace safety. It has the power to fine and even shut down businesses in violation of its safety regulations, something Melissa's company was doing on a regular basis. Hoping to avoid major fines, negative publicity, and the possibility of being shut down, the CEO pressured Melissa to drastically underreport the company's accident and injury record. When Melissa refused, she was fired on the spot.

Too smart to admit he fired Melissa for refusing to file fraudulent reports, the CEO created a false scenario in which he claimed she was fired for stealing from the company's petty cash account. As a result, Melissa was unable to collect unemployment payments, and she became a leper in the job market. Nobody wanted to hire a thief. After explaining the situation to her pastor, Melissa got some help. He hired her as a part-time secretary in their church, which allowed her to eke out enough of a living to get by. An attorney in their church filed a wrongful termination suit on Melissa's behalf pro bono. The case dragged on for years with the CEO and his company using every legal trick in the book to wear Melissa down and make her give up. But Melissa did not give up.

After years of fighting her case in the court and getting nowhere, Melissa finally got a break, a tragic break. An employee at her former company was killed in a workplace accident. The fatal accident triggered an OSHA investigation. The deeper OSHA's inspectors looked into the case, the more disturbing the evidence became. Eventually their investigation led them to Melissa. She was able to testify she was pressured by the company's CEO to file false reports with OSHA. Further investigation revealed the company had a history of serious accidents not reported. The findings of the OSHA investigators became evidence in Melissa's lawsuit against her former employer, and she was eventually awarded a major financial settlement. In addition, the CEO who pressured her to file false reports and fired her for refusing to do so was brought up on criminal manslaughter charges for ordering personnel to ignore OSHA's safety regulations.

Melissa's perseverance was eventually rewarded, but it took years of enduring near-poverty living conditions, a seemingly endless court battle, and heartbreaking frustration. Throughout her ordeal, Melissa was comforted by the promise in Matthew 5:11–12. She knew she might never be rewarded on earth, that her reward might come only in heaven. But knowing this gave her the strength and courage to persevere. It took years, but she eventually received an earthly reward in addition to the greater reward she will receive in heaven.

Refuse to Give In to Adversity

When facing adversity, follow Melissa's lead from the previous example: don't quit and never give up. Use the Bible, prayer, and wise counsel of fellow Christians to give you the strength to hang on when you feel like giving up. God is bigger than the problems you face. He knows you are suffering, and He knows exactly how much you can endure. God is like the coach who knows how far he can push athletes without pushing them too far. Coaches also know athletes must be pushed to their physical, mental, and emotional limits if they are going to excel. This is why Paul gave us the assurance in Romans 8:28 that God will work things out for those who love Him. Run to God not away from Him during times of adversity. He knows what you are facing, and He knows your limits. As He did with Melissa, God will see you through the adversity you face.

Reach Out to Someone Else Who Is Suffering through Adversity

One of the best ways to relieve or at least mitigate your own suffering is to help someone else who is hurting. This is what is meant in Galatians 6:2, where we are told to bear one another's burdens. Invariably, when we reach out to others who are suffering, we gain a more positive, more thankful perspective on our own problems. No matter how badly we are hurting, there is always someone who is hurting worse. In times of adversity, help yourself by helping others.

Cherie's life revolved around helping others. Ironically, Cherie endured more suffering in her life than anyone I knew. She lost a baby in childbirth and nearly died herself. Before she recovered from that tragedy, Cherie lost her husband in an automobile accident. Then shortly after the funeral, she was notified her twin sister was diagnosed with an aggressive form of brain cancer. To me, Cherie's life seemed to be the personification of adversity. Yet she spent all her free time and much of her income helping others.

When I asked her about devoting so much of herself to helping others when she had to endure so much adversity herself, Cherie taught me a humbling lesson. She told me anytime she begins to feel sorry for herself, she visits the cancer ward of the hospital where her twin sister is being treated. No matter what she was enduring in her life, those visits always put things in perspective for her. She told me when she helped others who are hurting, she gets more help in return than she gives. When you are suffering, think about Cherie and how she copes. No matter how bad your circumstances may be, there are always others who are suffering, too. Help yourself by helping them.

Take the Long View

In times of adversity, it is easy to get so caught up in the pain of the moment we cannot see beyond the present. This is why it is important to learn to take the long view. When you think the current adversity will never end, remember what is said in James 1:2–4. These verses tell us to be joyful even when suffering through adversity because the trials we face will strengthen us. Cling to God in times of trouble, and you will eventually emerge from the darkness stronger and better.

I saw an example of taking the long view many years ago when I worked with a Christian man whose boss was a petty, mean-spirited bully. This ogre of a boss seemed to take pleasure in browbeating subordinates. The stress of working for a tyrant was so intense my friend would end each workday physically and emotionally spent. On several occasions, he approached me for counsel. My friend wanted to find another position and thumb his nose at his boss on the way out, but he was place-bound. He needed to live in our community to be near his aging parents who relied on him for care. Unfortunately, the career opportunities in our small town were limited.

Finally, after listening to my friend vent on several occasions, I gave him the following advice: "Hang tough and wait him out. People like him eventually self-destruct." This turned out to be good advice. Within a year my prediction came true. The company eventually accumulated so many formal grievances against this tyrant he was terminated. I still run into my friend from time to time, and when we meet his greeting is always the same. With a big smile, he says, "Wait him out!"

As you face temptation and adversity in your career, take comfort from the words of Lamentations 3:19–24. When suffering, we can have hope in the Lord because His mercy endures forever and His compassion for us is unlimited. No matter how difficult your problems may be, the Lord is bigger than the adversity you face, and his compassion will not fail you.

DISCUSSION CASE 11.1: "I NEED HELP—TEMPTATION IS GOING TO RUIN ME."

Mark felt immense relief, but at the same time, he felt enormous guilt, even shame. He was a Christian less than a year when his old sinful outlook seemed to be raising its ugly head. Mark began to weaken in saying "no" to the seductive tug of temptation. An office romance almost ended his marriage two years before. In fact, it was the intervention of a good friend who introduced him to a Christian counselor that saved Mark from divorce. Mark and his wife reconciled after six months of marriage counseling, and his family life was better than it had ever been.

But a new sales representative in his company was becoming a problem for him. Mark knew better, but he started making excuses to spend more and more time with her. She was receptive to his attention and before long asked him to join her for a "business lunch" at her apartment. Aware he was making a mistake, Mark let temptation overcome his judgment and accepted the invitation. Torn by guilt but ensnared by temptation, Mark reached for the doorbell. However, before ringing it he was overcome with shame and self-loathing. Instead of ringing the doorbell, Mark bounded down the steps and ran as fast as he could for several blocks. His heart pounding and chest heaving, Mark burst into the office of his Christian counselor and said: "I need help—temptation is going to ruin me."

Discussion Questions

1. Have you ever worked with people who let temptation get the better of them on the job? If so what happened?
2. If you were Mark's counselor, what would you tell him concerning how he might stand up to temptation?

DISCUSSION CASE 11.2: "WHAT ELSE COULD GO WRONG?"

Gary was beginning to feel like his biblical hero, but he didn't think he was up to following Job's example of perseverance. Gary experienced adversity in his life. In fact, Gary always thought of himself as a person who could handle adversity. Lately, he was beginning to wonder. Everybody had an opinion concerning what he should do, but as the company's CEO, he had to make the hard decisions. Gary was facing some tough decisions. Just that morning he found himself thinking, "A man can take only so much."

Gary's company was struggling. Global competition was taking a serious bite out of corporate profits. Frankly, things never looked so bleak. Gary knew he could hold things together for a while by ignoring quality standards and resorting to some of the unethical practices competing companies adopted in response to the crisis. However, Gary was an honest man and a devout Christian who took the long view. He did not want to stoop to practices that might help in the short run but be destructive in the long run.

First, Gary was forced to tell employees there would no longer be Christmas bonuses or performance incentives. When sales figures continued to dwindle, he cut back on the work hours of all wage-earning personnel. As sales continued to decline, Gary asked all personnel to take a week off without pay. He continued to work during the week when all the company's personnel were off, but he forfeited his pay. When even this drastic measure was not sufficient to stem the tide of red ink, Gary finally took the step he most dreaded: layoffs.

Laying off loyal employees, many of whom were with the company more than twenty years, broke Gary's heart. He knew every one of his employees well and thought of them as family. In fact, he was Godfather to several of their children. To see people who served him so well for so long out of work and with few options in their one-company town was almost more than Gary could bear. The husband of his wife's best friend was laid off as was the father of his son's best friend.

Then, just when Gary thought he reached the end of his emotional rope, he got word his father, the founder of their company, suffered a stroke. Apparently, the stress of watching his company decline and his long-time employees suffer was more than he could bear. As Gary sat at the desk he occupied for fifteen years and his father occupied for more than thirty years before him, Gary wondered: "What else can go wrong?"

Discussion Questions

1. Have you ever faced a situation in which it seemed the world was caving in on you? Have you ever felt overwhelmed by adversity? How did you face this crisis?
2. Assume Gary is your friend. What would you tell him about persevering in the face of overwhelming adversity?

REVIEW QUESTIONS FOR INDIVIDUALS AND GROUPS

1. Is feeling tempted a sin? Why or why not?
2. How would you define the concept of "temptation"?
3. Is everyone tempted? Explain your response.
4. How can Christians use the mistakes and success of others to help them stand up to temptation in the workplace?
5. How can Christians use the Word of God as their armor against temptation?
6. How can Christians use prayer to fortify their hearts against temptation?

7. Why should Christians avoid trying to fight temptation alone?

8. Does being a Christian exempt you from adversity? Explain your response.

9. Will your perseverance in the faith always bring the results you want on earth?

10. How can reaching out to someone else who is suffering through adversity help you stand up to the adversity you face?

CHAPTER 12

RESPOND TO PERSECUTION AND CYBER-BULLYING IN A CHRIST-LIKE MANNER

"If the world hates you, know that it has hated me before it hated you."

John 15:18

Myra knew she was alone in her Christianity. There were seven other people on her work team and not one of them accepted Christ as Lord and Savior. Although her coworkers were unbelievers, Myra didn't think they were hostile to her beliefs. Unfortunately, events one morning changed her perception. Upon arriving at work, Myra was summoned to the company's human resources (HR) office. The HR director informed Myra her fellow team members—all seven of them—submitted a petition demanding she remove all Christian plaques, symbols, and quotes from her cubicle. The HR director was apologetic but said Myra would have to comply. She told Myra, although there was no company policy against the material displayed in her cubicle, the company's CEO made it clear he did not want this kind of trouble. He wanted any and all Christian materials removed from Myra's cubicle that day.

Most faith-related dilemmas believers have to cope with in the workplace result from rejection of the Christian faith by coworkers and superiors. The actions causing those dilemmas can be frustrating and even demeaning, but they rarely amount to persecution. The first eleven chapters of this book are devoted to helping you learn to deal effectively with those kinds of dilemmas. However, more and more frequently, the Christians who come to me for counseling are describing situations in which opposition to the Christian faith crosses a line and becomes persecution. Persecution is the systematic mistreatment of individuals or groups because of a specific factor. In the current context, that factor is Christianity. I do not refer to this issue as *religious persecution* because the cases I deal with are not about religion per se. Rather, they are about Christianity specifically.

Here are just a few examples of persecution of Christians on the job occurring during the course of writing this book:

- A Christian T-shirt printer was sued for refusing to produce a shirt for a gay pride festival.
- A Christian baker was sued for refusing to inscribe a cake with a message that violated his beliefs.
- A Christian photographer was sued for refusing to photograph a same-sex marriage.
- A Christian teacher was reprimanded for saying "God bless you" to a fellow teacher.
- A Christian businessman was told to stop wearing neckties with Christian verses on them to work.
- A Christian professor was told to remove a bumper sticker from her car emblazoned with the Bible verse John 3:16.

- A Christian engineer was the victim of anti-Christian cyber-bullying, and his supervisor refused to take corrective action on his behalf.

These situations represent more than just rejection of or opposition to Christianity. These are clear-cut cases of persecution of individuals because of their Christian faith. Although being persecuted for your Christian beliefs is an abomination, it should come as no surprise when it happens. After all, persecution of Christians is not new. If you are being persecuted in the workplace for your Christianity, you are in good company. Never forget what Christ said about persecution of Christians in John 15:18–19. In these verses Christ made it clear His followers should expect to be persecuted. Those who hate Christ are bound to hate His followers.

Consider the suffering of Christ and His Apostles at the hands of those who rejected the Gospel. Christians throughout history have been subjugated, abused, and persecuted because of their faith. Many became martyrs. However, in the United States, we have historically suffered little in the way of Christian persecution. Because the original European settlers came to America seeking religious freedom and because our Founders built religious freedom into the Constitution, the level of Christian persecution in the United States has been minimal. But that is changing.

Since the 1960s, those opposed to Christianity have become more vocal in their opposition. Our Founders sought to guarantee freedom of religion in the First Amendment, but increasingly, opponents of Christianity have lobbied to transform that clause into freedom from religion. Unfortunately, politically pliable courts have cooperated in this endeavor. Secular humanists have made substantial inroads into American culture. In fact, it sometimes seems those who seek freedom from religion have gained the upper hand. They have accomplished this by infiltrating and gradually dominating the courts, educational institutions, the entertainment industry, the media, government, and even some churches.

Because the workplace tends to reflect contemporary societal trends, secular humanism has made inroads there too. Secular humanists are determined in their opposition to Christianity, a fact making the workplace an increasingly difficult and sometimes even hostile environment for Christians. The most publicized instances of persecution involve Christian owners of flower shops, photography studios, T-shirt shops, and bakeries. When these owners exercise their Constitutional right to refuse to participate in same-sex marriages and other activities sponsored by LGBTQ groups, they are quickly pounced on by the courts and government agencies.

These agencies, in conjunction with various anti-Christian groups, combine their resources to prosecute and persecute the owners. However, as bad as these attacks on Christian businesses are, they represent a small percentage of the instances of persecution Christians face on the job every day. Consequently, it is important for Christians to know how to respond to persecution in the workplace. This chapter provides specific strategies.

RESPONDING TO PERSECUTION AT WORK

The first eleven chapters of this book explained strategies for standing firm in the faith when confronted by coworkers who reject Christianity and by situations that might tempt you to reject your Christian faith. All those strategies apply when confronting persecution in the workplace, but there are two additional strategies that might come into play when you are being persecuted because of your faith. The first of these is a long-term strategy. The second is for immediate relief. These strategies are:

- Getting engaged in the political process
- Seeking a legal remedy

I understand some Christians will be put off by these two strategies. However, if you are reluctant to engage in the political process or seek legal assistance, I encourage you to read on. One of the main reasons your coworkers are emboldened to persecute you in the first place is because Christians shying away from politics and the legal system. By ceding the public square to those who reject Christ, we have given them the upper hand. Remaining silent in the face of Christian persecution just encourages more persecution.

The question I am asked most often by Christians who are being persecuted on the job is "What about turning the other cheek?" (Luke 6:29). That is a good question, but it is based on a misinterpretation of this verse from Scripture. In the context of the workplace, this verse means we should avoid responding in-kind, seeking vengeance, or pursuing retribution. Luke wanted to make sure his brothers and sisters did not become like the people who mistreated them. Consequently, if you are forced to seek immediate relief from your persecutors by filing a lawsuit or long-term relief through political engagement, it is important to do those things in a spirit of justice, not retribution. Accordingly, before getting into legal remedies and political engagement, there are several foundational strategies to be reviewed.

SEEK JUSTICE NOT RETRIBUTION OR VENGEANCE

Maggy was applauded by several of her coworkers for standing up to their boss, an avowed humanist who recently demanded she remove the Twenty-third Psalm from the wall of her office. When Maggy respectfully but firmly refused, her boss removed the framed verse himself and threw it in a trash can. He then took disciplinary action against Maggy. Maggy responded to this blatant act of persecution by filing a First Amendment lawsuit against her boss. When her Christian coworkers took Maggy aside and encouraged her to give their boss what he deserved, they were surprised by what she told them.

Maggy made it clear to her coworkers she wanted justice, not retribution. If her boss replaced the framed Bible verse on her wall and refrained from further acts of persecution, she would be happy to drop the lawsuit and move on. Maggy's coworkers seemed disappointed she refused to attack her boss or even speak poorly of him. Each of them was mistreated at one time or another by this same supervisor. Maggy explained that his poor behavior was not an excuse for her to follow suit. She wanted justice, but she also wanted to reflect the image of Christ in how she pursued it.

What Maggy understood and her coworkers apparently did not is the appropriate response to Christian persecution on the job is a biblical response. What is a biblical response? The Bible is replete with verses answering this question. For example, in Romans 12:14, we are told to bless those who persecute us. In Luke 6:27–28, we are admonished to love our enemies and to do good to those who hate us. In Acts 5:41, we are reminded to rejoice when God deems us worthy to suffer for His sake. There are many additional verses on this subject. Collectively they make the following point: When suffering for Christ, the appropriate response is one reflecting the image of Christ. We are not called to accept the abuse of Satan's minions, but we are called to confront them in Christ-honoring ways.

When responding to persecution in the workplace, begin by applying the following strategies. These strategies will help ensure you are pursuing justice, not vengeance or retribution:

- *Run to God, not from Him.* Like any form of adversity faced by Christians, persecution can drive us to God or push us away from Him. Make the choice to run to God when suffering Christian persecution at work. With God at your side, you can do what is necessary to withstand and overcome the persecution. But if you try to face your persecutors alone, they will have the upper hand.
- *Pray for guidance, wisdom, and perseverance.* There will never be a time when Matthew 10:16 is more important to you than when you are subjected to persecution because of your faith. When beset by persecutors, pray constantly. Ask God for three things: (1) guidance concerning how best to handle the situation you face, (2) wisdom to handle

the situation in a manner both biblically sound and workplace appropriate, and (3) courage to stand firm while showing those who mistreat you the image of Christ.

- *Remind yourself constantly God, not Satan, is sovereign.* People who persecute you because of your faith are doing the work of Satan. Although you are suffering at their hands now, the battle is not really between you and your persecutors. You and they are just players in a much larger drama, the age-old clash between good and evil. Fortunately, this is a battle already won. God is sovereign, and against Him Satan can do nothing (see Acts 4:23–35, Luke 2:29, and 2 Peter 2:1). When facing persecution in the workplace, remind yourself constantly God is sovereign and will prevail at the time and place of His choice. The temptation is to want to see Satan and his minions conquered right now. This may, in fact, happen. But that is not the promise. The promise is God will prevail. Your persecutors will be defeated. It may happen in your time, and it may not. Regardless the timing, know it will happen. Like all things, it will happen in God's time. Your job and mine is to remain faithful in the interim, no matter how long it takes for God's promise to come to fruition.

- *Search the Bible for help and apply what you learn.* There are libraries and bookstores full of literature containing various strategies for dealing with adversity of every kind, but your best source is the Bible. It always has been and always will be. The answers you need concerning persecution in the workplace will be found in the Bible. The key is to take the guidance provided in God's Word and apply it to your situation in ways that conform to Christ's message in Matthew 10:16. Read Psalm 2, making note of how Herod and Pontius Pilate persecuted God's people. Then reread verse 4, where we are told God scoffs at those who oppose Him. Be wise in how you respond to persecution. Be faithful to your beliefs and continue to reflect the image of Christ in all you do. Then let God do the rest. Proverbs 1:24–33 warns of what happens to scoffers and fools who ignore God's wisdom. Your persecutors are scoffers and fools.

- *Seek the wise counsel and assistance of fellow Christians.* Don't keep what is happening to you at work bottled up. Share your fears, frustrations, and facts with fellow believers. Christian brothers and sisters can provide the support you need to persevere against maltreatment on the job and help you stand firm in ways that reflect the image of Christ. In 1 John 3:17, we are admonished to open our hearts to brothers and sisters in need. You have Christian brothers and sisters who are waiting to help and want to be called upon. Let them help you.

Once you have internalized the strategies just explained, you are ready to implement the two additional strategies I recommend for Christians who are being persecuted in the workplace: (1) engage in the political process and (2) seek legal redress.

ENGAGING IN THE POLITICAL PROCESS

There is disagreement among Christians concerning the issue of political engagement. Summarizing the various arguments for and against political engagement by Christians would require a volume the size of the Oxford English Dictionary. I do not propose to undertake that project at this point. Rather, I will simply observe that Christ told us to "occupy" until He comes (Luke 19:13). We do not "occupy" the world God has given us by ceding it to those who reject Him. Engaging in the political process is one of the ways we "occupy" until Christ comes.

Frankly, if Christians were more actively engaged in the political process over the past fifty years, there would be no need for this book. If you are being persecuted at work, one of the main reasons is Christians have emboldened those who reject Christ by ceding the public square to them rather than occupying it. All Satan and his minions need to win the battle of religious freedom is for Christians to remain silent. For the past five decades, too many have.

On the other hand, there are Christians who believe if they can just elect the right candidates, pass the right laws, and install the right judges, Christian persecution will go away. Doing these things will certainly have a mitigating effect on Christian persecution in the workplace. This is why I recommend political engagement as a strategy for Christians. However, we should not forget that hearts are not changed by the ballot box. As long as there are people who reject Christ, there will be persecution of those who worship Him. It is vitally important to reflect the image of Christ in how we engage in the political process.

Having consistent Christians in positions of authority throughout society is a good thing, something to be desired and worked for. For example, it matters who sits on the Supreme Court as well as the lesser courts. It also matters who serves in Congress, the White House, and down the line to the county commission and city council. Christians should work hard to place fellow believers in these important positions. By electing Christians to high office, we can do our part to keep our country from becoming like others where Christians are openly and systematically persecuted for their faith.

As Christians, we are also American citizens who enjoy the relative freedom that comes from living in our constitutional republic. The fastest way to lose our freedoms—including freedom of religion—is to cede the public square to those who deny Christ. As Christians, it is our duty to be good citizens. As citizens, it is our duty to engage in the political process. On the other hand, we should never rely exclusively on political engagement to solve a problem that, ultimately, will require the kind of heart change only Christ brings. The ballot box is one of the tools available to us for combating persecution, but an even better tool is the Bible.

A caveat is in order at this point concerning political engagement. Although part of being a good Christian is being a good citizen, it requires much more than just being a good citizen. Being a good Christian requires we put our faith in God for all things. Even weak faith in God will serve us better than strong faith in those who run for political office. This is what is meant by that old maxim about crossing a wooden bridge. Strong faith in a weak plank will land you in the river. But even weak faith in a strong plank will get you across. The strong plank for Christians is Jesus Christ, not people who hold political office.

As citizens, we should engage in the political process and work hard to elect people who will be guided by the Holy Spirit in their endeavors, but we should never make the mistake of substituting faith in politics for faith in God. Abraham Lincoln coined the now-revered phrase about a government "of the people, by the people, and for the people." As Christians, we should never forget a government of, by, and for the people is a government of sinners, by sinners, and for sinners. Like anything we do, our involvement in politics should be to glorifying God.

SEEK LEGAL ASSISTANCE IF IT BECOMES NECESSARY

Engaging in the political process is a long-term strategy. For immediate relief, you may have to seek legal assistance. Persecution of Christians can take many forms in the workplace. Actions of persecutors that violate the law are becoming more common. When your legal rights to live according to your faith are denied, being both wise and innocent might mean seeking legal assistance. If this becomes necessary, make sure the legal assistance you receive comes from an individual or group specializing in religious freedom cases.

America's system of justice and law was originally based on a foundation of Christian morality, but the trend in our country and, correspondingly, our justice system is to replace Christian morality with secular humanism. Consequently, with every victory they win in the courts, those who reject Christ become increasingly bold in their attacks on Christians on the job and elsewhere. Fortunately, there remain sufficient remnants of Christian morality in the body of law, so you and I can still have our day in court and often prevail.

There are religious freedom organizations specializing in defending Christians who are being persecuted because of their faith. These organizations know the Constitution and the long-standing legal precedents relating to religious freedom that are supposed to guide the decisions of judges and juries. Consequently, they are adept at applying the Constitution and legal precedent to protect the religious freedom of Christians. If you ever find it necessary to seek legal redress against persecutors, make sure you are represented by an individual or organization with expertise in handling religious freedom cases.

There are numerous organizations as well as individual law firms specializing in religious freedom cases. However, it is important to be careful in selecting the firm or group to represent you because many advertising themselves as religious freedom groups are, in fact, freedom-from-religion advocates. Two groups specializing in helping Christians who are being persecuted because of their faith are Alliance Defending Freedom (ADF) and the Center for Law & Religious Freedom:

- *Alliance Defending Freedom (ADF).* ADF funds legal cases, trains attorneys, and represents Christians who are being persecuted because of their faith. ADF has an admirable track record of winning approximately 80 percent of its cases and has played a key role in forty-seven victories for Christians in the Supreme Court. ADF is an organization to approach if you are seeking immediate assistance and relief. ADF may be contacted at the following web address: www.adflegal.org.
- *The Center for Law & Religious Freedom.* The Center is an advocacy ministry that argues high-impact cases and advises Congress on legislation relating to religious freedom. The Center advocates on behalf of religious student

groups, faith-based social services, religious educational institutions, and pro-life healthcare providers. The Center is better suited to helping groups than individuals. Its services tend to be broader and less immediate than those of the ADF. The Center may be contacted at the following web address: https://clsnet.org.

Both these are examples of organizations playing vital roles in protecting the religious freedom of Christians. Which group would be more appropriate for a specific case depends on the nature of the case. ADF is effective at assisting in cases affecting individual Christians. The Center is more inclined to take on cases affecting groups. However, both organizations can guide Christians to help in the event a given case does not fit their missions. If you are experiencing persecution yourself or are beginning to see other Christians persecuted in the workplace, make sure you have the websites of these two organizations stored for ready access.

RESPONDING TO PERSECUTION IN THE WORKPLACE: AN EXAMPLE

Alice was a good fit from the outset at ABC Real Estate, Inc. She was a committed Christian who lived her faith on the job and off. Serving God was at the forefront of Alice's life. Alice's supervisor, Milos, was also committed—not to God but to himself. Milos had nothing but disdain· for Alice's Christian beliefs. His religion was secular humanism, and his God was self. From the outset, Milos went out of his way to demonstrate his disdain for Alice's beliefs.

He complained about Alice keeping a Bible on her desk and reading it at lunch. Several times Alice came to work only to find that someone, probably Milos, had tossed her Bible into the trash can next to her desk. Milos complained that the cross-shaped necklace Alice wore every day was "offensive." He also made it clear he resented Alice's steadfast refusals to join him and the other members of the sales team in sampling the local nightlife after work. This, in his eyes, made Alice a poor team player.

What started out as minor harassment eventually morphed into persecution. Before long, Milos was actively trying to undermine Alice's sales figures and to deny her incentive bonuses. He also gave her poor ratings on performance appraisals. His favorite tactic was to schedule Alice for weekend duty on Sunday instead of Saturday. Milos knew by doing so he was denying Alice the opportunity to attend church. All sales agents in the company had to cover the office on either a Saturday or Sunday once every six weeks, but the others typically got to choose which day worked. Not Alice. She was given no option. Although she was happy to cover the office when her turn in the rotation came up, Alice thought she should be able to choose between Saturday and Sunday like everyone else. But Milos refused to hear her requests and made it obvious he delighted in forcing her to miss church services.

Despite the abuse, Alice persevered. Not only that, she outperformed her fellow agents month after month on sales. The one thing her boss could not take away from Alice was her relationships with customers. Buyers and sellers liked Alice and they trusted her. Alice quickly established a well-deserved reputation for being an honest, trustworthy, and helpful real estate agent. She went out of her way to help potential buyers find homes that were a good fit for them. Alice would guide customers to the best deals even if it meant lower commissions for her. Because of her work ethic, honesty, integrity, and helpfulness, Alice was a top performer month after month. Her excellent work made it difficult for Milos to continue giving her low ratings on performance appraisals. But this just made Milos resent her even more. In fact, the better she performed, the more determined Milos became in mistreating her.

When potential buyers began to specifically request Alice as the sales agent they wanted to work with, Milos decided to turn up the heat. He filed a trumped-up grievance against Alice claiming she violated the company's policy against religious evangelizing on the job. Milos listed the following facts in support of his grievance: (1) Alice kept a Bible on her desk at work, (2) she read the Bible during her lunch break, (3) her purse had a Bible verse stitched into the side of it, and (4) she often said "God bless you" in conversations with customers.

In keeping with company policy, a grievance committee was formed to hear both sides of the argument. Although Alice was warned by the committee to avoid evangelizing at work, the committee ruled the grievance brought against her had no merit and dismissed it. Milos became enraged and stomped out of the meeting. Not even waiting for the end of the workday, he sped off in his car. Less than an hour later, a call from the local police department informed ABC's HR Director that Milos lost control of his car and crashed into a retaining wall. He was in the hospital in intensive care. Milos was expected to live, but his recovery would take an extended period.

In the weeks after the accident, the personnel at ABC responded in different ways to Milos's absence. Several of his fellow sales agents began to actively lobby for the position Milos held: sales supervisor. Others simply ignored the situation and went on with their lives. But Alice's response was different. She knew Milos was married and had two young children. Knowing the wife, Svetlanna, would be traumatized and probably needed help, Alice paid her a visit. Her suspicions were correct. Svetlana was struggling to manage the household, care for the children, and visit her husband in the hospital. There were just too many responsibilities to juggle. She needed help.

Seeing this, Alice offered to babysit for the children two nights a week, so Svetlana could visit Milos in the hospital. She also organized a group of friends from her church to provide meals, do the grocery shopping, babysit when Svetlana needed to get out, and clean the house. With help from Alice and her fellow church members, Svetlana was able to manage. Alice also spent time talking with Svetlana, praying for her, and listening when she needed to talk. Svetlana told Alice several times she would not have been able to cope without her help.

Six weeks later, Alice was sitting in her usual pew waiting for the Sunday morning service to begin. She spent the few minutes before the service praying for Milos, Svetlana, and their children. Just before the call to worship sounded, Alice sensed someone taking a seat beside her in the pew. When she looked up, Alice was surprised to see Milos, Svetlana, and their children sitting beside her. Milos was pale, bruised, and thin, but his eyes sparkled as he shook her hand and said just two words: "Thank you."

At work, Milos was a changed man and, needless to say, Alice was never again subjected to religious persecution by Milos or anyone else at ABC Real Estate, Inc. A bad situation had a happy ending because Alice stood firm in the faith when she was being persecuted but, at the same time, she did what was necessary to reflect the image of Christ in how she responded to her persecutor.

RESPONDING TO CYBER-BULLYING

Marisa could not believe it. She knew her coworker, James, was no fan of her views on transgender restrooms in the workplace, but she never thought he would stoop to cyber-bullying. Unfortunately, she was wrong. One morning Marisa learned James posted a series of misleading insinuations about her on a social media site. Too smart to make specific allegations about Marisa, James posted his comments as questions. His questions included these: "Is it true that our resident Christian, Marisa, had an adulterous affair?" "Is it true that Marisa was once arrested for child abuse?" "Is it true that Marisa has a drug problem?"

Although it is usually thought of as a problem among teenagers, cyber-bullying is a growing phenomenon often directed at adults. Predictably, it has invaded the workplace. Not surprisingly, those who reject Christianity have found it to be a convenient and effective weapon. The tactics of cyber-bullies include sending threatening or offensive emails to Christian coworkers and using social media to spread malicious gossip, rumors, and lies about them. When those who reject your faith stoop to cyber-bullying, it is important for you to know how to respond. What follows are several specific actions I recommend to Christians I counsel who are victims of cyber-bullies:

- *Apply the First-Response Model.* As always, when being attacked because of your Christianity, it is important to apply the First-Response Model explained in Chapter

One. Begin by taking a few moments to compose yourself so you do not respond out of anger, fear, or frustration. These are not Christ-like responses. However, on the other hand, it is important you respond. Turning the other cheek (Matthew 5:39) does not mean allowing yourself to be continually abused. Rather, it means refusing to respond in kind. Pray for God's help, seek additional guidance in Scripture, ask for the wise counsel of Godly men and women, and translate Scriptural guidance and wise counsel into practical, workplace-appropriate action. Applying the First-Response Model will help you respond appropriately to cyber-bullying without becoming like the person who is harassing and persecuting you. The remaining strategies explained in this section will help you translate the guidance and counsel you receive into workplace-appropriate action.

- *Make screenshots or hard copies of all messages and images posted about you by cyber-bullies.* One of the reason bullies like to use email and social networking sites to attack Christians is the supposed *invisibility* these media provide them. Bullies will say things via electronic media they would never say face-to-face. Further, when challenged, their first response is likely to be denial. Therefore it is important to make screenshots or hard copies of the messages cyber-bullies send you or post about you. In addition, because some cyber-bullies disguise who they are by setting up accounts under assumed names; you might need copies to help authorities identify the culprits.

- *Confront the cyber-bully face-to-face with a witness present.* Arrange a meeting with the individual who is attacking you, preferably in the HR office of your employer with a witness present. Let the individual know you do not appreciate his or her actions and they have to stop. Be firm but not aggressive or threatening. Simply let the individual who is trying to bully you know there can be serious consequences for his or her actions, and a continuation of the attacks will result in those consequences. It is not uncommon for cyber-bullies to claim they were just kidding. For this reason, it is important for them to hear directly from you that you are not amused and do not interpret their actions as harmless fun.

- *Meet with your supervisor and the HR department about instances of cyber-bullying.* Use the chain of command in your organization to report instances of cyber-bullying. Provide people in positions of authority with the evidence you have copied. Many organizations have adopted policies prohibiting cyber-bullying and making it a punishable offense. Your employer's HR department will have a copy of the policy if one exists. If no such policy exists, recommend through the chain of command that the organization adopt one.

- *Contact the local police if cyber-bullying crosses a line into threats.* It is not uncommon for cyber-bullies—especially those who operate accounts under assumed names—to threaten their victims. If this happens, contact the local police department even before you make the threat known to your supervisor and your employer's HR department. Cyber threats should always be taken seriously. Follow up by bringing your supervisor and the HR director into the loop, and let them know you have already contacted the police.

- *Contact your employer's IT Department.* The IT department in your organization may be able to install filters to block some of the offensive material you receive from cyber-bullies. This strategy is intended to minimize cyber-bullying.

It will not eliminate it. However, all the strategies presented in this section, when taken together, will be effective in stopping cyber-bullying aimed at attacking your faith.

Now let me return to the case of Marisa introduced at the beginning of this section. Marisa was certain she knew who was posting the offensive, suggestive material about her on a social networking site. The culprit was James. But James established the account in question under an assumed name, so he denied any knowledge of the posts. However, when Marisa went to the local police, their specialist in cybercrime was able to determine James was, in fact, the bully. Armed with this information, Marisa approached James and politely but firmly told him the offensive posts had to stop. When he continued to maintain his innocence, Marisa approached her supervisor and the director of HR with the evidence she collected. She also had the cyber-expert from the police department join them for the meeting.

When Marisa's employer realized the police were involved, they moved immediately to solve the problem. James received a written reprimand placed in his personnel file. The letter of reprimand made it clear further instances of cyber-bullying would result in his termination. Marisa suspected from comments she heard during the meeting with the supervisor and the HR director her employer was more concerned about negative publicity in the local newspaper than about protecting her from harassment, bullying, and persecution. However, regardless of his motivation, the employer did take the necessary steps to stop the harassment and prevent future instances of it. Marisa's handling of the situation worked because it was in keeping with Matthew 10:16 being wise and innocent.

DISCUSSION CASE 12.1: "I AM NOT GOING TO TAKE THIS ANYMORE . . ."

Keenan was beyond angry. He was livid. First someone took the Bible off his desk, ripped pages out of it, and threw it into a trash can. Then someone stole the cross that hung on the wall of his office. He later found it in the company's parking lot, broken after a car ran over it. These two outrages were just the latest in a long list of incidents aimed at denigrating his Christian faith. After enduring that kind of treatment for more than six months, Keenan was fed up. He walked into his supervisor's office, slammed the door, and shouted, "I am not going to take this anymore. You know exactly what is going on around here, yet you do nothing about it. Well, I've had it. I am going to find out who is pulling these stunts, and when I do, he is going to pay, and so are you for letting this nonsense continue."

Discussion Questions

1. Have you ever faced a situation at work in which others tried to bait you into responding inappropriately? If so, how did you respond?
2. Keenan persevered against incidents of minor persecution for more than six months. Was he justified in getting angry? Did Keenan handle the situation appropriately?
3. Had Keenan approached you for wise counsel before shouting at his supervisor, what would you have told him concerning how to handle this situation?

DISCUSSION CASE 12.2: "IF THAT'S WHAT YOU BELIEVE, YOU SHOULD GO WORK SOMEWHERE ELSE!"

Linda worked for the local public-school system for twenty-eight years. Her latest position was administrative assistant to the principal of an elementary school, the same school her children once attended. Linda came to Christ only in recent years and was committed to her faith. This is where the problems began. As a Christian, she was concerned about the changes she observed in public schools over the years. When her children were in school, they prayed and then recited the Pledge of

Allegiance at the beginning of every school day. But those things were now strictly forbidden. And bans on prayer and the Pledge represented just the tip of the iceberg.

Linda was so disturbed by the religious discrimination in her school she considered resigning, even though she was just two years from her scheduled retirement date. But common sense prevailed. Linda decided to tough it out. She continued doing her job and setting a Christ-like example in spite of the growing hostility toward Christianity. However, Linda was adamant on one point: The granddaughter she and her husband were raising after the tragic death of the child's parents was not going to attend a public school in her district. Instead, Linda and her husband enrolled little Emma in a local Christian school.

When Linda's principal found out Emma was attending a Christian school, he was livid. Linda explained openly and forthrightly why she and her husband chose the Christian school, but that just made matters worse. After debating the issue with Linda for almost an hour, the exasperated principal shouted, "If that is what you believe, you should go work somewhere else!" Two days later, Linda learned her principal had initiated termination procedures against her.

Discussion Questions

1. Have you ever known an individual who worked in a public educational institution but sent his or her children to a Christian school? If so, did this individual ever experience persecution from colleagues who resented that choice?
2. Should a Christian who works in the public education system be required to enroll his or her children in public school?
3. If you were Linda, how would you handle this situation?

REVIEW QUESTIONS FOR INDIVIDUALS AND GROUPS

1. Why are bitterness, anger, and frustration not appropriate responses to Christian persecution at work?
2. Should Christians engage in the political process? Why or why not?
3. Should Christians put their faith solely in political engagement to end Christian persecution? Explain your view.
4. Explain how the following maxim applies to Christians who are facing persecution at work: When crossing a wooden bridge, strong faith in a weak plank will land you in the river. But even weak faith in a strong plank will get you across.
5. List and explain several Bible verses that provide guidance concerning how Christians should respond to those who persecute them.
6. List and explain six strategies Christians can use for dealing with persecution in the workplace.
7. When is it appropriate for Christians who are facing persecution at work to seek legal assistance?
8. Describe the services provided by Alliance Defending Freedom (ADF).
9. Describe the services provided by The Center for Law & Religious Freedom.
10. Describe the approach you might take in dealing with attacks on your Christianity by a cyber-bully.